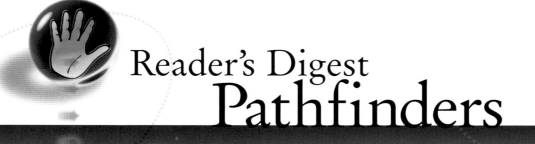

Reader's Digest
Pathfinders

Wonders
of Science

Published by Reader's Digest Children's Books
Reader's Digest Road, Pleasantville, NY, U.S.A. 10570-7000 and
Reader's Digest Children's Publishing Limited, The Ice House
124-126 Walcot Street, Bath UK BA1 5BG

Reader's Digest Children's Books is a trademark and Reader's Digest
is a registered trademark of The Reader's Digest Association, Inc.

Conceived and produced by Weldon Owen Pty Limited
59 Victoria Street, McMahons Point, NSW, 2060, Australia
A member of the Weldon Owen Group of Companies
Sydney • San Francisco • Auckland

© 2003 Weldon Owen Inc.

WELDON OWEN PTY LTD
Chairman: John Owen
Publisher: Sheena Coupe
Creative Director: Sue Burk
Design Concept: John Bull
Editorial Coordinator: Jennifer Losco
Production Manager: Caroline Webber
Production Coordinator: James Blackman
Vice President International Sales: Stuart Laurence

THE HUMAN BODY
Author: Laurie Beckelman
Consultant: Jonathan Stein, M.D.
Illustrators: Susanna Addario, Marcus Cremonese, Sam & Amy Collins,
Christer Eriksson, Peg Gerrity, Gino Hasler, Jeff Lang, Siri Mills,
Spencer Phippen, Kate Sweeney/K.E. Sweeney Illustration, Rod Westblade
© 1999 Weldon Owen Inc.

ROCKS AND MINERALS
Author: Tracy Staedter
Consultants: Robert Coenraads, Ph.D., Carolyn Rebbert, Ph.D.
Illustrators: Andrew Beckett/Illustration, Chris Forsey, Ray Grinaway,
David McAllister, Stuart McVicar, Michael Saunders, Kevin Stead,
Sharif Tarabay/Illustration, Thomas Trojer
© 1999 Weldon Owen Inc.

SPACE
Author: Alan Dyer
Consultant: Roy A. Gallant
Illustrators: Julian Baum/Wildlife Art Ltd, Tom Connell/Wildlife Art Ltd,
Christer Eriksson, Murray Frederick, Chris Forsey,
Lee Gibbons/Wildlife Art Ltd, Ray Grinaway, David A. Hardy/Wildlife Art Ltd,
Oliver Rennert, Chris Stead, Marco Sparaciari, Tony Wellington, Rod Westblade
© 1999 Weldon Owen Inc.

ISBN 0-7944-0352-2

Color Reproduction by Colourscan Co Pte Ltd
Printed by Imago Productions (F.E) Pte Ltd
Printed in Singapore

10 9 8 7 6 5 4 3 2 1

A WELDON OWEN PRODUCTION

Reader's Digest
Pathfinders

Wonders
of Science

Reader's
Digest
Children's Books™

Pleasantville, New York • Montréal, Québec

The Human Body

Contents

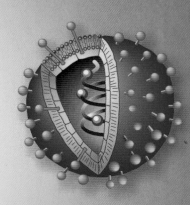

Control Centers 8

The Framework 34

Supplies and Demand 48

Pick Your Path!

PREPARE YOURSELF FOR a journey through *The Human Body* like no other. You can read straight through to the end to discover what we now know about our amazing bodies—and what we might learn in the future. Or follow your interests. Want to know how the brain works? Jump straight to "The Sensing Brain," and move through the book from there.

You'll find plenty of other discovery paths to choose from in the special features sections. Read about the heroes of human biology in "Inside Story," or get creative with "Hands On" activities. Delve into words with "Word Builders," or amaze your friends with fascinating facts from "That's Amazing!" You can choose a new path with every reading—READER'S DIGEST PATHFINDERS will take you wherever *you* want to go.

INSIDE STORY
Heroes of Science

Picture yourself alongside a doctor who dips food into an open stomach wound to learn more about digestion. Share a scientist's excitement as he discovers X-rays. Learn why a child with diabetes must give herself a shot each day. Explore life in the womb. INSIDE STORY introduces you to the men and women behind the science, and gives you an insider's look at new tools and treatments. Read about them and make yourself a part of the discoveries that have changed the world.

HANDS ON
Things to Do

Trick your brain into seeing a hole in your hand. Use buckets of water to understand how much blood the heart pumps each day. Assemble straws and cardboard into a "bone" and test it for strength. Find out how long it takes for a yawn to catch on. The HANDS ON features suggest experiments, projects, and activities that demonstrate how the body works.

Word Builders

What a strange word!
What does it mean?
Where did it come from?
Find out by reading
Word Builders.

That's Amazing!

Awesome facts, amazing records, fascinating figures—you'll find them all in *That's Amazing!*

Pathfinder

Use the *Pathfinder* section to find your way from one subject to another. It's all up to you.

Ready! Set!
Start exploring!

Control Centers

YOUR BODY IS a familiar friend. You know it so well that you probably don't think about it much. But beneath your freckles, dimples, or knobby knees is a world as vast as the universe. Trillions of cells work together so you can breathe, move, eat, think, talk, and grow. How does your amazing body make this teamwork possible? You're about to find out.

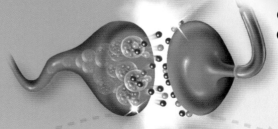

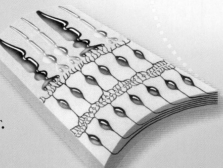

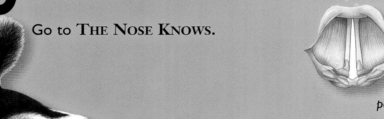

THEN...
500 years ago, Italian artist and scientist Leonardo Da Vinci was one of the first to cut apart dead bodies in order to understand how we work.

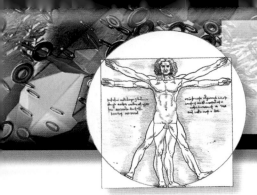

...AND NOW
Today, imaging machines make living organs visible. This digital brain scan helps doctors locate areas damaged by disease.

Amazing Us

HAVE YOU WONDERED how you grow? Why you get sick? Why people die? If so, you share a curiosity as old as humankind. People in every age have wondered how the body works. And in every age, they've tried to find answers.

For most of history, people had only one tool with which to study the body. That tool was the body itself. Their senses were their instruments. They listened to the heart and felt the heat of fever. They smelled the odor of decaying flesh or watched a wound heal. They studied healthy bodies and sick ones. In the 16th century, they began studying dead ones, too. Scientists peeled away flesh and fat to reveal muscle. They separated muscle from bone. They removed bones to examine the heart, lungs, liver, and gut. Knowledge grew.

As tools improved, knowledge grew even further. Microscopes revealed cells. Machines gave doctors X-ray vision and recorded the rhythms of the heart. If you become a scientist, your tools will be even better. But you still won't have all the answers. The more people learn about the human body, the more there is to know. Amazing us.

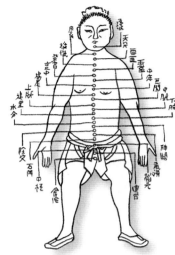

MYSTERIOUS FORCES
Chinese healers believe that life energy flows through invisible channels. They stimulate points in these channels in the body to treat illness and block pain. This practice is called acupuncture. No one knows why it works, but it often does.

HANDS ON

A New Look

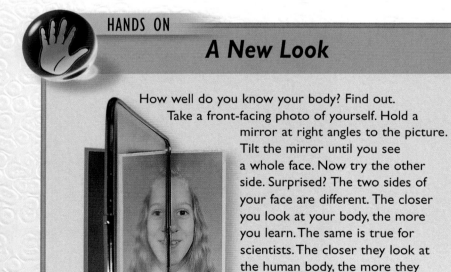

How well do you know your body? Find out. Take a front-facing photo of yourself. Hold a mirror at right angles to the picture. Tilt the mirror until you see a whole face. Now try the other side. Surprised? The two sides of your face are different. The closer you look at your body, the more you learn. The same is true for scientists. The closer they look at the human body, the more they discover about us.

BODY KNOWLEDGE
The ancients had little understanding of how the body worked. They blamed demons for illness. Today, we know that germs can cause illness. We know that our genes and habits influence health and growth.

AMAZING DISCOVERIES
In 1674, Anton van Leeuwenhoek discovered bacteria by cleaning his teeth. He put the stuff under a microscope he'd made and saw a world swarming with life. Two hundred years later, scientists realized that germs such as these could cause disease.

Word Builders

- **Anatomy** is the study of body parts. It comes from the Greek word, *anatome*, which means dissection.
- **Physiology** is the study of how body parts work. It comes from the Greek word *physis*, which means nature.

That's Amazing!

- Touch your thumb to your middle finger. No other animal can do that! This is one of the main things that distinguishes the human body.
- The oldest known human skeleton is Lucy. She was found in 1974 and is about 3.2 million years old.

Pathfinder

- In the Middle Ages, people believed that bad smells caused disease. What do we know about bad smells now? To find out, go to pages 26–27.
- Take a microscopic look inside the body to find out all about cells. Go to pages 12–13.
- Who discovered X-rays? How did this discovery change our understanding of bones? Find out on pages 42–43.

PAIN SAVER

Early surgeons could do little to relieve their patients' pain. But in the 1840s, doctors discovered gases that allowed their patients to sleep right through surgery. We now know that anesthetics like these block pain messages to the brain. Modern anesthetics make long operations, like heart transplants, possible.

Cell City

YOU HAVE 75 TRILLION living factories inside you. These factories are your cells, some of the smallest units of life. They make up bone, skin, hair, and every other part of you. If you could watch your cells work through a microscope, you'd see that they are constantly busy. They absorb nutrients from the fluid around them. They turn these nutrients into energy. They respond to messages from other cells. They churn out chemicals your body uses when you throw a ball, eat a burger, or dream. Each cell completes trillions of actions a second!

Like all living things, cells come into being, grow, reproduce, and die. Unlike you, they don't need two parents. Cells are clones. They form when a single parent cell divides in two. This process is called mitosis. How often a cell divides and how long it lives depends upon its type. You have about 200 types of cells. Some, like skin cells, wear out quickly. They must be replaced quickly, too. They divide every 10 to 30 hours. Millions die and form every minute. Most brain cells, however, must last a lifetime. They do not reproduce. When you remember these words years from now, you'll use the same cells you're using today.

TEAM WORK

Cells are team players. They join with others like themselves to form tissues, and tissues form organs that together carry out life's work. Each cell's shape is perfect for its job. Most cells have a nucleus and the other parts shown in the drawing of the cell on page 11.

Nerve cells have long, tail-like structures called axons to carry messages from one nerve cell to the next.

Red blood cells look like Frisbees. They zip through your bloodstream, bringing oxygen to other cells and removing carbon dioxide.

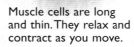

Muscle cells are long and thin. They relax and contract as you move.

Fat cells look like bubble wrap. They protect your joints and some organs, store energy, and provide warmth.

Skin cells stack together like bricks. They form a protective wall around your body.

INSIDE STORY

Wanted: DNA

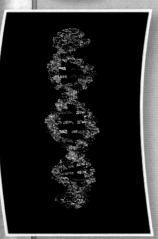

The Crime: David's bubblegum—stolen!
The Evidence: A chewed wad of bubblegum stuck under Sally's desk.
Your Job: Find the thief! Impossible? Not with DNA testing. DNA (see left) is the chemical that makes up your genes. It is stored on 46 chromosomes that are twisted in pairs inside a cell's nucleus. Every nucleus holds a complete set of DNA. But the cell "reads" only those genes it needs to do its job. Scientists can read a person's genes, too. All they need is a drop of saliva or a single hair, and a DNA sequencer. To solve your crime, match DNA from saliva on the gum with DNA from a suspect. You'll get your thief!

Word Builders

Gene comes from *genea* the Greek word for "generation" or race. Genes are the instructions for making you. You inherit them from your parents. They are stored on 46 chromosomes, half from mom and half from dad. If you were a frog, you'd have 26 chromosomes. If you were a garden pea, you'd have 14. But simpler plants and animals don't always have fewer chromosomes. A goldfish has 94.

That's Amazing!

• All the DNA in your body could stretch to the moon and back 37,585 times. It fits inside you because chromosomes have an amazing shape. They are like tightly coiled and twisted ladders. Unwind a Slinky to see how much space coils save.

• Blood cells live about 120 days. Liver cells live 18 months. Nerve cells can live for more than 100 years.

Pathfinder

• Sex cells (sperm and eggs) have only half the chromosomes of other cells. They form through a process called meiosis. Find out more on pages 14–15.

• Red blood cells are the smallest cells in the body. Mature ones don't have a nucleus. Learn more about blood on pages 58–59.

Cell membrane. This gatekeeper lets supplies in, wastes and products out.

The parts of a cell are called **organelles**. Each has a different job.

Vacuoles. These storage vessels ferry supplies of nutrients.

Lysomes. The cell's digestive organs destroy wastes and dangerous substances.

Cytoplasm. This jellylike maze of fibers throughout the cell supports organelles inside the cell.

Endoplasmic reticulum. The cell's proteins and fats move through these long, squiggly tunnels.

Microtubules. These tracks transport chemicals and give the cell shape.

ibosomes. nese factories ake proteins r the ll's use.

Nucleolus. This organelle makes and stores ribosomes.

Nucleus. The cell's "brain" holds genes and directs cell activities.

Mitochondria. These powerhouses make energy to fuel cell activities.

Golgi bodies. These long sacs prepare cell products for export.

ALIENS ABOARD

Billions of beings call your body home. They live on your skin and inside you. They enter your body through food, air, and cuts in your skin.

BAD BREATH?

B.O.? Blame bacteria. These one cell beings can cause such problems and much worse. A few bacteria, like those pictured above, can become millions in hours. They destroy healthy tissue and keep the body from working properly.

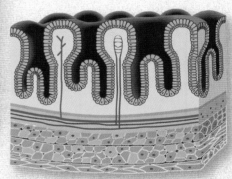

GOOD GUYS

Not all bacteria are bad. Good-guy bacteria in the folded lining of your stomach (pictured above) help your body use vitamins from foods. Some also fight their bad-guy cousins.

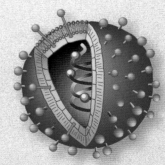

TRICKSTERS

Viruses invade your cells. They trick the cells into making more viruses. This process changes the cells chemically. They are damaged or die.

NASTY NEIGHBORHOOD

Cancers are cells out of control. Unlike healthy cells, they divide without limit. They crowd out normal cells, destroying healthy tissue.

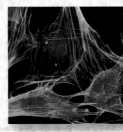

*Elephant—18 to 22 months
from conception till birth*

*Whale—11 to 16 months
from conception till birth*

*Small bat—40 to 60 days
from conception till birth*

Life Begins

WHAT A MIRACLE you are! You began life as a single cell smaller than the dot on this *i*. But in less than a school year, you were born!

The story of you began with a sperm and an egg. Sperm and eggs are sex cells, or gametes. They form through a process called meiosis. Each carries 23 chromosomes, half the instructions for a human being. As a result of sexual intercourse, egg and sperm unite to form a new life. This is called conception.

Females are born with all the eggs they'll ever have. However, these eggs don't mature until puberty, which is the age of sexual maturity. Then, once a month, an egg bursts from the ovary in which it ripens. It slides into a Fallopian tube. It stays there for 10 to 15 hours, awaiting a sperm.

Males begin making sperm at puberty. Their testes, epididymus, and seminal vesicles form an assembly line in which sperm develop, mature, and are stored. During sex, males ejaculate. Semen, which is a mix of fluid and sperm, shoots down the urethra and out the penis, into the woman's vagina. The sperm then swim to the Fallopian tubes. Some 300 million sperm start this journey. Just a few hundred survive. Only one fertilizes the egg. From this tiny beginning, a baby forms and is born. The human race goes on.

PRIVATE PARTS

Some reproductive organs make the sperm or the eggs. Other organs transport them. But only one can house and nourish new life. This is the woman's uterus, or womb. Each month this 3-inch (7.6-cm) wide organ gets ready to house new life. Its lining thickens. If no pregnancy occurs, the woman menstruates. She sheds this blood-rich lining. If pregnancy does occur, the lining combines with the placenta, which supplies nutrients to the unborn child. As the baby grows, the womb's muscles stretch. The cervix is the opening of the womb.

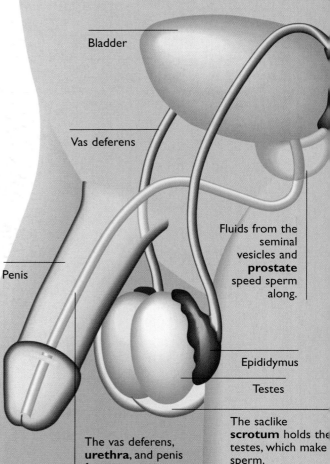

Seminal vesicles

Bladder

Vas deferens

Fluids from the seminal vesicles and **prostate** speed sperm along.

Penis

Epididymus

Testes

The vas deferens, **urethra**, and penis form a sperm delivery system.

The saclike **scrotum** holds the testes, which make sperm.

HANDS ON

Jellybean Genes

The instructions for making you are your genes. Like these jellybeans, genes for eye color come in pairs. You inherit one gene from each parent. The front row of jellybeans represents this boy's parents. One parent has two brown-eye genes. The other has one brown-eye gene and one blue-eye gene. But both parents have brown eyes. Why? Here's a simple explanation: genes for darker eye colors are dominant over those for lighter colors. Get one of each, and you get the darker colored eyes. The second row of jellybeans represents the boy and his siblings. What are their eye colors?

Use some colored candy or beads to give an imaginary family their genes for eye color. If each parent has a brown-eye gene and a blue-eye gene, might any of the children have blue eyes?

FERTILIZATION
Sperm cells meet the egg and burrow in. The first sperm to penetrate fertilizes the egg. By hardening its outer wall, the egg locks out other sperm. The egg is now called a zygote.

IMPLANTATION
The zygote divides and divides again. But it does not grow in size! In about seven days, this tiny cell ball attaches to the wall of the uterus.

EMBRYO
At seven weeks, the unborn child is called an embryo. It grows quickly. Its umbilical cord brings the embryo oxygen and nutrients from the placenta.

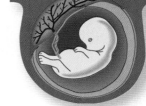

Fraternal comes from the Latin word *frāternus*, which means "brotherly." **Fraternal twins** share the same womb but not the same genes. They develop when two sperm fertilize two eggs at the same time. **Identical twins** share the same genes. They develop when one fertilized egg splits in two and each half grows into a whole human being.

• Imagine swimming 25 miles (40 km) in choppy seas. That's equivalent to the journey each sperm makes.
• Smell might guide sperm toward the egg. Sperm have odor receptors like those in the nose.
• Sperm develop best below body temperature. That's why the testes hang outside the body.

• Your brain and spinal cord formed before almost all the rest of you. Learn more about these bundles of nerves on pages 16–17.
• The testes and ovaries make hormones that partly control sexual maturity. The story of your hormones is on pages 30–31.
• The muscled wall of the uterus stretches as the baby grows. Read more about muscles on pages 40–41.

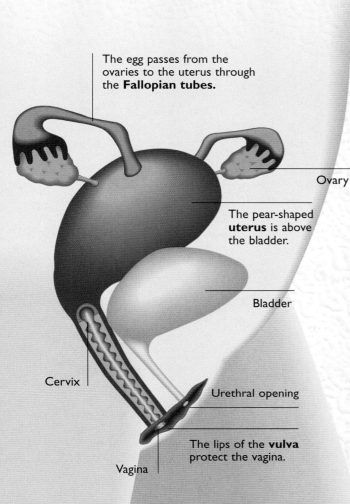

The egg passes from the ovaries to the uterus through the **Fallopian tubes.**

Ovary

The pear-shaped **uterus** is above the bladder.

Bladder

Cervix

Urethral opening

The lips of the **vulva** protect the vagina.

Vagina

INSIDE STORY
Life on the Inside

That could be you on the screen. Like the baby-to-be in the ultrasound, you started life floating in your mother's womb. Warm amniotic fluid surrounded and protected you. Your umbilical cord delivered oxygen and food from your mother's blood. It also carried wastes away. Two months after conception, you were already on the move. You waved. You kicked. You sucked your thumb. By seven months, you could hear your mother's voice and see light through her abdomen. You were almost ready to be born.

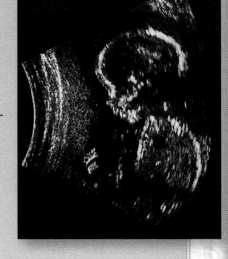

RECIPES FOR LIFE
Humans are more alike than not. But our genes make each of us unique. Sometimes, errors in genes or chromosomes cause major differences in the way humans look, think, and act. This child has an extra chromosome, which causes Down syndrome.

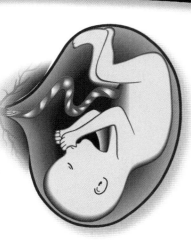

FETUS
At two months, the embryo becomes a fetus. It has all its organs but isn't much bigger than a walnut. By seven months, it will look just like a baby and will be able to survive outside the womb.

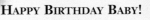

HAPPY BIRTHDAY BABY!
At nine months, strong uterine movements push the baby through the vagina and into the world. The baby's first cry clears its lungs. It breathes.

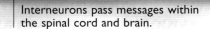
Interneurons pass messages within the spinal cord and brain.

Nerve Central

SHOULD YOU BREATHE? Digest your food? Sweat? You have no choice. These happen automatically because of your nervous system. Should you dance? Smile? Shout? Now you're in control, thanks also to your nervous system. The nervous system is your body's decision and communication center. It makes sure you respond appropriately to changes in your world.

Your nerves, brain, and spinal cord make up your nervous system. Nerves reach from your brain to your face, eyes, ears, nose, and spinal cord. They stretch from the spinal cord to every corner of your body. All day, every day, sensory nerves gather information. They sense the warmth of the sun. They detect changes in your body temperature or energy level. They flash this information to your spinal cord, which speeds it to your brain. Your brain makes sense of the messages. It fires off a response. Motor nerves deliver the instructions. Your body acts.

Your brain and spinal cord are your central nervous system. Your nerves are the peripheral nervous system. Together, they control all the things you do without thinking and all those you do think about. Breathe, burp, blink, or think—your busy nervous system is always hard at work.

Spinal cord

INSIDE STORY

Sensing the World

A breeze brushes your cheek. You hear a friend call. You inhale the woodsy scent of a campfire and lick sweet, sticky marshmallow from your lips. Special nerve cells bring you all the sensations of your world. They are sense cells called receptors. They change pressure, light, sound, scent, or taste into electric pulses. Some receptors, such as the taste cells shown above, have hairlike parts that do the sensing. When the hairs come in contact with taste molecules from food, they send a signal to nearby nerves.

WHAT A NERVE!

Each nerve is made of thousands of nerve cells called neurons. These long, thin cells fire messages at amazing speeds—a nerve message can travel 300 feet (91 m) a second! Electric pulses zap each message down an axon, a neuron's long "arm." At the end of the axon, chemicals ferry the message across the tiny gap between nerve cells. The gap is called a synapse. The chemicals are neurotransmitters. The dendrites of the next cell receive the message. It is passed along in this way until it has reached its destination.

NIGHT DUTY

Your nervous system is on duty even as you sleep. It lets you breathe, turn, and dream. It responds to danger signals and can wake you up.

Word Builders

- **Paralysis** comes from the ancient Greek word, *palsy*, meaning "to loosen from grip or disable."
- A **paraplegic** is a person whose legs are paralyzed. The word comes from an ancient Greek word, *paraplegie*, which means "paralysis on one side."
- A **quadraplegic** is someone who cannot move his or her arms or legs. *Quadri* means four.

That's Amazing!

Your arms or legs can "go to sleep" if there is pressure on a nerve. When the pressure is removed, the nerve sends a flood of signals to the brain. You then feel a sensation known as "pins and needles."

Pathfinder

- What happens to sense information when it reaches the brain? Find out on pages 18–19.
- Your spine protects your spinal cord. Find out what other bones protect on pages 44–45.
- Discover how nerves tell you that your bladder is full on pages 52–53.

Interneuron

A fatty material called myelin coats the axon. It speeds messages along.

Dendrites are the parts of neurons that receive messages from other cells.

Motor neurons carry the brain's instructions to the body.

The axon flashes messages to the next nerve cell.

Neurotransmitters ferry the message across the synapse, a gap between cells.

GETTING THE MESSAGE

The spinal cord is a superhighway, speeding messages to and from the brain. It is a bundle of nerves that runs down the center of the protective backbone, or spine. Spinal fluid cushions the nerves. Sensory nerves send information from the senses and organs to the brain. Motor nerves whisk the brain's instructions back to the body. Block the highway and messages can't get through. The result is paralysis.

Spinal cord

Sensory nerves

Motor nerves

Spinal fluid

HANDS ON

Reflex Action

Ask a friend to clap near your face. Try not to blink. Impossible, right? That's because blinking is a reflex. It's an instant response that you can't control. Reflexes are your nervous system's shortcuts. A nerve signal that triggers a reflex never makes it to your brain's thinking centers. As soon as the nerve signal reaches the spinal cord or brain stem, it causes a response. You react. You pull your hand from a hot plate, for instance. Sneezing, coughing, and breathing are all reflexes. Here are two more reflexes to have fun with.

1. Stroke the bottom of your friend's foot with a ruler. The foot will curve away.

2. Try yawning in front of your friends. See how long it takes until they're yawning, too. Yawning is catchy, but no one knows why.

SENSORY NEURONS

Sensory neurons like this one speed messages to the brain. When flavors excite taste cells in your tongue, for instance, the cells pass the message to sensory neurons. The neurons flash the message to taste centers in your brain.

The Sensing Brain

DUMP SEVERAL JIGSAW puzzles on the floor. Imagine that this is your world, a jumble of light and sound and ever-changing things around you. Now pick out just the pieces you need to make a picture. That's what your brain does hundreds of times a second. Your eyes, ears, nose, mouth, and skin take in the world. But your brain makes sense of it. Your brain combines colors and smells, tastes and sounds, so you know the difference, for instance, between a skunk and a cat.

When you come upon a skunk, your senses awaken a great many nerve pathways to your brain. Information about the skunk's color jogs down one path. Messages about its size, shape, or scent race down others. Each message lands in a separate area of the brain. These messages are like scattered puzzle pieces. But they don't stay separate long. Different brain regions have specialties, but they also work together. Your brain combines messages from all the senses and runs them through its memory banks. It makes an ID: "Skunk!" Instructions zoom to your muscles: "Don't move!" In less time than it takes to say "Awesome!" your brain saves you from getting sprayed.

SMALL WONDER

Your brain weighs only three pounds (1.4 kg). It looks like a wrinkled mass of gray jelly, but it's the world's most powerful information processor. It's made up of more than 100 billion nerve cells and ten times as many support cells. It has three main parts: the cerebrum, cerebellum, and brain stem. The cerebrum, which is the largest part of the brain, combines information from all your senses. It controls thought and action.

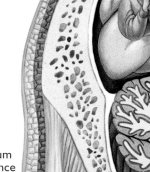

Sight

H

Balance

The cerebellum controls balance and smooth movement.

The brain stem regulates vital life functions such as breathing.

The spinal cord connects your brain to the rest of your body.

HANDS ON

Picture This

Your memory and imagination rely on information from sound, touch, smell, and taste as well as from sight. How well do these senses serve you? Try this activity to find out.

Have a friend make a picture with clay. Don't look. Put on a blindfold, then trace the picture with your finger. Now take off your blindfold, but don't look. Draw what you felt. How do the pictures compare?

PAIN AND THE BRAIN

A cut scalp hurts. A cracked skull hurts. But injury to the brain doesn't. So what does the brain have to do with pain? Everything.

WARNING!

Special nerves carry pain messages to your brain. These nerves are in skin, muscle, blood vessels, bone, and organs. They make sure you know when something's wrong.

SIGNAL SPEED

The sharp pain of a bee sting takes the express lane to your brain. Signals sprint up "fast" nerve fiber at up to 100 feet (30 per second. Dull, aching pains move i awareness more slo

Word Builders

Brain waves are regular patterns of brain activity. They are named for the wave-like pattern they make when recorded. They result from the millions of tiny bursts of electricity that move messages through your brain. Your brain waves are different when you are awake or sleeping. Brain waves are even different during different stages of sleep, as the pictures to the top left show.

That's Amazing!

• There are more nerve cells in the human brain than stars in the Milky Way.
• Your brain's wrinkles may be ugly, but they're efficient. They pack more nerve cells into your skull.
• Information comes into the brain in pieces. It is also stored in pieces. Your brain stores colors separately from numbers, for instance.

Pathfinder

• How do you remember that a skunk is a skunk and not a cat? Find out on pages 20–21.
• What connects your ear to your brain? Go to pages 24–25.
• Your brain uses 10 times as much energy as any other body part. Learn how energy-rich blood reaches the brain on pages 56–57.

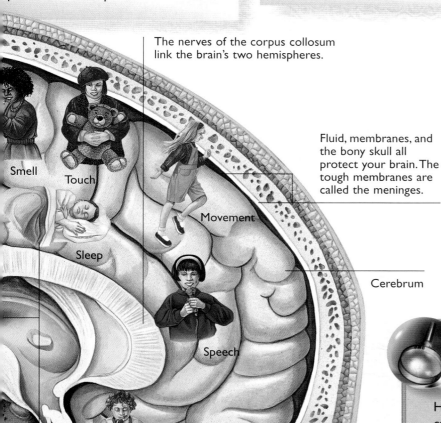

The nerves of the corpus collosum link the brain's two hemispheres.

Smell

Touch

Sleep

Movement

Fluid, membranes, and the bony skull all protect your brain. The tough membranes are called the meninges.

Speech

Cerebrum

Taste

The pineal gland controls sleep.

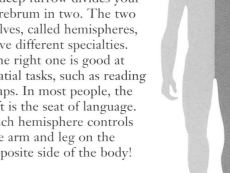

TWO FOR ONE

A deep furrow divides your cerebrum in two. The two halves, called hemispheres, have different specialties. The right one is good at spatial tasks, such as reading maps. In most people, the left is the seat of language. Each hemisphere controls the arm and leg on the opposite side of the body!

INSIDE STORY

Windows on the Brain

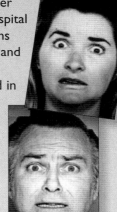

Frightened

Have you ever wondered why most adults can control reactions to emotions better than kids can? Scientists at McLean Hospital may have the answer. They showed teens and adults these pictures of frightened and worried faces. Then the scientists used brain imaging to record what happened in the brain as their subjects looked at the pictures. They found a difference. In teens, one of the brain's emotion centers responded more than the reasoning center. In adults, the opposite was true. The younger the teen, the greater the difference. Imaging studies like this help us understand how the brain develops.

Worried

NATURAL PAINKILLERS

Severe injury often causes no pain at first. That's because the brain makes its own painkillers. But these work only for a while. Pain is important. It forces you to rest the parts that hurt, which helps healing.

NERVE BLOCKS

Pain medicines work in the brain. Some keep pain signals from getting through. They block the places on nerve cells that usually receive messages of pain. Others lessen reactions, such as swelling, that cause pain.

The Thinking Brain

YOUR BRAIN IS doing something amazing right now. It's reading about itself. Your dog's brain can't do that. Your cat's brain can't do it. And certainly your pet guppy's can't, either.

The human brain is like no other. It can admire the stars and imagine life on other planets. It can design spaceships and thrill as they hurtle toward the moon. It owes these remarkable abilities to the cerebrum. This walnutlike mass of nerve cells is more developed in humans than in any other animal. It is the largest part of your brain. It transforms the rush of information from your senses into thoughts, hopes, and feelings. It makes you who you are.

Both genes and experience shape your brain. Genes lay down the basic road map, the connections between nerve cells. But experience determines which "roads" get used and which don't. When you practice your bassoon or read a nightly story with your parent, some connections strengthen. As you learn new facts or skills, new connections form. You lose connections you do not use. This process continues throughout life. But scientists don't yet know what changes in the brain's cells to strengthen connections. Perhaps your cerebrum will someday figure it out.

EMOTION AND LEARNING

Emotion is the glue that makes learning stick. You may love baseball but hate math. If so, chances are you learn batting statistics more easily than times tables. Your pleasure helps you remember. Many parts of the brain play a role in this learning. The limbic system (parts of which are shown in yellow) and prefrontal area (in pink) are important ones. The limbic system is the group of brain areas in which emotions form. Emotions are combined with thoughts in the prefrontal area.

HANDS ON

Shaping Memory

A

Glance at the shapes to the left (A). Now glance at those below left (B). You'll most likely remember the bottom ones longer. Here's why: You have two types of memory. Working memory lasts a minute or so. It lets you remember a message to give your brother, for instance. Long-term memory is your brain's hard disk. What it records can last a lifetime. To enter long-term memory, however, an experience needs to be repeated and linked to other, similar items. The house shape has more staying power because it's familiar.

B

ACCIDENTAL KNOWLEDGE
Ouch! A rod damaged poor Phineas Gage's frontal lobe, changing his personality. From this accident, scientists learned that the frontal lobes help control emotion.

WHEN THE BRAIN BREAKS

Illness can damage the brain areas involved in thinking and feeling. These mental illnesses often change a person's behavior and personality. Most cannot be cured, but many can be treated.

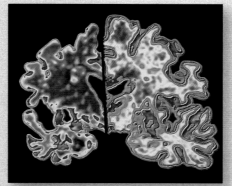

CHANGING PICTURES
People once thought mental illness was "all in the head." But it isn't. It's as real as a broken ankle or chicken pox. The brain scan on the left is from a person with Alzheimer's disease. The one on the right from a healthy person. The Alzheimer's brain is much smaller because the disease kills brain cells. Images like these are helping scientists see how the brain changes during mental illness. New knowledge will lead to better treatments.

Word Builders

Cerebrum is the Latin word for "brain." **Cerebellum** is Latin for "little brain." The word cerebral comes from the Latin, too. It means "of or relating to the brain." **Cerebral** also means "relating to the intellect." When you puzzle through a tough problem, you're being cerebral, or intellectual. You're putting your cerebrum to good use.

That's Amazing!

• Babies who are badly neglected have brains that are 20–30 percent smaller than those who are well cared for.
• Words shape the brain. The more an infant hears each day, the more likely he or she will learn well later on.
• Children who learn two languages from birth store them in the same brain center. When someone learns a second language later on, however, the brain stores it separately.

Pathfinder

• One nerve fiber connects your brain to every two eye muscles. What else can you learn about how the eye works? Go to pages 22–23.
• Brain cells die as you get older. Can you keep learning without them? Find out on pages 32–33.
• Your brain helps you decide what to eat and when to eat. Then a different "brain" in the digestive system takes over. If you want to know more, turn to pages 50–51.

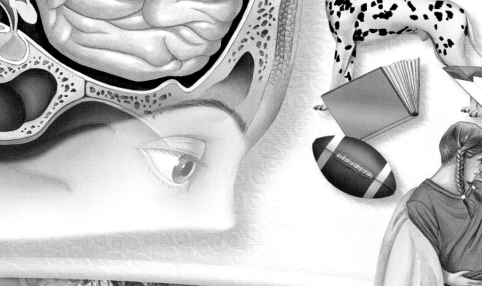

INSIDE STORY

Famous Mind

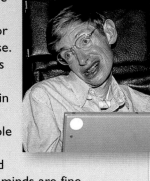

Not all brain diseases damage the mind. Stephen Hawking has ALS, or Lou Gehrig's disease. This disease attacks nerve cells connecting the brain to the spinal cord. Like Hawking, people with ALS have trouble walking and speaking. But their minds are fine. Hawking, one of the greatest physicists ever, has done most of his work since becoming ill.

I KNEW IT!
People can't read minds, but we do get "hunches," or gut feelings. Our brains seem to know something before we do. Scientists suspect this is because our brains remember experiences and emotions we only think we've forgotten.

COMMON ILLNESS
The most common mental illness is depression. It drains happiness, hope, and laughter from life. But many people with this disease lead successful lives. Abraham Lincoln was one.

DIFFERENT BRAINS
Some victims of crime or war cannot forget these terrible events. The memories invade without warning. Others have had similar experiences but don't have the same problem. Scans show that the brains of these two groups are different.

The Eyes Have It

YOUR EYES GLANCE up to watch a bird. They dart right and left as you cross a street. They adjust automatically to the dim light of dusk and the bright light of the summer sun. They focus on objects near and far. Protected within their bony perch, your eyes are always on the move, feeding your curious brain.

Light bounces off every object in your sight. Your eyes gather and focus this light. They then transform it into millions of nerve signals. These hurtle down the optic nerve to your brain at 248 miles (400 km) an hour. When your brain interprets the messages, you see.

The world you see and the one your eyes record are not identical. The back of your eyeball, which is called the retina, is covered with light-sensing cells called rods and cones. Rods detect movement and let you see in dim light. Cones provide clear, sharp, color vision. The cones cluster together in the macula, which is the center of your retina. Only this part of your eye records detailed images. Your brain fills in the rest from memory. Though your eyes focus light, your brain makes sense of what your eyes record. Can't find your math book even though you're staring right at it? Your brain, not your eyes, is at fault.

NATURE'S LAUNDRY
Each blink sweeps cleansing tears across your eyes. These tears contain germ-fighting chemicals. They form in the tear, or lacrimal, glands above your eye and wash out through tear ducts into your nose.

NO GYM NEEDED
Your eyes get a constant workout. Six muscles move each eyeball every time you shift your gaze. Other muscles adjust the lens and pupil. These are always on the move to keep your world in focus.

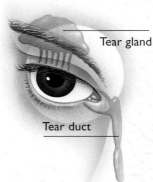

Tear gland

Tear duct

HOW WE SEE
Light bends as it passes through the cornea. It then enters the pupil and hits the lens. The lens thins to focus far-off objects and thickens for close-up ones. Then the lens projects an upside-down image on the retina, which changes the image into nerve signals. Your brain reads the signals and shows you the world right side up.

INSIDE STORY
Windows on the Soul

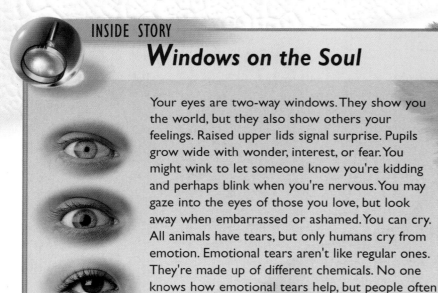

Your eyes are two-way windows. They show you the world, but they also show others your feelings. Raised upper lids signal surprise. Pupils grow wide with wonder, interest, or fear. You might wink to let someone know you're kidding and perhaps blink when you're nervous. You may gaze into the eyes of those you love, but look away when embarrassed or ashamed. You can cry. All animals have tears, but only humans cry from emotion. Emotional tears aren't like regular ones. They're made up of different chemicals. No one knows how emotional tears help, but people often feel better after a good cry.

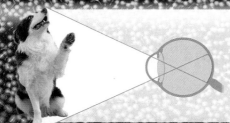

NORMAL VISION
When the lens focuses light directly on the retina, a person can see clearly. Genes, illness, and aging can interfere with normal vision.

NEARSIGHTED
The shape of some people's eyes makes light focus in front of their retina. Objects far away look blurry.

Word Builders

• The **iris**, which is the colored part of the eye, gets its name from the ancient Greek rainbow goddess, Iris.
• The gel that gives the eye its shape is called **vitreous humor** because it is clear. Vitreous comes from the Latin word *vireus*, which means "glassy."
• A protective membrane lines the eyelid, then covers the eyeball. It is called the **conjunctiva**, from the Latin word *conjunctus*, which means "joined."

That's Amazing!

• The spot on the retina where nerves meet has no light-sensing cells. It's your blind spot.
• Your fingerprints have 40 features that are unique to you. But your iris has 266. It's the perfect ID. Will eye scans someday eye-dentify you?
• You can't see for one-half hour a day. Why? You're blinking!

Pathfinder

• You inherit eye color from your parents. How does this work? Find out on pages 14–15.
• Eye color comes from a pigment called melanin. So does skin color. For more on melanin, turn to pages 36–37.
• Someone who is blind must rely on other senses. Hearing, especially, becomes very strong. Take a look at ears on pages 24–25.

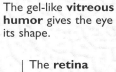

The gel-like **vitreous humor** gives the eye its shape.

The clear **cornea** helps focus light.

The **retina** converts the image into nerve signals.

Blood vessels in the **choroid** feed the retina.

The **optic nerve** connects the eye and the brain.

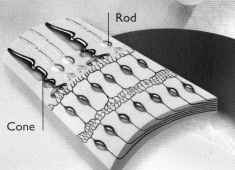

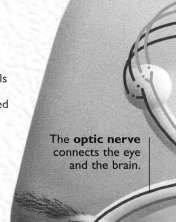

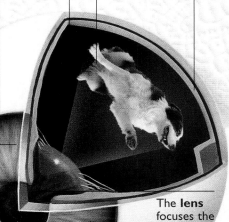

The **lens** focuses the image.

Light enters through the dark opening of the **pupil**.

The **sclera** is the tough white coating of the eyeball.

The **iris muscle** controls how much light gets in.

Rod

Cone

HANDS ON

Eye Can't Believe It!

Your eyes are in different positions, so they record slightly different images. Your brain combines these to create a single image with depth. See how this works. Hold a tube to your right eye. Place your left hand as shown. Look straight ahead. One eye sees your hand. The other sees the hole. What does your brain see? A hole in your hand!

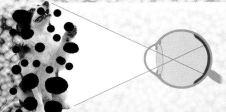

SEEING COLOR

The three types of cone cells in your retina detect red, blue, and green. Light stimulates different combinations of these cones to produce all the colors you see. In some people, one type of cone cell is missing or faulty. The person can't see that color. We say that he or she is colorblind.

FARSIGHTED

As people age, the eye's lens stiffens, and it cannot focus on close objects. Light falls behind the retina, causing close objects to look blurry.

DIABETIC BLINDNESS

Diabetes can damage blood vessels in the retina. The damaged parts can't send messages to the brain. This can be treated.

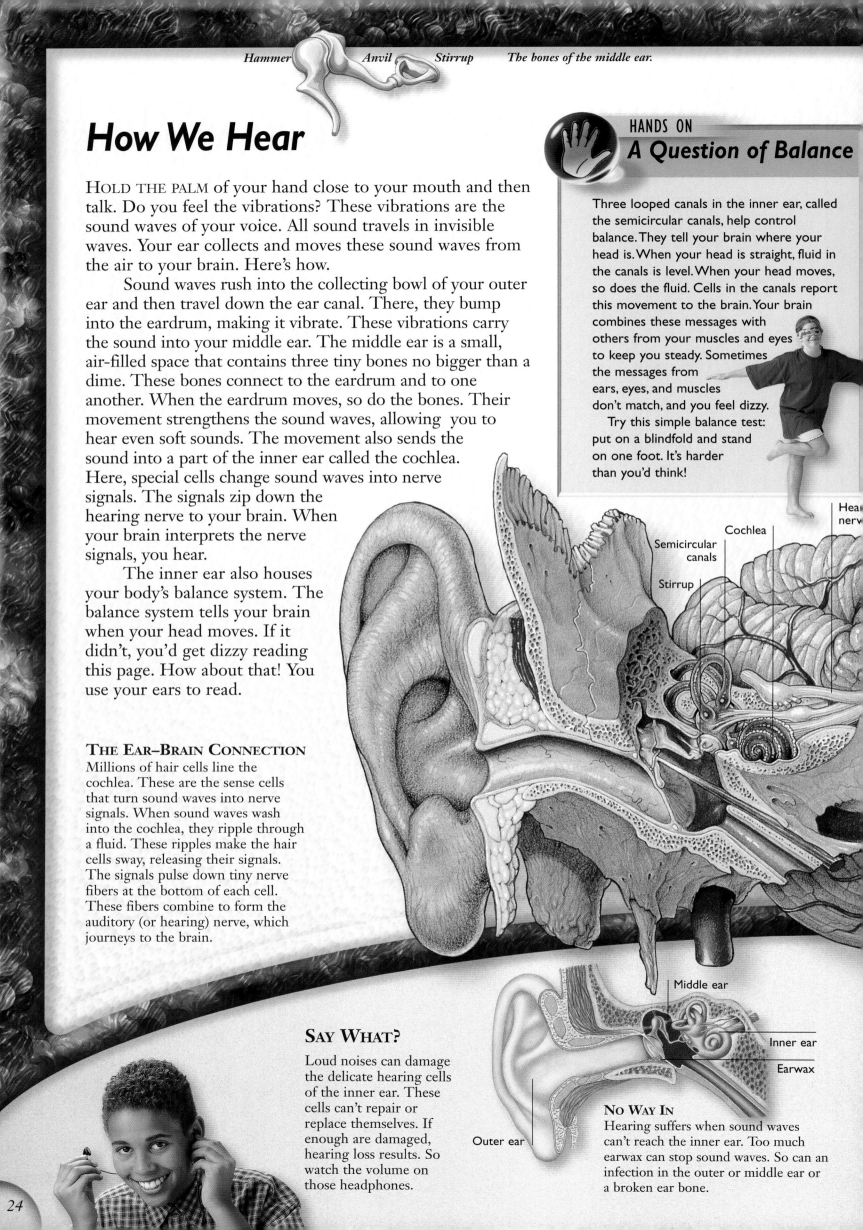

Hammer　　*Anvil*　　*Stirrup*　　The bones of the middle ear.

How We Hear

HOLD THE PALM of your hand close to your mouth and then talk. Do you feel the vibrations? These vibrations are the sound waves of your voice. All sound travels in invisible waves. Your ear collects and moves these sound waves from the air to your brain. Here's how.

Sound waves rush into the collecting bowl of your outer ear and then travel down the ear canal. There, they bump into the eardrum, making it vibrate. These vibrations carry the sound into your middle ear. The middle ear is a small, air-filled space that contains three tiny bones no bigger than a dime. These bones connect to the eardrum and to one another. When the eardrum moves, so do the bones. Their movement strengthens the sound waves, allowing you to hear even soft sounds. The movement also sends the sound into a part of the inner ear called the cochlea. Here, special cells change sound waves into nerve signals. The signals zip down the hearing nerve to your brain. When your brain interprets the nerve signals, you hear.

The inner ear also houses your body's balance system. The balance system tells your brain when your head moves. If it didn't, you'd get dizzy reading this page. How about that! You use your ears to read.

THE EAR–BRAIN CONNECTION

Millions of hair cells line the cochlea. These are the sense cells that turn sound waves into nerve signals. When sound waves wash into the cochlea, they ripple through a fluid. These ripples make the hair cells sway, releasing their signals. The signals pulse down tiny nerve fibers at the bottom of each cell. These fibers combine to form the auditory (or hearing) nerve, which journeys to the brain.

HANDS ON
A Question of Balance

Three looped canals in the inner ear, called the semicircular canals, help control balance. They tell your brain where your head is. When your head is straight, fluid in the canals is level. When your head moves, so does the fluid. Cells in the canals report this movement to the brain. Your brain combines these messages with others from your muscles and eyes to keep you steady. Sometimes the messages from ears, eyes, and muscles don't match, and you feel dizzy.

Try this simple balance test: put on a blindfold and stand on one foot. It's harder than you'd think!

Hea
nerv

Cochlea

Semicircular
canals

Stirrup

Middle ear

Inner ear

Earwax

Outer ear

SAY WHAT?

Loud noises can damage the delicate hearing cells of the inner ear. These cells can't repair or replace themselves. If enough are damaged, hearing loss results. So watch the volume on those headphones.

NO WAY IN

Hearing suffers when sound waves can't reach the inner ear. Too much earwax can stop sound waves. So can an infection in the outer or middle ear or a broken ear bone.

Word Builders

• The word **cochlea** means "snail" in Latin. Take a look at the shape of the cochlea to see how the part got its name.
• The **eustachian tube** was named after the Italian anatomist Bartolomeo Eustachio. He published studies of the ear in the 1560s. He described the tube better than anyone before him.

That's Amazing!

• Sound waves in the air travel 1 mile (1.6 km) in five seconds.
• Tiny glands in your ear canals make wax. The sticky wax traps dust and germs, protecting your ear.
• Your voice sounds different on a tape recorder because the sound reaches you only through the air. When you talk, some of the sound travels through the bones of your skull.

Pathfinder

• The ear's eustachian tube leads to the throat. Where does the throat lead? Find out on pages 28–29.
• The bones in the ear are the smallest in the body. Where are the longest bones in your body? Go to pages 42–43.
• A mucous membrane lines your middle ear. What does mucus do for you? Turn to pages 26–27.

Hear, Fido

Dogs and many other mammals have wide, flattened ear flaps to pick up a large variety of sounds. They can "prick" their outer ears, moving them to catch sound waves. Our outer ears cannot move. They are shaped to capture passing sound waves. Shape isn't the only difference between dog and human ears. A dog's hearing is sharper. We can't hear many of the high, squeaky sounds or low, rumbling ones that Fido can.

Restoring Hearing

People who can't hear very much, or can't hear at all, can be helped by a device called a cochlear implant. A microphone and speech processor are worn behind the ear. They pick up sounds and turn them into electrical signals. These signals pass through the skin to a part of the device that is implanted inside the inner ear. The implant sends the signals on to the brain.

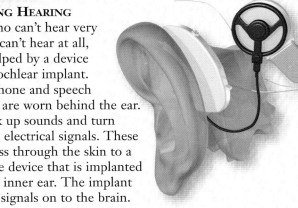

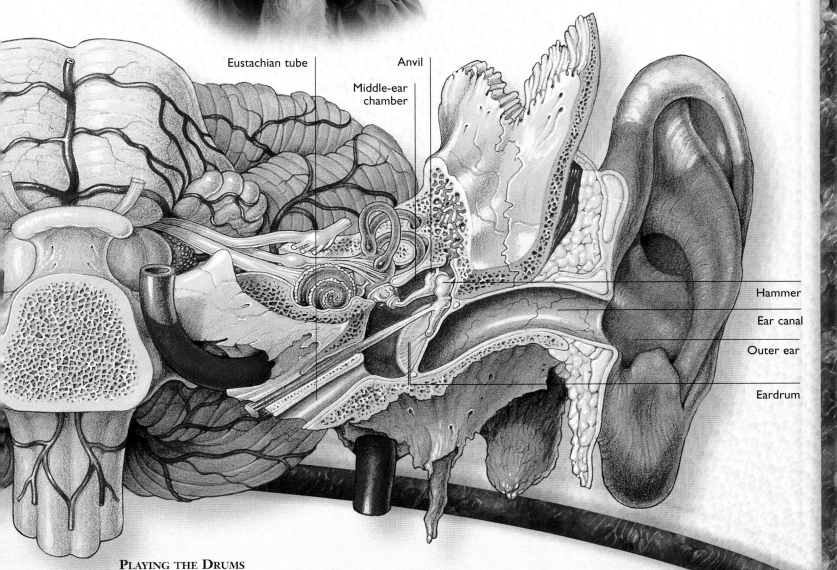

Eustachian tube

Anvil

Middle-ear chamber

Hammer

Ear canal

Outer ear

Eardrum

Playing the Drums

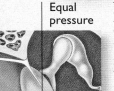

Equal pressure

Air inside the ear canal pushes against the eardrum. At the same time, air inside the middle ear pushes back. When the pressure on both sides is the same, the eardrum works normally. It vibrates, passing sound from the outer to the middle ear.

Bad Vibrations

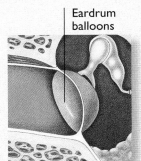

Eardrum balloons

The eustachian tube lets air from the nose into the middle ear. If the tube can't open, the pressure of air in the middle ear is no longer the same as in the ear canal. The eardrum suddenly balloons. Ouch! It can't work well and you can't hear properly.

Relief!

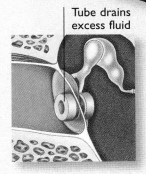

Tube drains excess fluid

During a middle ear infection, fluid presses against the eardrum. It hurts. Doctors can insert tiny tubes to drain the fluid.

The Nose Knows

WANT TO KNOW about mucus and nose hairs? Before you say "Gross!" and turn the page, consider this. Without mucus, you couldn't enjoy the scent of a rose. And without nose hairs, objects like dust, pollen, and tiny flying things would skitter right up your nose.

Your nose has two important jobs. It cleans and warms the air you breathe. It also brings you life's odors—foul and fair. Your nose is well made for these tasks. It sticks out from your face to take in air. It has blood vessels inside to warm the air passing through. It is protected by bone up high, but it has flexible cartilage at the tip. The cartilage lets you widen your nostrils to breathe more deeply.

Your nose filters enough air each day to fill 500 balloons! Nose hairs allow air in but keep debris out. Bits of pollen or dirt small enough to sneak by can trigger a sneeze. Otherwise they suffer the same fate as germs, which mucus inside your nose traps and helps destroy. Mucus also dissolves scent molecules so that you can smell. It saves you from chugging sour milk or wearing yesterday's socks. So now you know about mucus and nose hairs. S'not as bad as you thought, was it?

INSIDE STORY

Ah-ah-ah-choooo!

Dust mites are just one of the unwelcome visitors that can make you sneeze. They're microscopic animals that live in dust (this one's enlarged so you can see it). If mites irritate your mucous membrane, nerve cells there sound an alarm. Your brain's breathing center responds. It signals the lungs. They fill with air. *Ah-ah-ah....* Then the air passages close. Pressure builds up until— *chooo!* Air explodes from your lungs with hurricane force, taking mites and mucus with it.

HANDS ON
Yum! Smells Good

If you love chocolate, thank your nose! Much of what you experience as taste is really smell. The same molecules in food trigger both senses. But your nose is at least 20,000 times more sensitive than your tongue. Find out for yourself.

❶ Hold your nose while you eat a piece of chocolate. You'll taste the candy's sweetness but not its flavor. Now do the same while chewing an apple and then a carrot. Can you tell the difference between the two?

❷ To make a taste stronger, breathe out through your nose after swallowing. When you breathe out, odor molecules travel a back alley from your mouth to the smell area in your nose.

SMELLS WELCOME
Your smell cells occupy two patches about the size of raisins, high in your nose. They stretch hairlike cilia through the mucous membrane to detect smells. Smell cells can pick up about 1,000 different odors.

HOW WE SMELL
Flowers, dogs, spinach, people—all of these things give off different scent molecules. The scent molecules travel through the air into your nose. At the top of your nose, under the bridge, they bump into smell cells. Odors from spinach will turn on one set of smell cells. Odors from dogs or people will turn on others. The turned-on cells send messages to one of your olfactory bulbs. These are two button-sized clumps of nerve cells just above the smell receptors. They relay messages between nose and brain. Your brain combines thousands of scent messages into a single smell, then compares this odor with those already on file. Mmm! Get a whiff of that rose.

SMELLY BUSINESS
Few smells please, or displease, all people all of the time. A person's genes and upbringing influence what smells good or bad. So does experience. A sanitation worker might not even notice garbage smells that others think are foul.

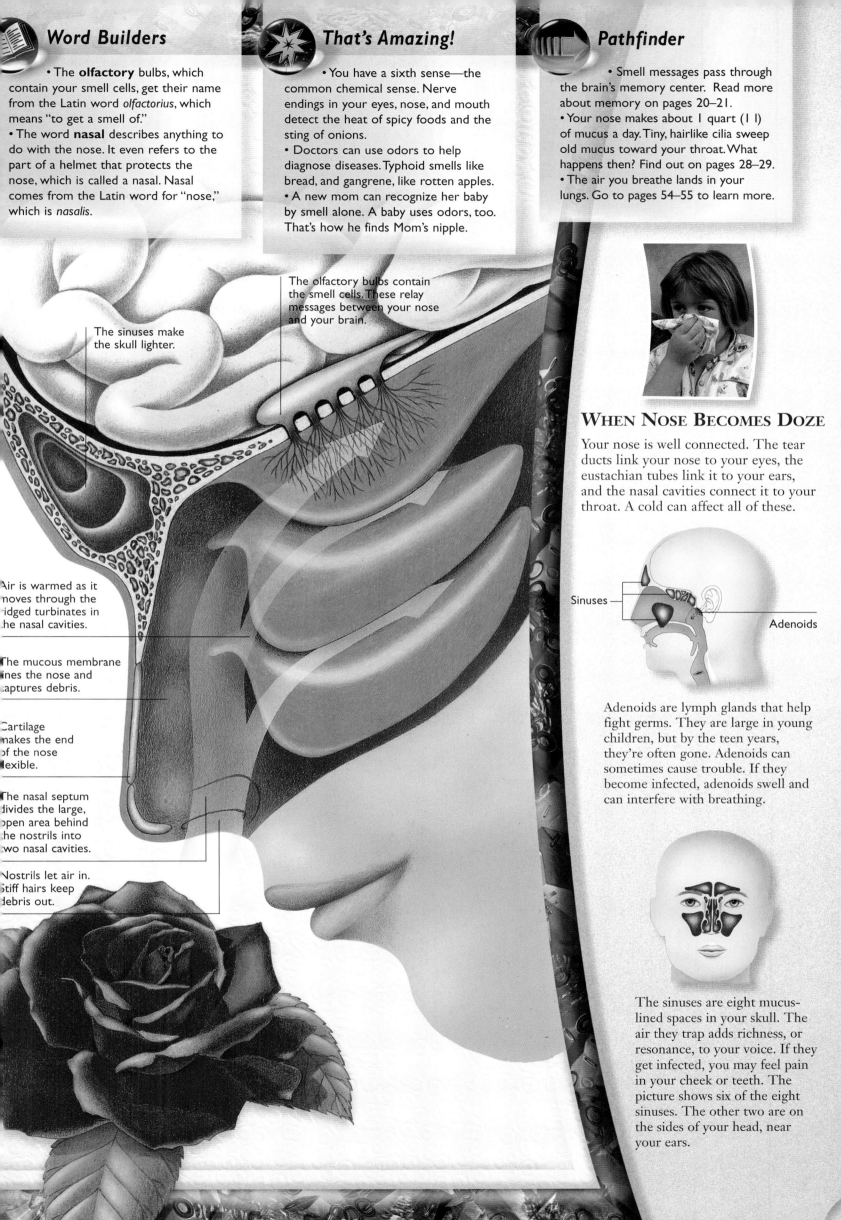

Word Builders

- The **olfactory** bulbs, which contain your smell cells, get their name from the Latin word *olfactorius*, which means "to get a smell of."
- The word **nasal** describes anything to do with the nose. It even refers to the part of a helmet that protects the nose, which is called a nasal. Nasal comes from the Latin word for "nose," which is *nasalis*.

That's Amazing!

- You have a sixth sense—the common chemical sense. Nerve endings in your eyes, nose, and mouth detect the heat of spicy foods and the sting of onions.
- Doctors can use odors to help diagnose diseases. Typhoid smells like bread, and gangrene, like rotten apples.
- A new mom can recognize her baby by smell alone. A baby uses odors, too. That's how he finds Mom's nipple.

Pathfinder

- Smell messages pass through the brain's memory center. Read more about memory on pages 20–21.
- Your nose makes about 1 quart (1 l) of mucus a day. Tiny, hairlike cilia sweep old mucus toward your throat. What happens then? Find out on pages 28–29.
- The air you breathe lands in your lungs. Go to pages 54–55 to learn more.

The sinuses make the skull lighter.

The olfactory bulbs contain the smell cells. These relay messages between your nose and your brain.

Air is warmed as it moves through the ridged turbinates in the nasal cavities.

The mucous membrane lines the nose and captures debris.

Cartilage makes the end of the nose flexible.

The nasal septum divides the large, open area behind the nostrils into two nasal cavities.

Nostrils let air in. Stiff hairs keep debris out.

WHEN NOSE BECOMES DOZE

Your nose is well connected. The tear ducts link your nose to your eyes, the eustachian tubes link it to your ears, and the nasal cavities connect it to your throat. A cold can affect all of these.

Sinuses

Adenoids

Adenoids are lymph glands that help fight germs. They are large in young children, but by the teen years, they're often gone. Adenoids can sometimes cause trouble. If they become infected, adenoids swell and can interfere with breathing.

The sinuses are eight mucus-lined spaces in your skull. The air they trap adds richness, or resonance, to your voice. If they get infected, you may feel pain in your cheek or teeth. The picture shows six of the eight sinuses. The other two are on the sides of your head, near your ears.

These are the organs of the throat. If infected, tonsils and adenoids can be removed.

 Tonsils Adenoids Uvula

Down the Hatch

YOUR TONGUE IS hairy. That's not an insult. It's a fact. Millions of microscopic "gustatory hairs" cover your tongue. These aren't real hairs. They're tips of taste cells, which cluster in onion-shaped bunches called taste buds. Your taste buds are too small to see. But stick out your tongue and you'll see a landscape of bumps called papillae. These house your taste buds as well as the nerve endings that scream "Hot!" when you attack a pizza.

While your tongue's out, look around your mouth. The tissue dangling from the back of your throat is your uvula. It closes the nasal passage when you swallow. The dark tube beyond the uvula is your pharynx, or throat. Food and air start their downward journey there. Lift your tongue to see your frenulum. This membrane anchors your tongue.

Your teeth and palate are more familiar. Your teeth cut and mash food. They mix it with saliva to form a bolus, the glob you swallow. Your tongue, lips, and cheek muscles push the bolus along your palate. From there, it slides into your throat. Together, your mouth and throat support some of your body's most vital and enjoyable functions. They let you breathe, eat, speak, and savor a bite of pizza.

INSIDE STORY
How We Speak

Your lips aren't all that move when you speak. Your vocal cords do, too. The vocal cords are two springy bands at the opening of your larynx, or voice box. They form a V. Air from your lungs flows through this opening. When you breathe, the V is open. When you speak, it narrows. Air causes the vocal cords to vibrate, creating sound. The more forceful the air, the louder the sound.

Larynx

Vocal cord

Although vocal cords produce sound, the mouth creates speech. Your teeth, tongue, and lips shape raw sounds into consonants and vowels. Air spaces in your skull give your voice its own unique tone.

You can feel your larynx at the very top of your throat. It is made up of nine cartilages. The biggest of these is the thoracic cartilage, or Adam's apple. Your vocal cords attach to the Adam's apple and to the smaller cartilages behind it.

HANDS ON
Gulp!

Your body has a life-saving trapdoor. It's a flap of cartilage above your windpipe called the epiglottis. When you swallow, the epiglottis swings shut, closing the windpipe so no food gets in. Place your fingers on your throat. The ridges you feel are your air passage. Now swallow. The saliva goes down your food tube, or esophagus, which lies behind the windpipe. The esophagus is a muscled tube. When you swallow, the muscles tighten and relax, sending food or saliva downward.

Epiglottis open

Epiglottis shut

PUCKER UP
Call them smoochers, smackers, or just plain lips—but you wouldn't want to be without them. You use your lips to eat, to seal your mouth closed while you chew, and to shape sounds so you can speak. Just try talking with them closed. Your lips are also the body's most sensitive thermometer. They detect food that's too hot or cold. And do you want to whistle or kiss? Well, pucker up!

THE MIGHTY TONGUE
Your tongue is a mighty and mobile muscle. It licks, lifts, and darts as it forms sounds, moves food, or teases your brother. It also springs up to guard your throat against objects that could choke you.

SAY "AHHH"
A peek at your throat reveals lots about your health. But your doctor must first get your tongue out of the way. Then the doctor can spot infection in your throat or tonsils. With a special tool called a laryngoscope, he or she can check your voice box, too. Tonsil infections are most common in childhood.

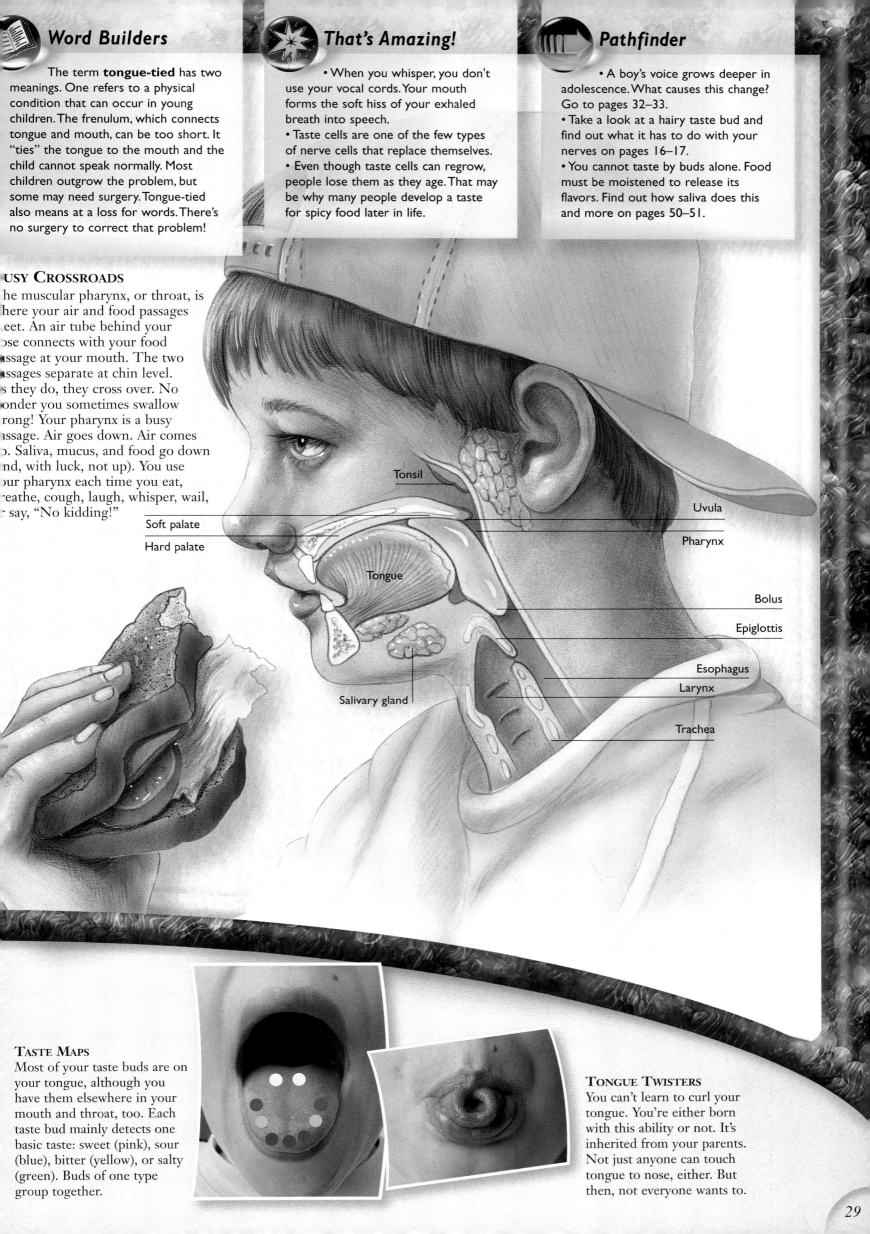

Word Builders

The term **tongue-tied** has two meanings. One refers to a physical condition that can occur in young children. The frenulum, which connects tongue and mouth, can be too short. It "ties" the tongue to the mouth and the child cannot speak normally. Most children outgrow the problem, but some may need surgery. Tongue-tied also means at a loss for words. There's no surgery to correct that problem!

That's Amazing!

• When you whisper, you don't use your vocal cords. Your mouth forms the soft hiss of your exhaled breath into speech.
• Taste cells are one of the few types of nerve cells that replace themselves.
• Even though taste cells can regrow, people lose them as they age. That may be why many people develop a taste for spicy food later in life.

Pathfinder

• A boy's voice grows deeper in adolescence. What causes this change? Go to pages 32–33.
• Take a look at a hairy taste bud and find out what it has to do with your nerves on pages 16–17.
• You cannot taste by buds alone. Food must be moistened to release its flavors. Find out how saliva does this and more on pages 50–51.

Busy Crossroads

The muscular pharynx, or throat, is where your air and food passages meet. An air tube behind your nose connects with your food passage at your mouth. The two passages separate at chin level. As they do, they cross over. No wonder you sometimes swallow wrong! Your pharynx is a busy passage. Air goes down. Air comes up. Saliva, mucus, and food go down (and, with luck, not up). You use your pharynx each time you eat, breathe, cough, laugh, whisper, wail, or say, "No kidding!"

Tonsil

Uvula

Pharynx

Soft palate

Hard palate

Tongue

Bolus

Epiglottis

Esophagus

Larynx

Salivary gland

Trachea

Taste Maps

Most of your taste buds are on your tongue, although you have them elsewhere in your mouth and throat, too. Each taste bud mainly detects one basic taste: sweet (pink), sour (blue), bitter (yellow), or salty (green). Buds of one type group together.

Tongue Twisters

You can't learn to curl your tongue. You're either born with this ability or not. It's inherited from your parents. Not just anyone can touch tongue to nose, either. But then, not everyone wants to.

Chemical Messengers

YOU CAN IMPRESS the next adult who says, "My, how you've grown." Just answer, "Yes. It's my hormones." Hormones are chemical messengers. Along with your nervous system, they keep your body in balance. They aid digestion and adjust body temperature. They help keep blood pressure steady. Hormones also regulate growth and reproduction. A boy's voice deepens. A girl's breasts grow. A woman's ovary releases an egg. You grow an inch. Hormones are at work.

Some hormones form in organs called endocrine glands. Others form in body tissues, such as the stomach or heart. Most of these hormones travel through your bloodstream to other body parts. Once they reach their targets, they cause changes. You feel the results when you get hungry, thirsty, or tired, for instance. When you eat, drink, or sleep, you bring your body back in balance.

A part of your brain called the hypothalamus monitors many hormones. If it detects too much of one, it alerts your pituitary gland. The pituitary sends a message to the gland that makes that hormone: Slow down! It does. If levels drop too low, the brain nudges the pituitary again and the cycle repeats. Your brain and hormones work together to keep your body running.

Chief controller, the **hypothalamus**.

The **pituitary** controls other glands and regulates growth.

The **thyroid** influences growth and energy.

The **thymus** makes a hormone that influences the body's defenses.

The **adrenals** make adrenaline and regulate the balance of water and salt.

The **pancreas** makes insulin, hormone that helps control blood sugar.

The **testes** in men and **ovaries** in women make sex hormones.

IN CONTROL
Seven main glands control many of the activities that keep your body running da in and day out.

INSIDE STORY
Life-Saving Hormones

This girl is saving her own life. She has a disease called type 1 diabetes and is giving herself a shot of insulin. Without this daily treatment, she would die. Insulin is made in the pancreas. It helps the body turn blood sugar into energy. People with type 1 diabetes don't make any insulin. That's why they need daily shots. This disease runs in families and starts in childhood. Another type of diabetes, type 2, usually develops late in life. People with type 2 diabetes make insulin, but their bodies can't use it properly.

A FRIENDSHIP HORMONE?
Might a hormone make you want to be with other people? Maybe. Just as one hormone readies the body to fight, so another helps it relax. This hormone is called oxytocin. It causes changes in a new mother's body that helps her to be calm and let her nurse her baby. But all people, not just nursing mothers, have oxytocin in their bodies. Some scientists think the hormone is at work when you feel like being with other people.

DAILY MESSAGES
Are you feeling hungry? Tired? Do you have a cut that is healing or a bug bite that's swelling? Hormones and other chemical messengers play a role in each of these everyday experiences.

HUNGER
At least three hormones curb appetite. One of these, urocortin, may shut off hunger during times of stress.

CLOTTING
Blood platelets, a type of blood cell, make a chemical messenger that helps blood clot. It's called thromboxane. It causes the platelets to stick together.

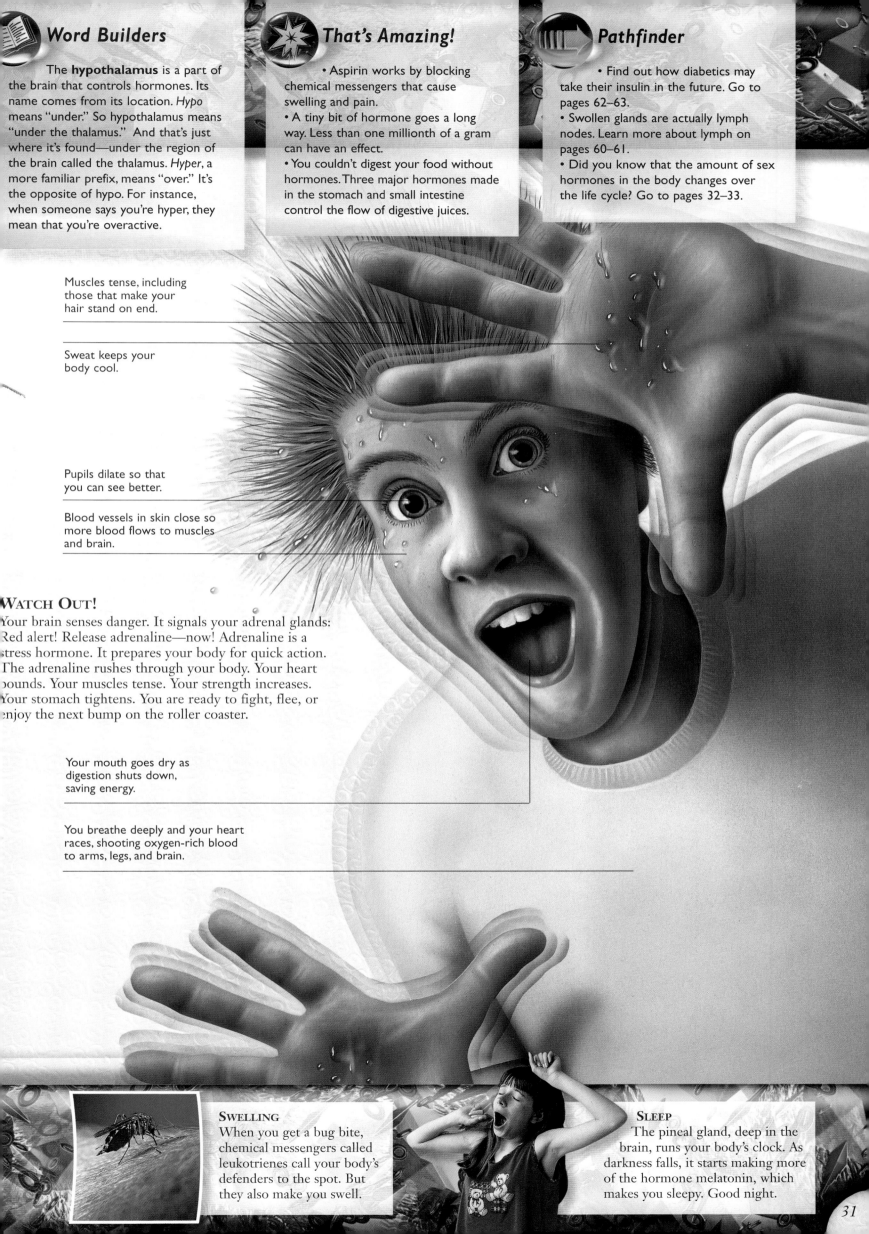

Word Builders

The **hypothalamus** is a part of the brain that controls hormones. Its name comes from its location. *Hypo* means "under." So hypothalamus means "under the thalamus." And that's just where it's found—under the region of the brain called the thalamus. *Hyper*, a more familiar prefix, means "over." It's the opposite of hypo. For instance, when someone says you're hyper, they mean that you're overactive.

That's Amazing!

• Aspirin works by blocking chemical messengers that cause swelling and pain.
• A tiny bit of hormone goes a long way. Less than one millionth of a gram can have an effect.
• You couldn't digest your food without hormones. Three major hormones made in the stomach and small intestine control the flow of digestive juices.

Pathfinder

• Find out how diabetics may take their insulin in the future. Go to pages 62–63.
• Swollen glands are actually lymph nodes. Learn more about lymph on pages 60–61.
• Did you know that the amount of sex hormones in the body changes over the life cycle? Go to pages 32–33.

Muscles tense, including those that make your hair stand on end.

Sweat keeps your body cool.

Pupils dilate so that you can see better.

Blood vessels in skin close so more blood flows to muscles and brain.

WATCH OUT!

Your brain senses danger. It signals your adrenal glands: Red alert! Release adrenaline—now! Adrenaline is a stress hormone. It prepares your body for quick action. The adrenaline rushes through your body. Your heart pounds. Your muscles tense. Your strength increases. Your stomach tightens. You are ready to fight, flee, or enjoy the next bump on the roller coaster.

Your mouth goes dry as digestion shuts down, saving energy.

You breathe deeply and your heart races, shooting oxygen-rich blood to arms, legs, and brain.

SWELLING
When you get a bug bite, chemical messengers called leukotrienes call your body's defenders to the spot. But they also make you swell.

SLEEP
The pineal gland, deep in the brain, runs your body's clock. As darkness falls, it starts making more of the hormone melatonin, which makes you sleepy. Good night.

The Cycle of Life

HAVE YOU SEEN a photo of your mother or your father at your age? It's hard to imagine that they were once that young. It's even harder to imagine that some day you will be as old as they are now. Yet you will. Life's stages unfold for us all.

Look at how far you've come already. When you were born, your foot was no longer than your mother's thumb. Your fist was no bigger than your father's nose. A year or so later you could walk. You could toddle to your toys, find a crayon, and scribble. But you could not yet draw. Or talk. Or catch a ball. These accomplishments awaited a later stage of childhood.

As tiny as you were, the instructions for your growth were inside you already. They were encoded in your genes. Genes direct the growth of cells and the flow of hormones that bring each human life from conception to death. Along the way, each person passes through known stages. These stages, the life cycle, are the same for everyone. But not everyone lives them with the same health and vigor. The choices you make and the experiences you have influence how you grow and age. What happens when the cycle ends? That's a mystery to us all.

CYCLING ON

Our bodies change throughout the life cycle. When we're young, we see that change in outgrown jeans and T-shirts. The changes are less obvious in early adulthood. But over time, our cells become less efficient. Levels of hormones and brain chemicals drop. We age. We die. Death is sad for the person, but it is necessary. Earth would be too crowded if we lived forever.

HANDS ON
My Family/Myself

You can trace the cycle of life within your own family by making a photographic time line. Can you find pictures of your relatives as babies? How about graduating high school or getting married? Look at how each person has changed. Then talk to your relatives about the changes they've experienced. How did they feel about those changes? What do they do to stay healthy? Your family can help you understand the stages that await you.

Word Builders

Life span means the amount of time between birth and death. Scientists believe that the maximum life span for humans is 120 years. The oldest person on record died at 122. The average is much shorter, however. A child born in the United States today can expect to live to be about 76.

That's Amazing!

• We need less sleep as we get older. A newborn baby sleeps about 20 hours a day. An 80-year-old may sleep as little as five hours a day.
• You grow more during the first year of life than at any other time.

Pathfinder

• You can't control your bladder when you are a baby. Learn why on pages 52–53.
• See pages 36–37 to find out what causes your skin to wrinkle as you age.
• Will scientists be able to make humans live longer? Find out on pages 62–63.

LIFE PRESERVERS
Science can help life along at both ends of the life cycle. Doctors can combine egg and sperm outside the womb, creating a life that otherwise would not have been. They are also able to replace damaged body parts with new ones, such as this plastic heart valve.

THE GROWTH FILES

The truth is out there. You're going to grow up. How will it happen? When will it happen? Read on.

COMING OF AGE
Girls become women and boys become men because of sex hormones. At around age 10 or 11 in girls and 12 or 13 in boys, sex hormones start flowing. Girls develop breasts and broader hips. They begin to menstruate. Boys' voices deepen. They grow facial hair. This stage of development is called puberty. By the end of it, both males and females are able to have children.

GROWING UP
Growth hormone brings you to your full height. It strengthens your muscles and bones. Your body makes growth hormone throughout life, but it makes less as you get older.

MAKING A DIFFERENCE
Identical twins, such as these boys, have identical genes. These genes will influence their growth in many ways. They may influence how tall the boys become, when they reach puberty, and even how long they live. Some diseases, such as heart disease, run in families. So does long life. Genes aren't everything, however. Healthy habits help people avoid disease and live longer. One of these twins may outlive his brother if he takes better care of his mental and physical health. People often live longer when they are close to others, have a positive outlook on life, and keep their minds active.

The Framework

WHAT HAS 206 BONES, more than 650 muscles, and enough skin to cover a small dining-room table? Why, your body of course. Skin, muscles, and bones give your body its shape and appearance. But that's not all they do. Skin protects you. Muscles move you. Bones shelter the soft inner parts of your body. How does each work? Read on.

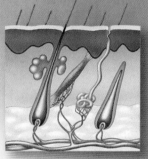

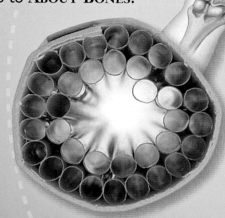

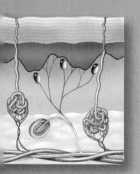

Skin Deep

TAKE A LOOK at your hand. In three weeks, the skin you see will be dust. A new batch will have grown to take its place. Your skin constantly renews itself. It must. You shed some each time you wash, dress, run, walk, scratch, clap, or turn over in bed. Even tickling takes its toll. But skin is tough. It's built to take the abuse.

Skin is the body's largest organ. Its main job is to keep good stuff in and bad stuff out. It is both waterproof and germproof. Skin also controls body temperature and absorbs sunlight you need to make vitamin D, which is essential for strong bones and teeth. And, of course, skin gives you your sense of touch.

You feel what you touch because skin is rich in nerve endings. The nerve endings are your body's alarm system. They sense hot and cold, pressure and pain. They warn that the bath is too hot or that a bee has just attacked. They crowd your fingers, toes, and lips—the parts of your body you use to test the safety of the world. Touch also brings you pleasure, which is vital for survival, as well. Babies who aren't held and stroked can suffer severe emotional damage. Skin's benefits are more than skin deep.

HANDS ON
Skin's Paintbrush

Your skin gets its color from melanin. This pigment is made in special skin cells. Other skin cells then absorb it, coloring you shades of brown or black, yellow or white. The more melanin you have, the darker your skin. People from hot places, such as Africa, need more melanin. It soaks up the sun's harmful rays, protecting the skin's lower layers.

You can see melanin at work in your own skin. Wear a bandage for a few days. When you remove it, you'll see a change in your skin color. Try this in different seasons.

Cold sensor

Oil gland

Hair follicle

Sweat gland

Fat under skin

HOT SKIN
Heat gets your sweat glands going. Your pores open. The sweat runs out. You cool off as the sweat evaporates. Heat makes blood vessels in your skin expand, too. As blood flows more freely, you turn red.

Word Builders

Some people have no color in their skin, eyes, or hair. They are called **albinos,** from the Latin word *albus,* which means "white." Their bodies don't make melanin, the pigment that colors skin. Scar tissue doesn't have melanin, either. It is made of collagen, not skin cells. Sometimes, one area of skin has more melanin than another. The result is freckles or a mole.

That's Amazing!

• Over your life, you'll shed about 105 pounds (47.6 kg) of skin.
• Humans are the only animals that blush with emotion. Anger or embarrassment can turn your cheeks red.
• The ridges and valleys of your fingertips help you get a good grip. They are uniquely yours. Not even identical twins share the same fingerprints.

Pathfinder

• As we age, the skin's springy fibers become stiff. That's why we wrinkle. Pages 32–33 tell more about aging.
• A substance called keratin makes skin, hair, and nails tough. Find out more on pages 38–39.
• What do your skin and skeleton have in common? The answer is on pages 42–43.

ZIT CITY

Pimples are proof that you can have too much of a good thing. Glands in your skin make an oily substance called sebum. Sebum helps keep skin moist. But too much of it can clog pores, causing pimples.

INSIDE STORY

Healing Skin

Skin repairs itself. But some burns and wounds are so severe the skin just can't make new cells fast enough. In these cases, doctors can sometimes take skin from another part of a patient's body to cover the wound. They can also use artificial skin made from shark cartilage, but the body may reject this. Now, though, they may have a better choice. Scientists can grow human skin in a laboratory. The patient's body accepts this lab-grown skin as its own.

LAYER UPON LAYER

Your skin is constructed like an iced cake. The "cake," the skin's thick lower layer, is the dermis. The thin "icing" is the epidermis. The epidermis constantly makes new skin cells. They form at its base and push their way to the top. Along the way, they become flat and tough. By the time they reach the surface, they're dead. The dermis is made mainly of collagen, the protein that gives skin its spring. Hair shafts, sweat glands, oil glands, and nerve endings fill this layer, too. So do blood vessels that nourish the epidermis.

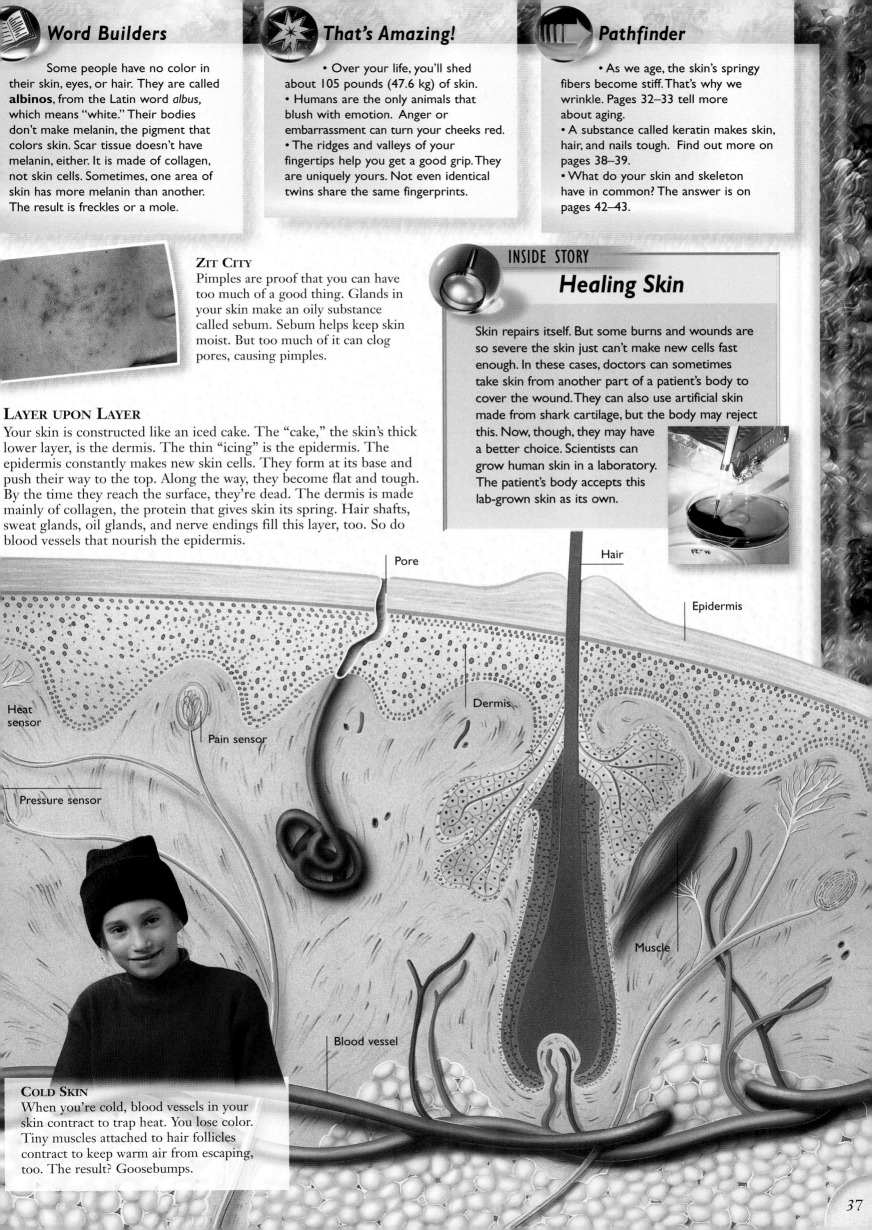

Pore

Hair

Epidermis

Heat sensor

Pain sensor

Dermis

Pressure sensor

Muscle

Blood vessel

COLD SKIN

When you're cold, blood vessels in your skin contract to trap heat. You lose color. Tiny muscles attached to hair follicles contract to keep warm air from escaping, too. The result? Goosebumps.

Straight hair

Wavy hair

Curly hair

Hair and Nails

RUN YOUR FINGERS gently over your cheek. Do you feel the soft, downy hairs? Now check out your stomach or thigh. Can you feel the hairs there, too? Hair covers almost all of your skin. The major exceptions are your lips, palms, and the soles of your feet. What does all this hair do? Let's take it from the top.

The thick mane on your head is a natural sunscreen for your scalp. It absorbs sweat, conserves heat in winter, and softens the occasional blow. Hairs in your nose and ears trap germs. Eyelashes blink away dust. What's more, all hairs are tiny sense organs. Bend one and it triggers a nearby nerve, enhancing your sense of touch.

Although they don't look it, your nails have a lot in common with your hair. Both are dead and toughened with keratin, a protein also found in skin. And like some of your hair, nails protect you by shielding sensitive skin. Have you ever smashed a finger or toe? Imagine how that would feel without a nail.

Genes determine the strength and shape of your nails. They also dictate whether you have curly blonde tresses or straight black ones. But fashion often overrules nature. Since earliest times, humans have changed their hair and nails to express personality and to attract mates. Have you ever changed yours?

HEAD TO TOE

Your hair grows about five inches (12.7 cm) a year. But every two to five years, each follicle takes a rest. It makes no new hair cells for about three months, then starts again.

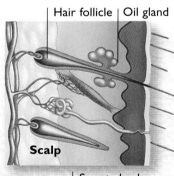

Hair follicle | Oil gland

Scalp

Sweat glands

Armpit

Pain and pressure sensors

Sole of foot

HOW HAIR GROWS

The base of each follicle is shaped like a bulb. Here, new hair cells form constantly. As these new cells press their way up, they drive older, dead cells to the surface. Glands on the side of the follicle coat the growing hair with an oil. This keeps it soft and flexible. Your hair is thicker in some places than others because you have more follicles there. Some places, such as the sole of your foot, have no follicles at all.

HANDS ON

How Fast Do Your Nails Grow?

Your nails never stop growing. Unlike hair, they get no time out. But they grow more slowly than hair. Fingernails grow about 1.5 inches (3.8 cm) a year. Toenails are twice as slow. Just how fast do your nails grow? Find out.

❶ Measure the length of your nails from base to tip once a week. Measure each fingernail and toenail. Ask a parent to do the same.

❷ Plot the results on a growth chart.

What differences can you see? How much faster do your fingernails grow than your toenails? Do the nails on one hand grow faster than those on the other? Whose nails grow faster?

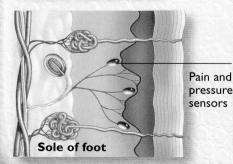

Word Builders

A **follicle** is the tiny pouch deep in your skin from which a hair grows. The word comes from the Latin *folliculus*, which means "little bag." Your follicles influence whether your hair is coarse or fine, curly or straight. The smaller the follicles, the finer the hair. If cells form evenly in the base of the follicle, hair is straight. If they form unevenly, hair is curly.

That's Amazing!

• You shed 50–100 hairs a day.
• By four months, a fine coat of hair covers the fetus. It is called lanugo. Many babies still have this hair at birth.
• Nails grow fastest during early adulthood. Growth is slowest during infancy and old age.
• Tiny mites can live in the follicles of your eyelashes. They feed on the oils in the skin.

Pathfinder

• Hairs in your ear canal trap dust and germs. What else keeps debris out of your ears? Find out on pages 24–25.
• Some hair follicles are present at birth but don't become active until puberty. Learn about puberty on pages 32–33.
• Goosebumps are caused by contractions of the tiny muscles around each hair. For more on muscles, go to pages 40–41.

CANCELED COLOR

Hair gets its color from melanin, the same pigment that colors skin. As people age, their follicles stop making melanin. Hair turns white or gray.

FOLLICLE FALLOUT

Genes influence balding. So do male sex hormones. That's why men go bald more often than women. Hair loss in women is usually less noticeable than in men. Because women's hair generally thins all over, most don't get bald spots.

NAILS TELL TALES

Nails grow from under the skin at their base. The area that makes new nail cells is called the matrix. The skin that covers and protects it is the cuticle. Even small changes in the shape and color of your nails can signal trouble. Liver disease turns the skin under the nail yellow, for instance. Heart disease can make it blue.

The matrix produces new nail cells.

The nail plate is the visible nail.

The cuticle covers and protects the matrix.

The nail plate covers the nail bed.

The white half circle is the lunule.

NASTY NAILS

Heart or lung disease can cause fingers to swell, which makes the nail bulge.

Frequent use of chemicals, such as detergents and hair dyes, can cause nails to curve.

A bang can cause harmless white spots in the nail. White spots *under* the nail may be from a fungus.

Illness can cause nails to grow poorly. The ridges disappear as the nail grows out.

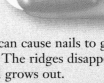

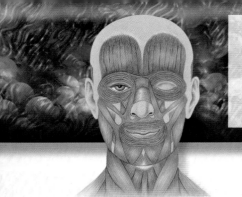

Frown *Surprise* *Smile*

Mighty Muscles

HAS ANYONE EVER told you not to move a muscle? It's impossible to do. You can decide not to tap your foot or wiggle your pinky. But your heart and stomach are muscles, too, and you can't control them.

Muscles are your body's power stations. They convert energy into pulling power. The ones you can control are skeletal muscles. You have about 650 of these. They attach to your bones with tough ropes of tissue called tendons. Skeletal muscles work in pairs to move you. One contracts, or tightens, to pull on a bone. At the same time, its sister muscle relaxes. Then the sister muscle contracts and the first one relaxes. The bone moves back. Whether you're jumping or plucking a guitar, the mechanism is the same.

The muscles you can't control are called smooth muscle because they look smooth under the microscope. Smooth muscle forms the walls of your blood vessels and intestines. It lets your stomach contract to process food. Your most powerful muscle is neither smooth nor skeletal. It's called cardiac muscle. What is it? Your heart.

Blood vessels and nerves feed all your muscles. The blood vessels supply fuel and oxygen. Nerves direct the muscles' actions. Think about this as you use your eye muscles to read on.

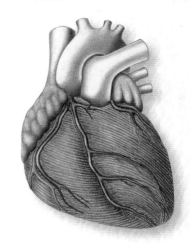

ONE TOUGH MUSCLE
Your tireless heart beats more than 4,500 times each hour. Its muscle is unique. The cells look striped, like skeletal muscle, yet you can't control it.

MUSCLE MAPS
Have you used your gluteus maximus lately? You have if you've stood up. How about your rectus abdominus? It gets a workout every time you cough. Look at the muscle maps below to find these and other major muscles. The maps can't show all your muscles. Each hand alone has 37. You even have muscles inside your ears to move tiny ear bones. One of these is the stapedius, your smallest muscle. It looks like a wisp of cotton.

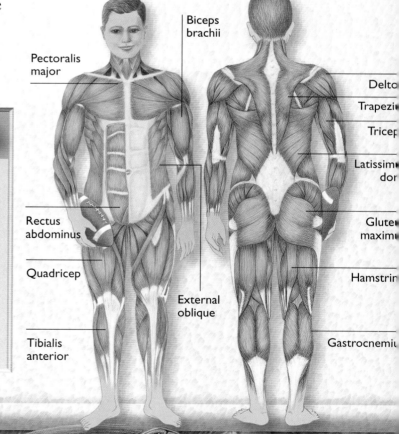

Pectoralis major

Biceps brachii

Delto

Trapezi

Tricep

Latissim dor

Rectus abdominus

Glute maxim

Quadricep

Hamstrin

External oblique

Tibialis anterior

Gastrocnemi

HANDS ON

Tricky Muscles

❶ A tendon attaches each finger to the muscles in your forearm. Place your hand as shown in the picture. Try to lift each of the extended fingers. Can't move your ring finger? That's because its tendon connects with the middle finger's tendon. This limits your ability to move the finger on its own.

❷ While your friend holds it down, try to raise your arm for 30 seconds. What happens when your friend lets go? Your muscle "remembers" that you were trying to lift it.

GETTING DOWN TO DETAIL
Bundles of muscle cells make up each of your muscles. Each muscle cell is, in turn, made up of smaller bundles of fibers called myofibrils. *Myo* means "muscle." Within each myofibril, thin strands of protein surround thick ones. When a muscle contracts, the thick strands pull the thin ones closer together. The cell, and the muscle, shortens. You flex your arm.

Muscle

Muscle cell bundle

Word Builders

When you and your brother fight, you are antagonists. You're enemies. But muscles are called **antagonists** when they work together. This is because they have opposite actions. When one contracts, the other relaxes. **Contract** means "to draw together," or shorten.

That's Amazing!

• Your muscle cells produce enough heat every day to boil almost 2 pints (1 l) of water for an hour.
• When you shiver, your muscles contract involuntarily. This releases energy that keeps your body warm.
• You use your muscles to stand still. Try it. Stand as still as you can. Gravity will make you sway, but your muscles will pull you straight again.

Pathfinder

• Your eye muscles are the most active in the body. To find out more, go to pages 22–23.
• Muscles move bones, but bones also protect muscles. To bone up on bones, turn to pages 42–43.
• Muscle cells are packed with mitochondria, which produce all that muscle energy. Learn more about cells on pages 12–13.

MUSCLE POWER

Muscles you don't use lose strength and size. Those you use a great deal grow strong and big. The repeated stress of swinging a bat or lifting weights, for instance, causes the muscle fibers to thicken. Body builders do special exercises to develop all of their major muscles. But you don't have to look like a body builder to be strong. Regular exercise will keep your muscles fit.

Muscle cell

Myofibril

Protein strands

Protein strands when muscle is relaxed

Protein strands when muscle is contracted

Bone-bending Fashions

Chinese women used to have their feet broken and bound.

Some women from Burma wore neck rings that stretched vertebrae.

Western women wore corset that squished lower ribs.

About Bones

YOUR BONES ARE so strong that just a small piece of one can support the weight of an elephant. A lot of bone supports *your* weight and protects your delicate insides. Your skull bones form a natural helmet for your brain. Ribs create a cage around your heart, liver, and lungs. The pelvis cradles your lower organs. The vertebrae of your spine encircle your spinal cord. While your bones are standing guard, they are also making your blood cells and storing minerals for the body's use.

Bone has three busy layers. A thin outer layer called the periosteum wraps around a hard shell called compact bone. Compact bone looks solid, but it isn't. The bone grows in circles around hollow canals. Blood vessels in these canals deliver food and oxygen to the bone cells. Beneath the shell of compact bone is a spongy web of minerals and marrow. The bone marrow is where blood cells are made.

Throughout life, bone makes and remakes itself. One type of bone cell constantly breaks old bone down while another builds new bone up. Hormones play a role in this process but so do your activities. As you move around each day, the push of gravity and the pull of muscles stimulate new bone growth. Strong muscles make strong bones.

HANDS ON
Build a Bone

Bone is so hard that surgeons must cut it with a saw. But it is also light because of air pockets in the core. Make a model bone using stiff paper, tape, scissors, and drinking straws. Then test its strength.

❶ Cut a piece of stiff paper 5.5 inches (14 cm) wide and the length of a straw.

❷ Using double-sided tape, line the paper with two layers of straws. Roll the paper into a tube with straws on the inside. Tape it firmly shut with regular tape.

❸ Stand your "bone" upright on a table. Now press hard with your hands or a book. How strong is your bone?

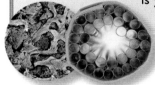

Real bone   Straw bone

SEE THROUGH ME
You have twice as many bones as a giraffe—and as most other mammals. The reason? Your hands and feet. Together, they contain more than half of your 206 bones. That's why they are so flexible. Bones tell a lot about a person. Even thousands of years after death, they reveal secrets of a person's health, lifestyle, height, and sex.

INSIDE STORY
A Glow in the Dark

On November 8, 1895, German scientist Wilhelm Roentgen was working with electricity when he discovered a new kind of light. It passed through paper, books, and tin. It made skin invisible and lit up the bones beneath. Roentgen stayed in his lab for the next two months, experimenting with this light he called an "X-ray." He found that he could take photos with X-rays, capturing images of the inside of the body. Within months, doctors around the world were using X-rays to diagnose broken bones and other problems.

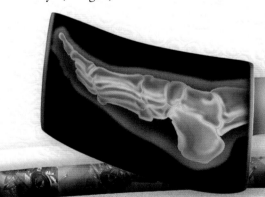

BROKEN BONES

Sticks and stones don't usually break bones, but falls and accidents do. A break in a bone is called a fracture. Doctors X-ray a fracture to see the amount and type of damage. Then they set the bone, making sure the broken pieces line up. The bone would heal without help, but it might not grow straight and strong. A cast keeps the bone still and in place while it heals.

BAD BREAKS
In a simple fracture, the bone breaks but the skin doesn't. In a compound fracture, the bone pierces the skin. This can be a more serious injury because germs can enter and infect the fractured bone.

Word Builders

• Doctors don't know whether bones cause **growing pains**, but they do know that growing doesn't. Children grow most during their first three years and in their teens, but they don't get growing pains then.
• Your **funny bone** is misnamed, too. It's really a nerve, not a bone. Its name comes from the nearby upper arm bone, the humerus. Get it?

That's Amazing!

• Bone is the second-hardest substance in your body. Only tooth enamel is harder.
• You don't need a cast for a broken rib. Your chest muscles hold it in place.
• Your bones hold 98 percent of the body's calcium supply. Your body uses these supplies if you don't get enough calcium in your diet. Over time, this can weaken bones.

Pathfinder

• Your bones make your blood cells. Find out more on pages 58–59.
• Learn how bones hold together to form your skeleton. Go to pages 44–45.
• Bone isn't the only body tissue that renews itself all the time. So does skin. Find out more on pages 36–37.

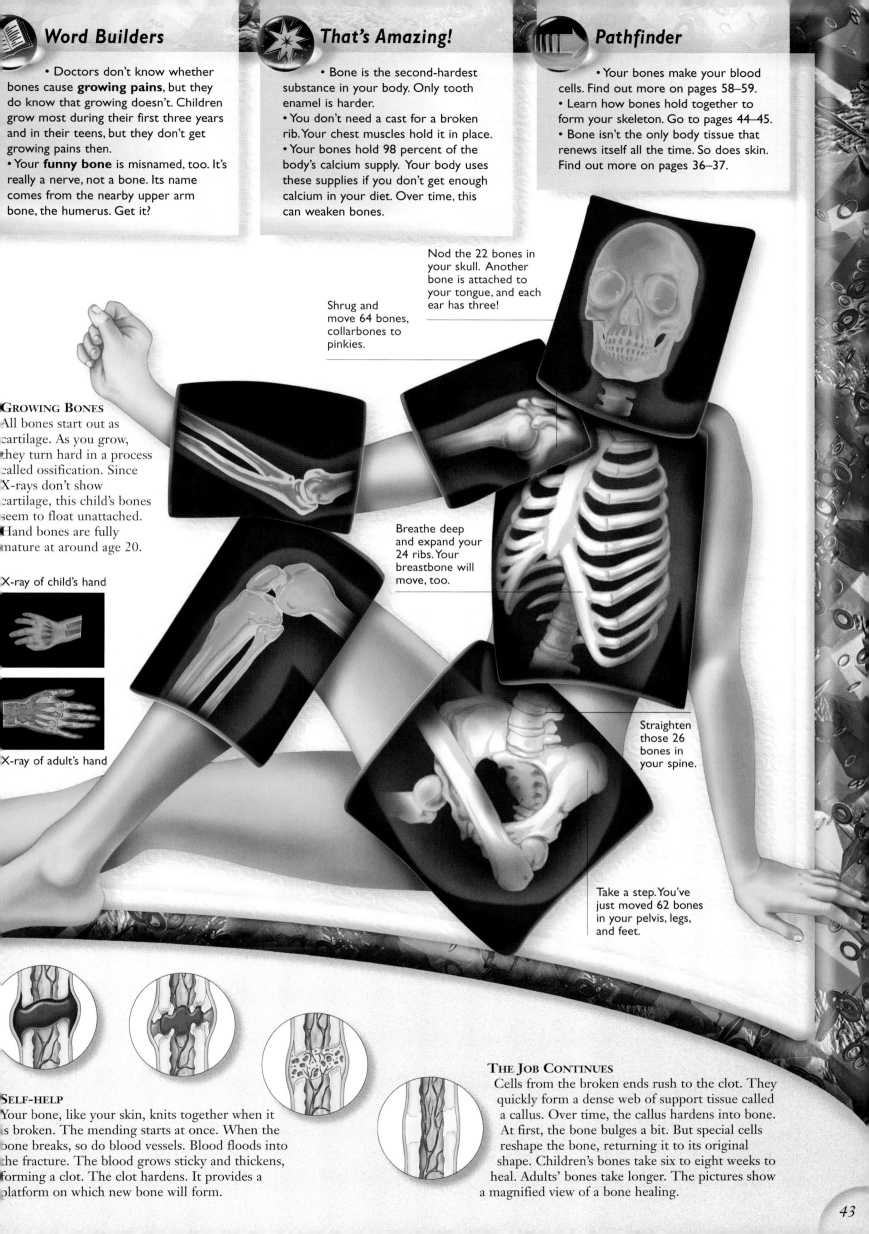

Nod the 22 bones in your skull. Another bone is attached to your tongue, and each ear has three!

Shrug and move 64 bones, collarbones to pinkies.

GROWING BONES
All bones start out as cartilage. As you grow, they turn hard in a process called ossification. Since X-rays don't show cartilage, this child's bones seem to float unattached. Hand bones are fully mature at around age 20.

X-ray of child's hand

X-ray of adult's hand

Breathe deep and expand your 24 ribs. Your breastbone will move, too.

Straighten those 26 bones in your spine.

Take a step. You've just moved 62 bones in your pelvis, legs, and feet.

SELF-HELP
Your bone, like your skin, knits together when it is broken. The mending starts at once. When the bone breaks, so do blood vessels. Blood floods into the fracture. The blood grows sticky and thickens, forming a clot. The clot hardens. It provides a platform on which new bone will form.

THE JOB CONTINUES
Cells from the broken ends rush to the clot. They quickly form a dense web of support tissue called a callus. Over time, the callus hardens into bone. At first, the bone bulges a bit. But special cells reshape the bone, returning it to its original shape. Children's bones take six to eight weeks to heal. Adults' bones take longer. The pictures show a magnified view of a bone healing.

Arm straight   *Bicep muscle relaxed*   *Arm bent*   *Bicep muscle contracted*

On the Move

TRY A FRANKENSTEIN walk. Hold your legs stiff and take a few steps. Now try running that way. You can't get very far or go very fast. What if your arm was a single bone? Could you scratch your back? Bring an ice cream cone to your mouth? And imagine a spine as straight and stiff as a ruler. You couldn't look over your shoulder or touch your toes, let alone ride a skateboard.

Your skeleton is cleverly constructed. It lets you bend, twist, and twirl. It protects your insides and supports as much as five times its own weight in muscles and organs. This sturdy frame is shaped differently in men and women. A woman's wide pelvis allows room for a baby to grow. A man's broad shoulder bones support his heavier muscles.

Bones can't bend, but you need to. Because of joints you can. A joint is where two bones meet. Your joints let bones move only in certain directions and prevent them from moving the wrong way. Some joints let bones move only up and down, while others let them swivel. Joints wouldn't work, however, without muscles. Tendons anchor muscle to bone. When the muscle contracts, it moves the bone in the joint. Your knees bend. Your arms extend for balance. You ride that skateboard.

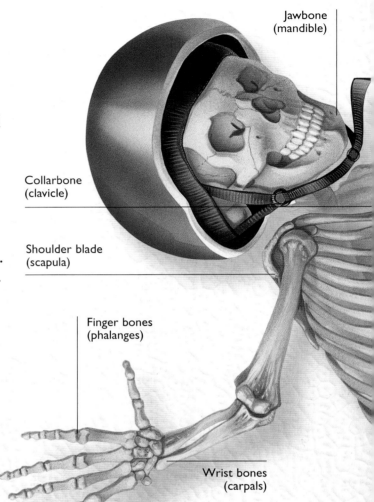

Jawbone (mandible)

Collarbone (clavicle)

Shoulder blade (scapula)

Finger bones (phalanges)

Wrist bones (carpals)

HANDS ON
Straight Talk About Spines

Your spine is your body's central support. It transfers the weight of your upper body to your pelvis and legs. When you stand straight, your weight is evenly distributed along your spine. When you slouch, the weight strains one part of your spine.

❶ Be aware of your body. Balance a book on your head and walk. Your head is high and your shoulders are slightly back. This is back-healthy posture.

❷ Keep your spine straight and your knees bent when you lift things. That way, your strong legs—not your spine— will absorb the extra load.

Pivot joint
Swivel your head. Pivot joints like the one in your neck let bones rotate.

Word Builders

Collagen is your body's glue. Its name comes from the ancient Greek *kolla*, which means "glue," and *gen*, which means "something that causes." Collagen is the main ingredient in the special tissues that hold your body together. These are called connective tissues. They are found throughout your body. Ligaments and tendons are connective tissues. So, too, are your bones, which form the frame that supports the rest of you.

That's Amazing!

• No one is really double-jointed. Some people simply have limber ligaments.
• Sensors in your joints tell your brain if the joint is bent. Your brain combines this information about your movement and position with messages from your senses to help you keep your balance.

Pathfinder

• What joints are the most active in the body? Find out on pages 46–47.
• Cartilage doesn't naturally replace itself. But scientists may be able to make it grow. Find out how on pages 62–63.
• Your skeleton protects your brain and spinal cord—the central nervous system. Learn about the nervous system on pages 16–17.

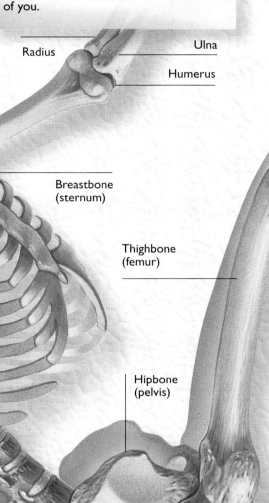

Radius

Ulna

Humerus

Breastbone (sternum)

Thighbone (femur)

Hipbone (pelvis)

Tailbone (coccyx)

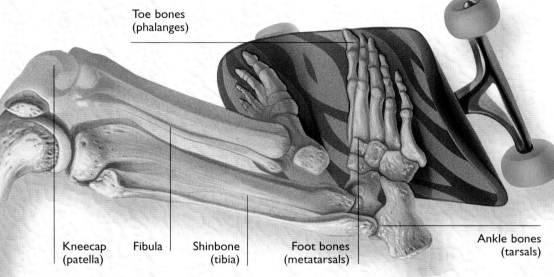

Toe bones (phalanges)

Kneecap (patella)

Fibula

Shinbone (tibia)

Foot bones (metatarsals)

Ankle bones (tarsals)

WIPEOUT!

Fortunately, a wipeout on your skateboard rarely wipes out your bones. That's because your skeleton is a natural shock absorber. The force of a fall radiates through the bone to the joint. There, cartilage and fluid absorb some of the shock. A bent elbow or knee, or the springlike curve of the spine, also softens the blow. Bones can still break, of course, especially if hit straight on.

Saddle joint
Thumbs up! A saddle joint, like the one in your thumb, gives movement two ways—up and down and across.

Ball-and-socket joint
Swing your arms. Ball-and-socket joints in your shoulders and hips let bones move all around.

Hinge joint
Flex your arm. Thanks to a hinge joint, your elbow bends up and down. Find other hinge joints.

INSIDE STORY

Where Bones Meet

Joints that move are built for a lifetime of action, with padding to protect bones from wearing out. Smooth cartilage coats the ends of each bone. Slippery synovial fluid moistens the joint and lessens friction. Tough, flexible ligaments lash the joint together and keep it from moving too much. In some joints, such as those of the spine, cushiony disks of cartilage separate the bones. All these parts work together. It's truly a joint effort.

Ligaments

Cartilage

Fluid

Talking Teeth

TAP YOUR FRONT teeth. You've just touched the hardest substance in your body. Your teeth are built to last. Over an average life, they will tear, chomp, grind, and mash some 30,000 tons of food. That's about 240 million hamburgers. Your chomping, grinding teeth begin the process of digestion. But that's not all they do. Teeth are a rigid gate, protecting the rest of your mouth from blows. They help shape speech from the sounds your vocal cords produce. And, of course, they contribute to appearance. Imagine a smile without any teeth.

Your teeth started forming before you were born. All 20 baby teeth and many of your adult teeth were present as tiny buds under the gums. They grew slowly, pushing into the open as your jaw developed. They are growing still. A child's jaw isn't big enough for adult teeth, which is why you get two sets.

Whether a tooth belongs to a baby or an adult, it is made of hard, shock-absorbing dentin. A layer of even harder enamel protects the dentin above the gum. Bonelike cementum covers the root. Nerves and blood vessels run through the tooth's soft core, the pulp. A sling of ligaments connects each tooth to your bony jaw. Together, ligaments and bone hold your teeth firmly in place. That should give you something to smile about.

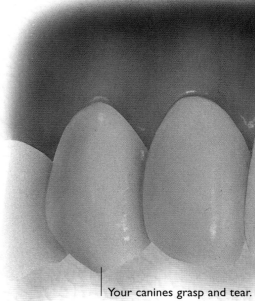

Your canines grasp and tear.

IN THE PINK
Gums cover and protect the bone that anchors teeth. If infected, the gums pull away from the teeth. Germs can move in and attack bone, loosening teeth. You can tell that gums are healthy when they are pink.

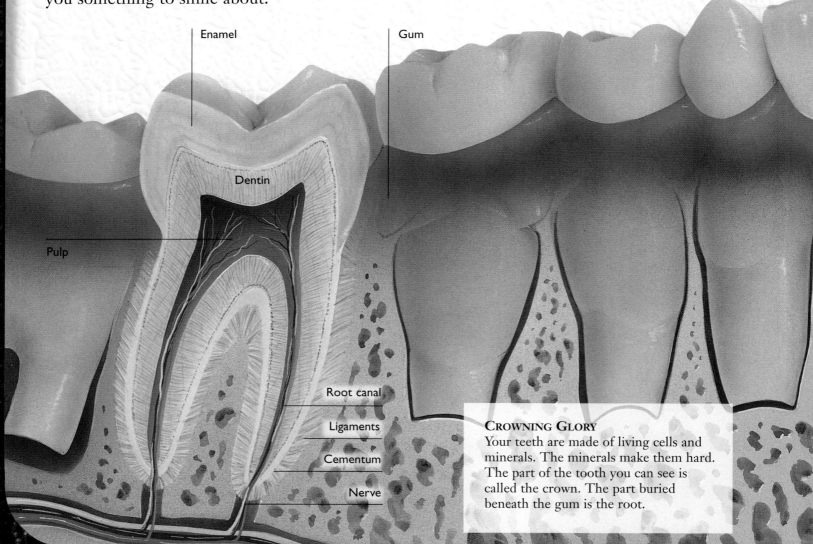

Enamel

Gum

Dentin

Pulp

Root canal

Ligaments

Cementum

Nerve

CROWNING GLORY
Your teeth are made of living cells and minerals. The minerals make them hard. The part of the tooth you can see is called the crown. The part buried beneath the gum is the root.

Word Builders

A thin slime of bacteria, mucus, and food debris constantly forms on teeth. It's called **plaque.** Brushing removes plaque. If plaque isn't removed, it hardens into tartar. The tartar can build up between the tooth and gum. This leaves pockets through which bacteria can reach and destroy bone. This condition is called gum disease, and it is the main reason people lose teeth.

That's Amazing!

• Tooth enamel is the second-hardest natural substance in the world. Only diamonds are harder.
• Saliva is a natural mouthwash. It kills bacteria. You produce enough saliva in your lifetime to fill a swimming pool.
• The backs of your front teeth are shaped like shovels so they can help move food into the mouth.

Pathfinder

• Your teeth start the process of digestion. Find out how it ends on pages 50–51.
• Your jaw joints are the most active in the body. You use them every time you smile, yawn, chew, or talk. Learn about other joints on pages 44–45.
• Without saliva, you couldn't taste your food. Find out why on pages 28–29.

Bite in with those incisors.

CHOMP!

When you chomp down on an apple, your top and bottom teeth should line up correctly. If they don't, it's hard to keep your teeth clean and healthy. You may also have trouble chewing or even speaking well. Braces can correct such problems.

INSIDE STORY

The Great Stain Mystery

These teeth were strange. They had stains as dark as chocolate. Stranger still, they had no decay. What was going on? A young dentist named Frederick McKay first asked this question in 1901. He had opened an office in Colorado Springs, Colorado, U.S.A. Many of his patients had this unusual staining. For 30 years, McKay tried to find out why. He finally found the answer in the water. The local water had lots of a chemical called fluoride. When children drank the water, the fluoride stained their teeth, but it also protected them from decay. Only tiny amounts of fluoride are needed to protect teeth. Today, it's added to toothpaste, mouthwash, and drinking water in many areas.

THE TOOTH EATERS

Most bacteria will brush right off your teeth, but some get trapped in tiny pits and grooves. These bacteria make acid that eats through the enamel. You get tooth decay.

Premolars hold and crush food.

Molars grind food to mush.

BRUSH THOSE TEETH

Baby teeth are good for more than money from the tooth fairy. They hold places for the adult teeth below. Without baby teeth as a guide, adult teeth would grow in crooked and crowded. So take good care of those baby whites.

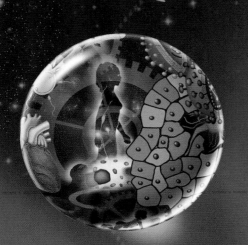

Supplies and Demand

BEFORE YOU HAD fingers, toes, eyes, or ears, you had a heart. It beat when you'd been in your mother's womb for just three weeks. It helped move life-giving oxygen and nutrients through your body. Before birth, these vital supplies came from your mother. Where do they come from now? What happens as your body uses them? What else moves through your blood? Turn the page.

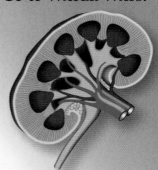

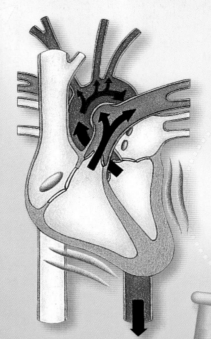
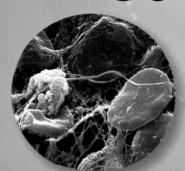

BUGS IN THE SYSTEM
Good bacteria live in your gut and help digest
food. The bugs and bacteria shown here can live
and breed in the digestive tract, too. But these
are harmful. They can make people sick.

Hookworm eggs   *Tapeworm*   *E. coli*

Digestion Alley

BURPS AND STOMACH growls may embarrass you. But they
signal that food is on the move. Your digestive system
squeezes food through 30 feet (9 m) of twisting, turning
tubes. This process begins the moment you sink your
teeth into a juicy sandwich. It ends 15 to 48 hours later.
In that time, churning muscles and powerful chemicals,
called enzymes, break the food into smaller and smaller
pieces. Your liver, gall bladder, and pancreas make or
release many of the enzymes.

Digestion breaks food into nutrients and wastes.
Wastes leave your body as feces and urine. Nutrients
seep into your blood. Some help build and repair cells.
Others get stored or burned for energy. You use energy
every time you tie a shoe, run a mile, breathe, sleep,
eat, think, or even digest your food.

Two sets of nerves help control digestion. One
links your gut and brain. These nerves can slow or
speed digestion depending on the body's needs. But
your gut also has a "brain" of its own. Nerves line your
entire digestive tract. They go into action when food
stretches the walls of the digestive organs. They control
the flow of enzymes and food with little help from above.
Now that's food for thought.

Esophagus

Bolus

Liver

Stomach

Pancreas

Gall bladder

Large
intestine

Small
intestine

Appendix

Rectum

Anus

INSIDE STORY

Ace in the Hole

In 1822, on Makinac Island in Michigan, U.S.A., a gunshot
wounded a young man named Alexis St. Martin. The wound healed,
but it left a hole into St. Martin's stomach. With the hole covered,
St. Martin could eat normally. With it open, his doctor, William
Beaumont, could study digestion up close. Dr. Beaumont
tied bits of meat, cabbage, and bread to a
string and placed them into the hole. He
pulled out the string from time to time
to see what was happening to the food.
Through this work, Beaumont discovered
digestive enzymes, the chemicals that
break down food.

ENERGY FROM FOOD
You need energy to read, to run—even to
breathe. Digestion releases this energy from
food. Your genes influence how quickly you
burn the energy. So do the things you do. The
more active you are, the more energy you use.

Word Builders

If you've ever washed a greasy pot with detergent, you know how your body digests fat. Your liver makes a "detergent" called **bile,** which dissolves fats in the small intestine. Your gall bladder stores the bile.

That's Amazing!

• The wastes from a meal can take up to five days to leave your body.
• You don't use your appendix. This part of the large intestine may have once broken down fibers in our ancestors' leafy diet.

Pathfinder

• Your stomach makes its own hormones to aid digestion. Learn more on pages 30–31.
• Your large intestine rids the body of solid wastes. How do you get rid of liquid wastes? Find out on pages 52–53.
• Your liver is a multipurpose organ. It makes sugar for energy, stores vitamins and minerals, and cleans your blood. Learn more on pages 58–59.

FOOD PROCESSOR

Two sets of powerful muscles form the walls of your digestive tract. Inner rings of muscle push food along. The pulsing, twisting outer muscles mash the food. Mucous glands, nerves, and blood vessels line the whole digestive tract. Mucous aids the food's passage and protects the stomach from its own acids. The glands make enzymes and hormones to break food down. Together, hormones and nerves control digestion.

A BUMPY RIDE

Three sets of crisscrossed muscles give your stomach its churning power. Its inner surface is folded and pitted. The folds flatten to make room for food. The tiny gastric pits squirt out enzymes and germ-killing acid. Food doesn't stand a chance.

Saliva and teeth transform the sandwich into mush, called a bolus.

Seconds later, a swallow sends the bolus hurtling down the esophagus, your food tube, to your stomach.

Your stomach churns. For three hours, it mashes the bolus with digestive juices, turning it into soupy chyme.

Chyme passes into the small intestine, which breaks it into nutrients and wastes. The nutrients seep through the intestine wall.

Blood carries the nutrients to the liver, which turns some into sugar for energy and stores others.

Wastes go into the large intestine, which sucks out the last water and minerals.

As solid waste called feces, this matter leaves the body through the anus.

HANDS ON

Open Wide

❶ Place a small ball inside a stocking. Imagine that the ball is some just-swallowed cheese and the stocking is your digestive tract.

❷ Hold the top of the stocking firmly in one hand. With the other hand, squeeze the stocking just above the ball, moving the ball down. Repeat until the ball reaches the end.

In the same way, the muscular walls of your digestive system contract in waves, moving food along. This is called peristalsis. Next time you take a bite of a sandwich, pay attention to the feeling as the food goes down your throat.

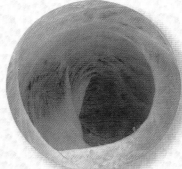

NOT SO SMALL

Your small intestine is small only in diameter. This narrow tube is about 18 feet (5.4 m) long. Thousands of folds and fingerlike villi make its surface even larger. Nutrients trickle through the villi into blood vessels. Blood carries the nutrients through your body.

YOU ARE WHAT YOU EAT

The foods you eat help your body in different ways. Fats give you long-term energy. Carbohydrates and sugars provide quick energy. Vitamins and minerals nourish cells, and proteins help repair them. Your body needs a balance of these.

ENERGY BANKS

Food energy is measured in calories (kilojoules). If you take in more calories than you use, your body stores the extra as fat. Exercise and balanced eating keep your weight healthy.

HARD AS STONE
Salts or minerals in urine can harden into kidney "stones". The stones can be different shapes and sizes, as shown here. Most pass out of the body.

Mulberries　　　　*Kackstones*　　　　*Gravel*

Water Ways

IMAGINE WHAT YOUR house would look like if no one drained the dishwater or took out the trash. Ugh! In no time at all, you'd need to move out. Your body must regularly get rid of wastes, too. If it didn't, you would die. Your kidneys and bladder flush out watery wastes. Along with two tubes called the ureters and another called the urethra, they make up your urinary system.

After your cells grab all the nutrients they need from your digested food, they return wastes to your blood. Blood carries these wastes to your kidneys. The kidneys are your body's recycling center. Each one has a million microscopic filters called nephrons. Each nephron is made up of a knot of tiny blood vessels and a twisted, looped tube. Fluid and wastes pass from the blood vessels into the tube. As they pass through the tube, needed water and chemicals return to the blood. Extra water, salts, and a waste product called urea don't. These become urine. Your kidneys can make more or less urine. In this way, they help keep the chemicals and water in your body balanced.

Urine dribbles from the kidneys into two long, muscled tubes—the ureters. The ureters' walls tighten and relax, pushing urine toward the bladder. The bladder expands. It stores the urine until you decide you've got to go.

Renal medulla
Renal cortex
Renal pelvis
Renal artery
Renal vein

THE KIDNEY
Each fist-sized kidney has three main parts. The outer renal cortex and the inner renal medulla are linked by millions of tiny filtration units. Urine exits through the renal pelvis. "Renal" means kidney.

DRIP, DRI
Your kidneys release urine every 10-15 second
The urine trickles down two thin tubes, calle
ureters, into the bladder. You can see this in th
colored X-ray. When half a cup of urine drip
down, you feel the urge to go. More than tw
cups and you'd better find a bathroom fas

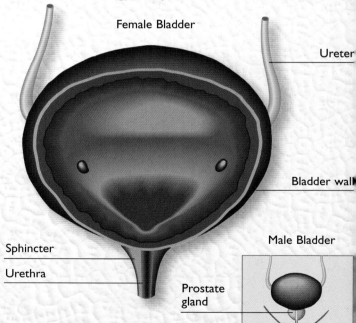

Female Bladder

Ureter

Bladder wal

Sphincter

Urethra

Male Bladder

Prostate gland

THE BLADDER
When your bladder fills with urine, its muscled walls stretch. Nerves sense this stretching and signal your brain that you've got to urinate. The bladder walls tighten. They squeeze the urine out as the sphincter muscles, which usually clamp the bladder shut, open. Urine gushes out the urethra. The bladders shown here are full. When empty, the bladder is the size of a walnut and shaped like a wine glass.

INSIDE STORY
Water World

It may feel solid, but your body is two thirds water. The balance of water and minerals in your body must be just right. Your kidneys maintain this balance by making more or less urine. They get their instructions from your brain. The brain monitors the amount of water in the blood. If there's too little, it releases the hormone ADH. ADH causes the kidneys to make less urine. It also makes you thirsty. You drink, restoring balance to your watery inner world.

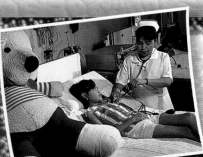

FAILED KIDNEYS
One kidney can do the work of two. But if both fail, poisons build up in the blood. Regular treatments, called dialysis, remove the poisons.

NEW KIDNEYS
A donated kidney can save a life. But not any kidney will do. It must match the receiver's tissue type. Many people die waiting for a matching kidney.

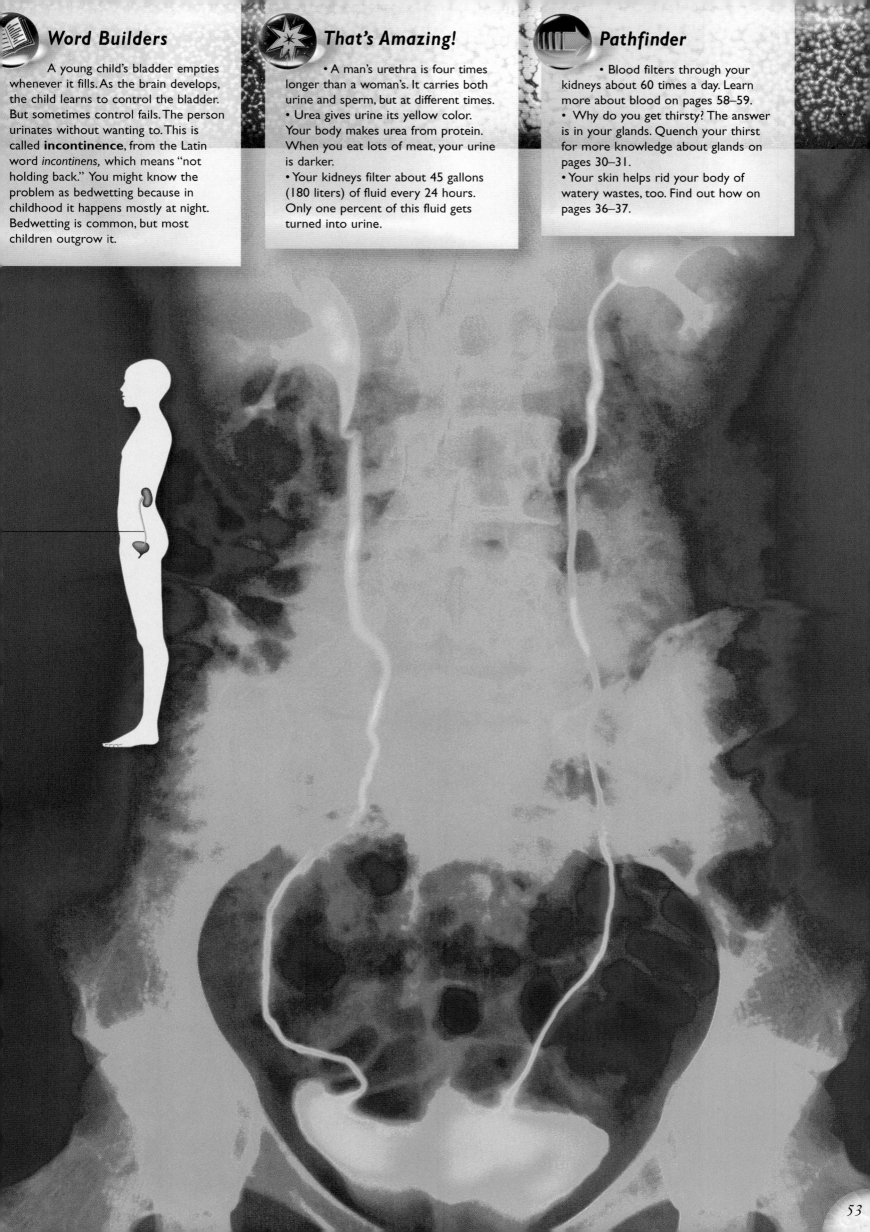

Word Builders

A young child's bladder empties whenever it fills. As the brain develops, the child learns to control the bladder. But sometimes control fails. The person urinates without wanting to. This is called **incontinence**, from the Latin word *incontinens*, which means "not holding back." You might know the problem as bedwetting because in childhood it happens mostly at night. Bedwetting is common, but most children outgrow it.

That's Amazing!

• A man's urethra is four times longer than a woman's. It carries both urine and sperm, but at different times.
• Urea gives urine its yellow color. Your body makes urea from protein. When you eat lots of meat, your urine is darker.
• Your kidneys filter about 45 gallons (180 liters) of fluid every 24 hours. Only one percent of this fluid gets turned into urine.

Pathfinder

• Blood filters through your kidneys about 60 times a day. Learn more about blood on pages 58–59.
• Why do you get thirsty? The answer is in your glands. Quench your thirst for more knowledge about glands on pages 30–31.
• Your skin helps rid your body of watery wastes, too. Find out how on pages 36–37.

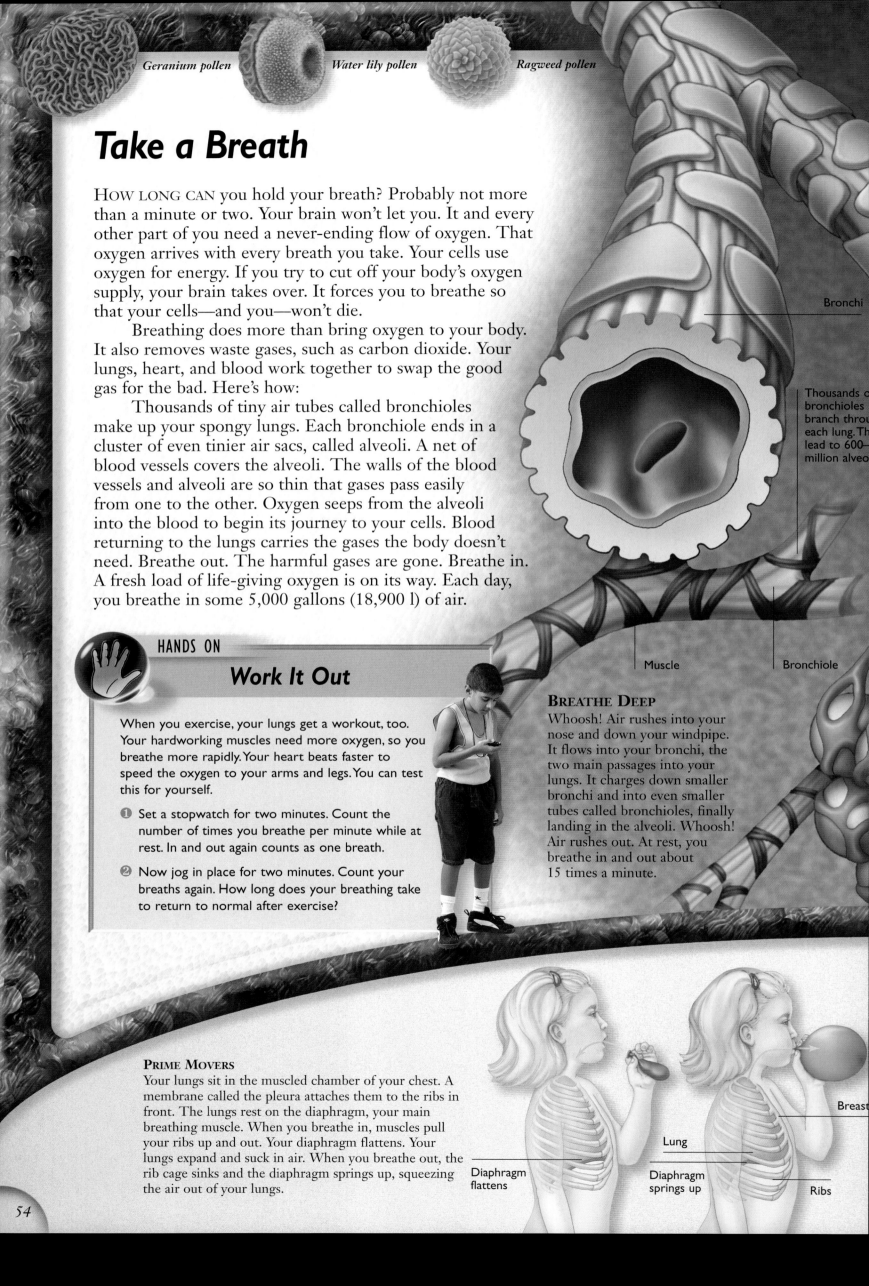

Geranium pollen   *Water lily pollen*   *Ragweed pollen*

Take a Breath

HOW LONG CAN you hold your breath? Probably not more than a minute or two. Your brain won't let you. It and every other part of you need a never-ending flow of oxygen. That oxygen arrives with every breath you take. Your cells use oxygen for energy. If you try to cut off your body's oxygen supply, your brain takes over. It forces you to breathe so that your cells—and you—won't die.

Breathing does more than bring oxygen to your body. It also removes waste gases, such as carbon dioxide. Your lungs, heart, and blood work together to swap the good gas for the bad. Here's how:

Thousands of tiny air tubes called bronchioles make up your spongy lungs. Each bronchiole ends in a cluster of even tinier air sacs, called alveoli. A net of blood vessels covers the alveoli. The walls of the blood vessels and alveoli are so thin that gases pass easily from one to the other. Oxygen seeps from the alveoli into the blood to begin its journey to your cells. Blood returning to the lungs carries the gases the body doesn't need. Breathe out. The harmful gases are gone. Breathe in. A fresh load of life-giving oxygen is on its way. Each day, you breathe in some 5,000 gallons (18,900 l) of air.

Bronchi

Thousands of
bronchioles
branch throu[gh]
each lung. Th[ese]
lead to 600–[?]
million alveo[li]

Muscle   Bronchiole

HANDS ON

Work It Out

When you exercise, your lungs get a workout, too. Your hardworking muscles need more oxygen, so you breathe more rapidly. Your heart beats faster to speed the oxygen to your arms and legs. You can test this for yourself.

❶ Set a stopwatch for two minutes. Count the number of times you breathe per minute while at rest. In and out again counts as one breath.

❷ Now jog in place for two minutes. Count your breaths again. How long does your breathing take to return to normal after exercise?

BREATHE DEEP

Whoosh! Air rushes into your nose and down your windpipe. It flows into your bronchi, the two main passages into your lungs. It charges down smaller bronchi and into even smaller tubes called bronchioles, finally landing in the alveoli. Whoosh! Air rushes out. At rest, you breathe in and out about 15 times a minute.

PRIME MOVERS

Your lungs sit in the muscled chamber of your chest. A membrane called the pleura attaches them to the ribs in front. The lungs rest on the diaphragm, your main breathing muscle. When you breathe in, muscles pull your ribs up and out. Your diaphragm flattens. Your lungs expand and suck in air. When you breathe out, the rib cage sinks and the diaphragm springs up, squeezing the air out of your lungs.

Breast[bone]

Lung

Diaphragm
flattens

Diaphragm
springs up

Ribs

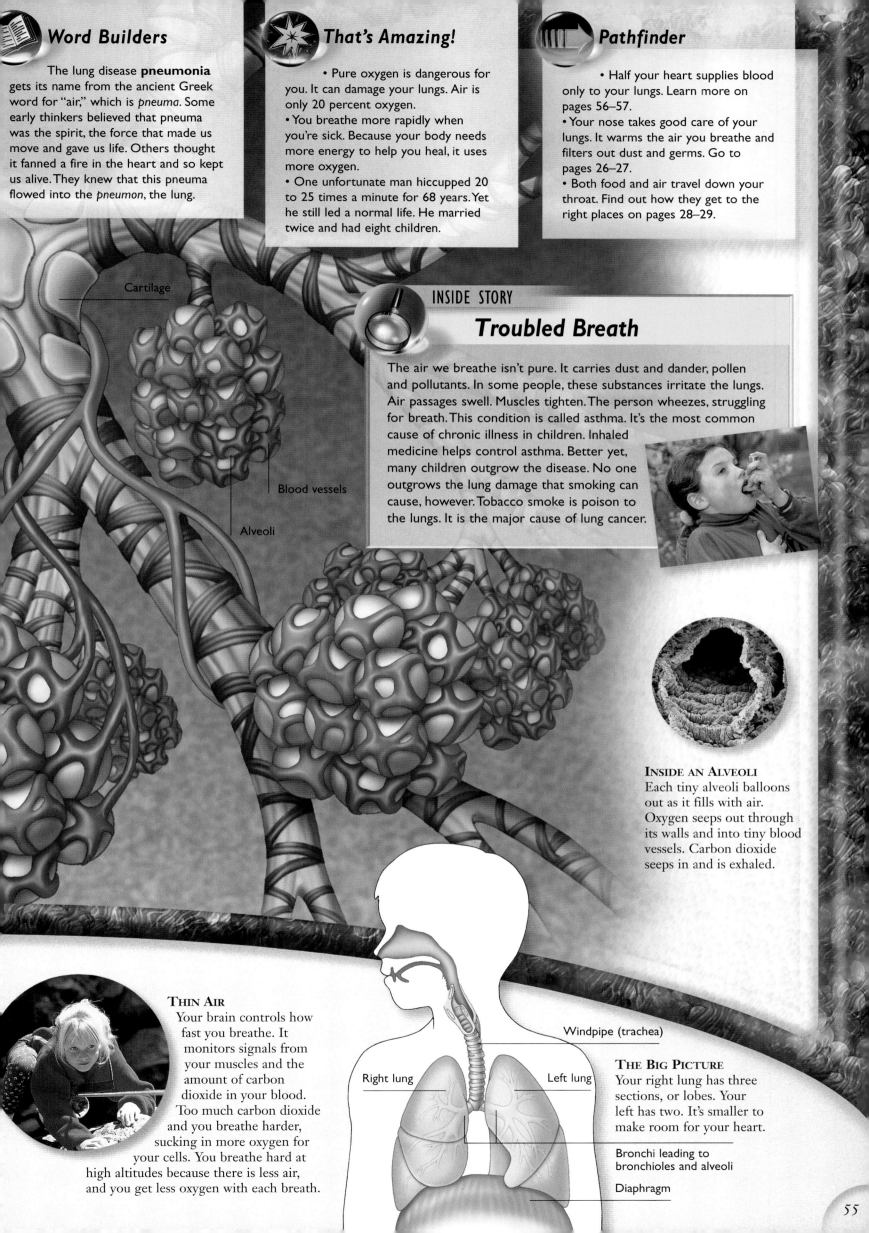

Word Builders

The lung disease **pneumonia** gets its name from the ancient Greek word for "air," which is *pneuma*. Some early thinkers believed that pneuma was the spirit, the force that made us move and gave us life. Others thought it fanned a fire in the heart and so kept us alive. They knew that this pneuma flowed into the *pneumon*, the lung.

That's Amazing!

• Pure oxygen is dangerous for you. It can damage your lungs. Air is only 20 percent oxygen.
• You breathe more rapidly when you're sick. Because your body needs more energy to help you heal, it uses more oxygen.
• One unfortunate man hiccupped 20 to 25 times a minute for 68 years. Yet he still led a normal life. He married twice and had eight children.

Pathfinder

• Half your heart supplies blood only to your lungs. Learn more on pages 56–57.
• Your nose takes good care of your lungs. It warms the air you breathe and filters out dust and germs. Go to pages 26–27.
• Both food and air travel down your throat. Find out how they get to the right places on pages 28–29.

Cartilage

Blood vessels

Alveoli

INSIDE STORY

Troubled Breath

The air we breathe isn't pure. It carries dust and dander, pollen and pollutants. In some people, these substances irritate the lungs. Air passages swell. Muscles tighten. The person wheezes, struggling for breath. This condition is called asthma. It's the most common cause of chronic illness in children. Inhaled medicine helps control asthma. Better yet, many children outgrow the disease. No one outgrows the lung damage that smoking can cause, however. Tobacco smoke is poison to the lungs. It is the major cause of lung cancer.

INSIDE AN ALVEOLI
Each tiny alveoli balloons out as it fills with air. Oxygen seeps out through its walls and into tiny blood vessels. Carbon dioxide seeps in and is exhaled.

THIN AIR
Your brain controls how fast you breathe. It monitors signals from your muscles and the amount of carbon dioxide in your blood. Too much carbon dioxide and you breathe harder, sucking in more oxygen for your cells. You breathe hard at high altitudes because there is less air, and you get less oxygen with each breath.

Windpipe (trachea)

Right lung

Left lung

THE BIG PICTURE
Your right lung has three sections, or lobes. Your left has two. It's smaller to make room for your heart.

Bronchi leading to bronchioles and alveoli

Diaphragm

Your pulse tells you how fast your heart is beating.

Heart of the Matter

PLACE YOUR FINGERS on your wrist. The beat you feel is the steady pumping of your blood. Each day, your blood circles your body over and over. It delivers food and oxygen to your cells and removes wastes. It carries hormones to their targets and helps you fight disease. It travels through a vast network of tubes called blood vessels, pumped by your powerful heart.

Your heart is slightly bigger than your fist. Its unique cardiac muscle never tires and never rests. It keeps blood streaming steadily through your body.

When your body needs more energy, your heart responds. Jog for a short time and you'll feel it pounding. The harder pumping speeds blood along. Oxygen-rich blood flows from your heart into arteries. It delivers the oxygen, as well as food, to hungry cells. It picks up carbon dioxide and other wastes, then flows back to the heart through veins. Along the way, your kidneys and liver filter the blood. The returning blood surges into your heart. A powerful contraction sends it to the lungs, where the blood dumps carbon dioxide and picks up oxygen. It flows back into the heart, then hits the road again.

LISTENING IN

Doctors use a stethoscope to listen to your heart. Unusual sounds can tell the doctor that the heart valves are not opening or shutting properly. If the valves are not doing their job, the heart can't pump efficiently.

THROUGH THICK AND THIN

Capillaries are the body's smallest blood vessels. Their walls are only a single cell thick. Nutrients pass easily through these walls into the cells of your tissues. Arteries and veins are much thicker and tougher. Their walls have three layers: an outer coat, muscle, and a lining. Thin membranes separate these layers.

Blood cell   **Capillary**

THE HEART'S HELPERS

Arteries carry blood away from the heart. Their thick, elastic muscles help push the blood along. They also make a gas—nitric oxide—that relaxes their muscles. When the artery muscles relax, blood flows more easily.

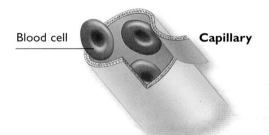

Artery

Outer coat

Muscle

Lining

FORWARD HO!

Veins carry blood back to the heart. Those in arms and legs have valves to keep blood from flowing backward.

Vein   Outer coat

Valve   Muscle

Lining

Word Builders

Your arteries throb with every beat of your heart. This is the **pulse** you feel at your wrist. The word pulse comes from the Latin *pulsus*, which means "beating." A knob of special heart tissue called a pacemaker sets and controls the beat. **Pace** comes from the Latin word *passus*, which means "step."

That's Amazing!

• Most of your capillaries are so thin that red blood cells must line up single file to get through.
• Growing takes work, so a child's heart beats faster than an adult's to supply extra energy. A child's heart rate is about 90 beats a minute. An adult's is 70. An infant's heartbeat is 120 times a minute.

Pathfinder

• Your heart beats almost 40 million times a year. Each beat pushes about five tablespoons (70 ml) of blood into your arteries. Learn more about blood on pages 58–59.
• Your body has a second transportation system. Find out more on pages 60–61.
• Your brain cells begin to die after just a few minutes without blood. Go to pages 18–19 to learn about your brain.

TWO PUMPS IN ONE

The four chambers of your heart form two pumps. The right side pumps blood from the body to the lungs. The left side pumps oxygen-rich blood from the lungs to the body.

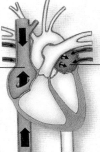

Right atrium — Left atrium

BLOOD IN

The top chambers of the heart, the atria, relax. Deoxygenated blood from the body pours into the right atrium. Oxygen-rich blood from the lungs fills the left.

Right ventricle — Left ventricle

VALVES OPEN

The atria contract. Blood pushes open the valves leading to the heart's pumping chambers. These chambers, the ventricles, fill with blood.

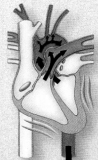

BLOOD OUT

The ventricles contract, forcing open the valves to the arteries. Blood shoots into the arteries. As the valves close, they make the familiar sounds of a heartbeat: *lub dub*.

Major vein
Major artery
Heart

PASSING THROUGH

Your blood vessels are your body's road system. The major veins and arteries are the wide freeways. They exit into smaller veins and arteries that supply each part of the body with its own local roads. Tiny capillaries are the country lanes. They connect veins and arteries and reach every tissue cell.

GO WITH THE FLOW

What's in your blood? What does blood do for you? What happens to the blood as it streams through your body? Find out below. Start with "Busy Blood," and then go with the flow.

It's in the Blood

LIKE A DROP of pond water, your blood teems with life. Trillions of blood cells cruise your body, traveling in a sea of straw-colored plasma. Plasma makes up most of your blood. It brings nutrients to your cells and carries wastes away.

Plasma's main passengers are red blood cells. These are your body's delivery people. They call on other cells, dropping off oxygen and picking up carbon dioxide. Red blood cells look like tires with dents instead of holes.

White blood cells prowl through your bloodstream too. They protect you against foreign invaders. Some travel to specific tissues and stand guard. Others keep sailing until you're injured or sick. Then they surge into your tissues to battle with germs.

Platelets, another component of plasma, aren't whole cells at all. They're fragments of certain white blood cells. When you bleed, they trigger clotting. This vital service helps you heal. It keeps your blood inside your vessels, streaming through your body on its life-preserving rounds.

INSIDE STORY

The Blood That Binds

The surgeon's tools lie on the tray. There are scalpels, tweezers, and glue. Glue? That's right. Surgical glue uses the same clotting chemicals as your body. These are fibrinogen and thrombin. When you bleed, they latch together to make fibrin. Threads of fibrin form the mesh on which blood clots. The glue makes fibrin, too. Surgeons use it to stop the flow of blood from small, hard-to-seal vessels and for skin grafts. And they don't have to remove the glue. The body absorbs it.

BUSY BLOOD
Blood carries hundreds of vital substances around your body. That's why blood tests reveal so much about your health.

WHY IS YOUR BLOOD RED?
Red blood cells give blood its color. A protein in the cells called hemoglobin latches onto oxygen. When it does, it turns bright red.

BLOOD CARRIES:
• sugar, proteins, and salts
• vitamins and minerals
• wastes
• hormones
• germ-fighting chemicals
• oxygen and carbon dioxide

THIN BLOOD
Anemia is a blood conditi… Someone with anemia can… make enough red blood c…

THE PUMP
Your heart keeps your blood moving through your body.

NEED RED CELLS?
As your kidneys clean your blood, they track oxygen levels. If levels fall too low, they tell bone marrow to make more red cells.

THE SUPPLIERS
Red blood cells ferr… oxygen to every cell… your tissues. They c… away waste gases. Yo… have 700 red cells fo… every white one.

Word Builders

If you ever need blood, your doctor will check your **blood group** before giving it to you. Your blood group tells which chemical markers your red blood cells carry. The markers are A and B. They are named for the order in which they were discovered. Your blood group can be A, B, AB (if you have both), or O (if you have neither).

That's Amazing!

• All the platelets in your body wouldn't fill two teaspoons. Yet you have billions of them.
• Dead red blood cells give feces most of its color.
• White blood cells aren't really white. They're clear.
• You have 60,000 miles (96,000 km) of blood vessels.

Pathfinder

• Your bones make your blood cells. What else does bone do? Go to pages 42–43.
• Each red blood cell makes its rounds 300,000 times before it dies. Learn more about cells on pages 12–13.
• Your white blood cells attack invading germs. Find out how they protect you on pages 60–61.

WHEN IS YOUR BLOOD BLUE?

When hemoglobin drops of oxygen, it loses its bright red color. The blood looks blue. You can see it in your veins.

ORGAN DUTY

The liver cleans the blood. It also grabs nutrients for processing, then returns them to the bloodstream.

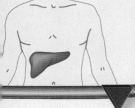

SPLEEN CLEANING

Your spleen removes dead red blood cells from circulation. It also makes some white cells.

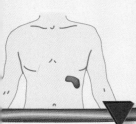

R. I. P.

Most blood cells have short lives. A red cell lives about 120 days. Some white cells live only about a week. They die protecting you.

A CLOT FORMS

Platelets release chemicals that make fibrin. The thread-like fibrin traps platelets and red blood cells (right). A clot forms, which stops the bleeding.

Splinter

BLOOD TO THE RESCUE

Ouch! Injured cells signal for help. Platelets stick together to plug the wound.

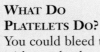

WHAT DO PLATELETS DO?

You could bleed to death without platelets. They bunch up at the site of an injury anywhere in your body. They plug the wound to stop the bleeding.

THE DEFENDERS

White blood cells are the body's protectors. They seek, round up, and destroy foreign invaders. They mop up after a battle with viruses, bacteria, or other aliens.

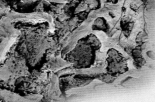

A TOUGH SCAB

The fibrin, trapped cells, and fluid from the blood harden into a protective scab. Healing begins.

GERM PATROL

White blood cells under a scab gobble up germs. They ward off infection.

REPLACEMENT BLOOD

Lost blood is replaced quickly. Bone marrow churns out millions of red blood cells a second.

HOW MUCH BLOOD DO YOU NEED?

◯ 3 pints (1.7 l)
◯ 20 pints (11.4 l)
✔ 8 pints (4.5 l)

That's how much is moving through your body right now.

BLOOD TYPES

The blood you get from a donor has to be compatible with your own. If not, your body will reject it. Your blood group tells which types of blood you can receive.

LIFESAVING BANKS

Blood banks test and store donated blood.

EMERGENCY!

This time you're badly injured. You're in surgery. You're losing more blood than your body can replace. You need new blood fast. Donated blood can help you.

Your Blood. Plasma makes up 55 percent of your blood. It's mostly water.

Red blood cells make up 45 percent of your blood.

White blood cells and platelets make up less than one percent of your blood.

Germs can gather in a hair follicle, causing an infection. This tender lump is called a boil.

Protecting Us

OUCH! A BEE STING. You feel pain. Blood rushes into your finger. The finger reddens. It swells. Your immune system is on the attack.

Your immune system protects you from poisons and germs. It helps heal injuries. It is made up of white blood cells, the chemicals they make, and the organs that produce them. Some white blood cells live in your tissues. They attack any harmful substance that comes near. Others patrol your body. They charge to an injury. They seek and destroy invaders like bacteria and viruses.

Any invader or injury can trigger your immune system's general alarm. Red, hot, swollen tissue is the result. But your body targets specific invaders, too. Invader cells display a unique chemical ID called an antigen. These IDs let your immune system tell the good guys—your cells— from the bad. Special immune cells recognize every possible antigen. Called B and T cells, each one prowls through the body, searching for a specific invader. If it finds its suspect, the cell reproduces rapidly. It creates an army to fight this one enemy. T cells kill directly. B cells mark the enemy with chemicals called antibodies, then other cells destroy it. The first time a foreign agent invades, you don't have many antibodies for it. You may get sick. But the next time, invaders beware. That's why you don't get diseases like chicken pox twice.

ARMED AND READY

An army of specialists is ready to protect you. These specialists are different types of white blood cells (they are colored cream in the picture so that you can see them). Each protects you in its own way. Neutrophils swoop in and destroy germs at the site of injury. Lymphocytes, which include B and T cells, hunt down specific invaders. Huge macrophages swallow germs. They also suck up the garbage left by an immune system attack.

Macrophages respond to the immune system's general alarm. The largest white blood cells, they gobble up invaders. This type of attack is called phagocytosis.

That's Amazing!

• Skin, mucus, and saliva are your body's front-line defenses. They keep germs from getting in.
• T cells mature in your thymus. But the thymus shrinks as you age. In children, it's the size of a lemon. In adults, it's the size of an acorn.
• The brain and immune system "talk" to each other. Your emotions and stress level can influence how well your immune system works.

Pathfinder

• You can inherit allergies. Go to pages 14–15 to learn more.
• The lymphatic system not only fights disease, it also helps maintain the body's fluid balance. To find out why this is important, go to pages 52–53.
• Your useful lymph aids digestion, too. It carries fats out of the digestive tract. Learn about digestion on pages 50–51.
• Is there veggie vaccine in your future? Find out on pages 62–63.

This **T cell** spies its suspect. It multiplies, forming an army of thousands. The army attacks. It makes chemicals that directly destroy its target.

Neutrophils attack any foreigner in sight. This one is lunching on a long bacterium.

B cells don't attack directly. They release antibodies into the area. This allows macrophages to recognize the invaders and gobble them up.

THE GERM FIGHTER
If you've had swollen glands, you've felt one of your body's top germ fighters. The glands are lymph nodes. A milky fluid called lymph flows around the body through its own system of vessels and nodes. This is called the lymphatic system. Packed with white blood cells, these nodes filter germs and debris. Your lymphatic system protects in other ways, too. T cells mature in the thymus. The spleen makes immune cells and filters blood. The lymph fluid itself carries foreign agents away from tissues. Cleansed lymph pours into the bloodstream through lymph ducts, carrying white blood cells with it.

Thymus

Lymph node

Spleen

Lymph vessel

DOWN TIME
Your immune system can sometimes let you down. It can overreact to pollen (below), dust, or even chocolate. The result? Allergies.

LOSING BATTLE
Your immune system can lose battles, too. When it does, you get sick. Some diseases attack immune cells themselves, and destroy the body's ability to defend itself. AIDS is one such disease.

MISTAKEN IDENTITY
Sometimes the immune system mistakes the body's own cells for aliens. It attacks. The body destroys its own tissues. This happens to the joints in rheumatoid arthritis. The disease causes joints to swell and fill with fluid. They become stiff and painful to move.

GENE-IES
Your genes may grant your future health wishes. One day, doctors will test your genes to choose the best medicine for you. They will replace bad or missing genes that play a role in diseases such as cancer.

COPY SHEEP
Cloned sheep may provide factories for human drugs. Genes are changed so that the sheep make these drug products in their milk.

Future Us

WHAT CAN A MUMMY tell us about the body of the future? More than you might think. Thanks to modern imaging, scientists have peeked beneath a mummy's wrapping. There lay the remains of a body much like ours. It showed signs of our diseases, too. Ancient Egyptians felt the pain of arthritis and tooth decay. They died of heart attacks and stroke.

Human bodies have changed little in the past 5,000 years. They aren't likely to change much in the next few thousand either. We will still walk upright. We will run five fingers through our hair. We will sleep and dream and fall in love. But we will live longer, healthier lives. As scientists unravel more of the body's mysteries, our ability to improve health grows. New vaccines may prevent killer diseases such as cancer or AIDS. Foods from cereals to chewing gum may be treated to help boost health and fight disease. A life span of 120 years won't be uncommon, and some scientists think we can expand even that.

No matter how long we live, our lives won't be illness-free. New viruses will outwit our immune systems. But the tools we'll have to fight them are as unknown to us now as vaccines and imaging machines were to our ancestors. Our bodies may stay the same, but we will learn more about ourselves and protect ourselves differently in the future.

FUTURE HEALING
Might plastic muscles replace damaged ones? Could nerve cells added to the brain repair damage from stroke or brain diseases? Could a person's own cells be grown in the lab then used to rebuild damaged tissues? Perhaps. Research in all these areas is underway. In fact, doctors can already grow cartilage-making cells in the lab. These cells are then put back into the body, where they make new cartilage.

INSIDE STORY

Remote Surgery

The surgeon prepares to operate. She slips her hands into her gloves. But these gloves aren't thin and sterile. They are threaded with wires that transmit pressure. The surgeon sits down at the computer. Her gloved hands grasp two joysticks. She is ready to begin. Her patient is ready, too. He lies in an operating room thousands of miles away. Robot arms hover above his kidney. As the surgeon guides the joysticks, the robot operates. Science fiction? No. Surgeons have already carried out remote surgery. One day, it will be routine.

Robots are aiding surgeons in another way, too. Robot fingers can fit through openings too small for human hands. They will be used to do more and more complex surgery.

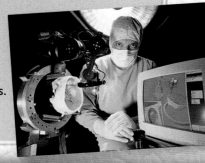

SUPER SCIENCE
A horseback-riding accident put Christopher Reeve, Hollywood's Superman, in a wheelchair. His spinal cord was damaged, paralyzing him from his neck down. Will he walk again? Perhaps. Scientists are looking for ways to heal damaged nerves and to make new ones grow. They are designing tiny computers to do the work of nerves and so move muscles. Super science may yet help Superman.

Word Builders

A **clone** is an exact copy of an individual. It is grown from a single cell of the original. Scientists have cloned adult sheep and cows. Might scientists someday clone humans? If they could, the clone and the original would never be exactly the same. Each person's life is unique. Every experience shapes both mind and body.

That's Amazing!

• People today are about 3 inches (8 cm) taller than 200 years ago. Why? Better nutrition.
• Our cells have built-in time clocks. They reproduce a set number of times, then die. In labs, scientists have reset these clocks, keeping cells alive longer. Someday they may be able to do this in the body to slow the aging process.

Pathfinder

• New contact lenses could give us better than 20/20 vision. To gain insight into eyes, turn to pages 22–23.
• Gene therapy may make bald heads and gray hair a thing of the past. Why do people lose their hair and turn gray? The answer is on pages 38–39.

BYE-BYE, NEEDLES
Some day, veggies might replace a shot in the arm. Scientists are working on special "veggie vaccines." Instead of getting a flu shot, you'll get a dose of the vaccine in your food. Diabetics may be able to say bye-bye to needles, too. Insulin inhalers are on the way.

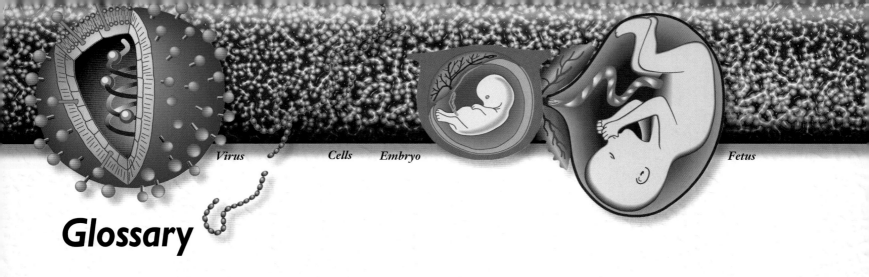

Virus *Cells* *Embryo* *Fetus*

Glossary

absorption The passage of a substance from one part of the body to another through a thin barrier, such as the passage of digested food into the bloodstream through the wall of the small intestine.

alveoli Tiny air pockets in the lungs that are covered with a net of blood vessels. Gases pass between the alveoli and blood vessels.

antibody A protein produced by special blood cells to help fight and destroy germs.

artery A muscular blood vessel that carries fresh (oxygenated) blood away from the heart.

atria The two chambers of the heart that collect blood as it comes in.

axon The long arm of a neuron that passes messages to the next cell. The messages travel down the axon as electric pulses.

bacteria One-cell beings. Some bacteria are germs that make people sick.

blood–brain barrier One of the brain's protections. It controls which substances enter the brain from the blood.

blood cells The two kinds of cells that make up some of your blood. Red blood cells deliver oxygen to other cells and pick up carbon dioxide. White blood cells fight off foreign invaders.

bolus A lump of chewed food that enters the throat during a swallow.

capillary The smallest kind of blood vessel. Capillaries reach every tissue cell in the body.

carbon dioxide A gas that is a normal waste produced by cells when they use energy. It is transported in the bloodstream to the lungs, then it is breathed out.

cardiac Anything to do with the heart.

cartilage A flexible but tough body tissue. It forms part of the framework of the body and covers the ends of some bones.

cell The smallest unit of life that is able to function independently. The human body is an organized mass of cells.

cerebral Anything to do with the brain.

chromosomes Structures containing DNA and proteins that carry genetic instructions. Humans have 46 chromosomes. They are stored in a cell's nucleus.

chyme Soupy lumps of partly digested food that move from the stomach into the small intestine.

cilia Fine, hairlike parts of cells that sway back and forth.

cochlea The part of the inner ear in which sound waves are turned into nerve signals.

cone A type of cell in the retina of the eye that picks up colors and fine details, then sends this information as nerve signals to the brain.

cortex The outer layer of a body part such as a kidney or the brain.

dermis The inner layer of skin that contains blood vessels, nerves, sweat glands, and hair roots.

DNA The molecule that contains genes. It looks like a twisted ladder. DNA stands for deoxyribonucleic acid.

embryo An unborn organism in the earliest stages of development. In humans, this is from about one week to eight weeks inside the womb.

enamel The hard outer coating of teeth.

endocrine system A network of glands that produce hormones.

enzyme A substance that acts on another to change it. Food is broken down with the help of enzymes.

epidermis The outer layer of skin. It is made of new skin cells at the base, and tough dead skin cells on the surface.

fertilization The union of female and male sex cells.

fetus An unborn individual during the later stages of development. In humans, this is from the ninth week of pregnancy through birth.

follicle A tiny opening, such as the one from which a hair grows.

gamete A sperm or egg; a sex cell.

genes The blueprints for life that individuals inherit from their parents. Genes are carried on chromosomes.

gestation The time a baby spends developing inside its mother's womb.

glands Parts of the body that produce hormones, sweat, saliva, and other substances.

gustatory Anything having to do with the sense of taste.

hormones The body's chemical messengers. They help control many body functions according to the body's needs.

immune Able to fight and destroy bacteria, viruses, or other germs so that they cannot harm the body.

implant To place in the body. For instance, an artificial pacemaker may be implanted.

inflammation A reaction of the body to a harmful substance or injury. This reaction usually involves swelling, pain, and warmth.

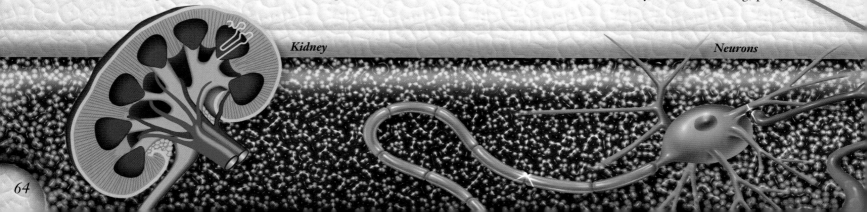

Kidney *Neurons*

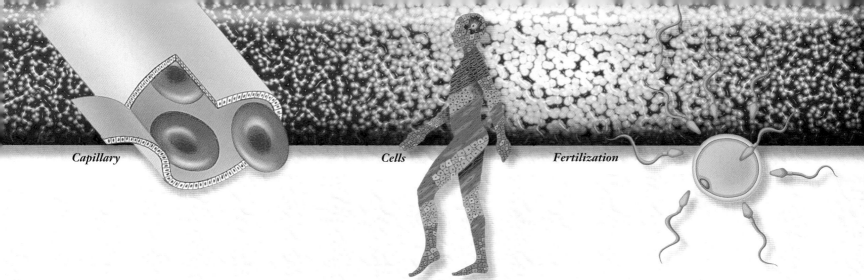

Capillary   *Cells*   *Fertilization*

keratin A protein that toughens skin, nails, and hair.

ligament A flexible band of tissue that attaches one bone to another at the joint. Ligaments also attach teeth to the jaw.

lymph A pale fluid that is made primarily of white blood cells. It is important in fighting infection. Lymph travels through the body in special vessels and pours into the bloodstream through lymph ducts.

lymph nodes Small organs that filter lymph and store white blood cells.

lymphocyte A type of white blood cell.

medulla The innermost part of an organ such as a kidney.

melanin The body's main natural coloring substance, or pigment, which gives skin, eyes, and hair their color. The greater the amount of melanin, the darker the skin's color.

membrane A thin protective barrier around cells or organs, such as the cell membrane around a cell or the mucous membrane lining the nose, mouth, airways, and digestive tract.

meninges The membranes that cover and protect the brain and spinal cord.

menstruation The breakdown and loss of the lining of the womb that happens every month if a woman's egg has not been fertilized.

mucus A thick, slimy substance that moistens and protects some body parts, such as the lining of the nose.

myelin A material that insulates the axons of many nerve cells.

myofibrils Fibers inside muscle cells.

nerves Bundles of long, thin neurons that connect the brain to the rest of the body.

neuron A nerve cell.

neurotransmitter A chemical that ferries messages across the gap between neurons.

nutrient A substance that the body can use for energy, growth, or repair.

olfactory Anything having to do with the sense of smell.

organ A collection of tissues that has a specific function. The brain, heart, stomach, and kidneys are organs.

organelle The parts of a cell. Each has a different job.

oxygen A gas that is breathed in and transported to every cell in the body through the bloodstream. Oxygen helps the cells release energy from food.

pacemaker A knob of specialized, electrically charged muscle that controls the heart's rhythm.

placenta The blood-rich organ that lines the mother's womb to provide nourishment for a developing fetus. The placenta comes out after the baby is born.

plasma The pale, watery fluid that makes up most of your blood. It brings nourishment, hormones, and germ-fighting substances to your cells. It carries away wastes.

proteins The chemicals that are the building blocks of cells.

renal Anything to do with the kidneys.

rod A type of cell in the retina of the eye that can pick up shapes in dim light. Rod cells cannot detect colors and fine details.

saliva A fluid made by glands in the mouth and throat to begin the process of digestion.

scan A computerized picture of the inside of the body created by a special machine.

synapse The gap between each nerve cell.

system A collection of organs that work together to carry out a job in the body. An example is the digestive system.

tendon A tough rope of tissue that attaches a muscle to a bone.

tissue Cells joined with others like themselves to carry out a specific function.

transplant To replace a damaged body part with a functioning one from a donor.

urea The chemical waste that gives urine its color.

ureter One of the two tubes that carry urine from the kidneys to the bladder.

urethra The tube that carries urine out of the body.

valve A flap in a blood vessel that opens only one way so that blood cannot flow backward.

vein A vessel that usually carries used (deoxygenated) blood back to the heart.

ventricles The two chambers of the heart that pump blood to the body (the left ventricle) and to the lungs (the right ventricle).

villi Tiny, finger-shaped projections from the lining of the small intestine.

virus A very simple microorganism that must invade living cells to grow and multiply. Viruses cause disease.

zygote A just-fertilized egg.

Ureter   *Rods and Cones*

Index

Rocks and Minerals

Contents

Pick Your Path!

ROCKS AND MINERALS is different from any other information book you've ever picked up. You can start at the beginning and learn about our rocky planet, then read through to the end and find out how to collect rocks and minerals. Or, if you have a special interest in crystals, jump right into the "Meet the Minerals" section and move through the book from there.

You'll find plenty of other discovery paths to choose from in the special features sections. Read about big discoveries and the scientists who made them in "Inside Story," or get creative with "Hands On" activities. Delve into words with "Word Builders," or amaze your friends with fascinating facts from "That's Amazing!" You can choose a new path with every reading—READER'S DIGEST PATHFINDERS will take you wherever *you* want to go.

INSIDE STORY
Great Moments in Geology

Investigate the spectacular canyons of the southwestern United States with explorer John Wesley Powell. Go rock hunting on the Moon with geologist Harrison Schmitt. Read photographer Brad Lewis's account of what it's like to have a volcano in your backyard. Read about great scientists and geology's historic events in INSIDE STORY. Imagine that you are there behind the scenes, and you will understand how it feels to witness or do something that changes the world.

Word Builders

What a strange word! What does it mean? Where did it come from? Find out by reading *Word Builders*.

That's Amazing!

Awesome facts, amazing records, fascinating figures— you'll find them all in *That's Amazing!*

HANDS ON
Create and Make

Squeeze a sugar cube and watch it glow in the dark. Fold layers of modeling clay into mountain ranges. Create seismic waves in a bowl of water. Grow your own crystals in a jar. Construct a simple display case for your rock and mineral collection. Learn how to identify minerals by examining their density, color, and hardness. The HANDS ON features showcase experiments, projects, and activities—each one related to that page's main subject.

Pathfinder

Use the *Pathfinder* box to find your way from one subject to another. It's all up to you.

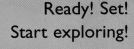

Ready! Set!
Start exploring!

Rocks

YOU ARE STANDING on an enormous rock. This rock is hurtling through space. Our planet, Earth, is a giant ball of rock—actually, many different kinds of rocks. These rocks are, in turn, made of minerals, which are naturally formed solids. You may not notice, but rocks are always changing. Hot, liquid rock—buoyed by heat from Earth's core—rises to the surface, where it cools and hardens. Ice, wind, and water constantly break down surface rocks into pieces. Rocks sink beneath the crust and melt again. This cycle, which has been going on for billions of years, creates three main kinds of rock—igneous, sedimentary, and metamorphic.

page **80**   Rocks have been around a lot longer than humans.

Go to THE ROCK CYCLE.

page **82**   Rocks like this one form when lava erupts from a volcano.

Go to RIVERS OF FIRE.

page **84**   Fragments of rock often join together to form new rock.

Go to LAYER UPON LAYER.

page **86**   How do some kinds of rocks turn into other rocks?

Go to SQUEEZED AND BAKED.

page **88**   Where did this weird rock come from?

Go to STRANGE ROCKS.

LIGHTBULBS
Most lightbulbs contain a wiry thread made from a metal called tungsten. Tungsten is extracted from a mineral called scheelite.

MIRRORS
Mirrors are made by painting silver or aluminum, two metals, onto glass. Glass is made from quartz sand—tiny grains of a mineral called quartz.

Rocks Around the Clock

STEP OUTSIDE, and you'll be surrounded—by rocks. Look down. Under the soil, the ground is made of many kinds of rock. Look up. Gigantic boulders and jagged slabs of stone make up hills and mountains. Some rocks formed just days ago. Some have been here for billions of years.

Pick up a rock and feel its weight. Ancient people noticed that rocks were tough as well, so they used them to build houses and roads. They also realized that some rocks contained useful minerals such as metals, which they soon learned to separate from rocks. Today we still process rocks. We extract metals used in bridges, cars, and skyscrapers. We crush rock to make railroad beds and to produce construction materials for buildings. We even extract the fuel to power trucks or heat our homes from rock layers below the ground.

We depend on rocks and minerals all day long. Faucets and water pipes are made of metals. The wires that carry electricity are made of copper, which is also a metal. We eat with metal utensils and flavor our food with rock crystals called salt. We write with pencils that contain a black mineral called graphite. Our computers wouldn't work without the crystals of quartz used to make silicon chips. Even plastic objects such as bottles and bowls are made with oil from rocks. Just where would we be without rocks and minerals?

A ROCKY LANDSCAPE

Rocks give shape to the land around us. You can see this most clearly on mountain peaks, streambeds, coastlines, and some roadways. Humans collect rocks from mines and quarries, using them to make buildings and machines, and turning them into all kinds of products from jewels to fuel.

The land around us is all rock. You can see this most clearly on mountain peaks and at coastal cliffs.

Most modern buildings are made of steel, concrete, and glass, all of which come from rocks.

HANDS ON

Rock Spotting

❶ Find a notebook and pen and take a look around your house. Make a list of all the things that you think are made of rocks and minerals. (The pictures at the top and bottom of this page will help you out.) Then go for a walk around your neighborhood. Again, try to guess which objects are made of rocks and minerals, and write them down in another list.

❷ Now, put your lists away for a while. When you finish reading this book, try the exercise again and make new lists. You'll be amazed how many more objects made from rocks and minerals you recognize.

FINE CHINA
Fine china is made of a clay called kaolin, which contains a mineral called kaolinite. Like other clays, kaolin can be molded into different shapes.

BLACKBOARDS AND CHALK
Blackboards are made from slate, a dark rock that forms in flat sheets. You write on blackboards with chalk, a soft, white rock.

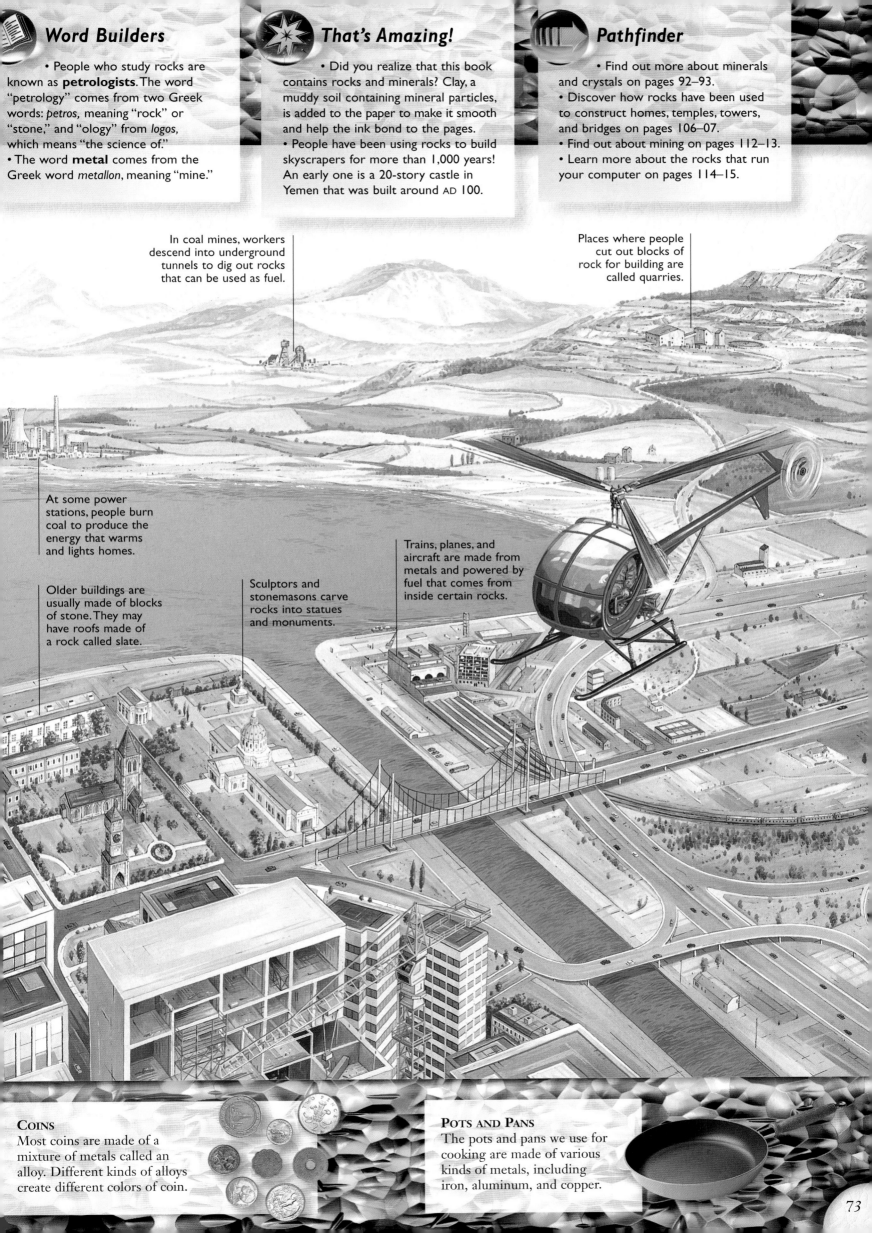

Word Builders

• People who study rocks are known as **petrologists**. The word "petrology" comes from two Greek words: *petros,* meaning "rock" or "stone," and "ology" from *logos,* which means "the science of."
• The word **metal** comes from the Greek word *metallon,* meaning "mine."

That's Amazing!

• Did you realize that this book contains rocks and minerals? Clay, a muddy soil containing mineral particles, is added to the paper to make it smooth and help the ink bond to the pages.
• People have been using rocks to build skyscrapers for more than 1,000 years! An early one is a 20-story castle in Yemen that was built around AD 100.

Pathfinder

• Find out more about minerals and crystals on pages 92–93.
• Discover how rocks have been used to construct homes, temples, towers, and bridges on pages 106–07.
• Find out about mining on pages 112–13.
• Learn more about the rocks that run your computer on pages 114–15.

In coal mines, workers descend into underground tunnels to dig out rocks that can be used as fuel.

Places where people cut out blocks of rock for building are called quarries.

At some power stations, people burn coal to produce the energy that warms and lights homes.

Older buildings are usually made of blocks of stone. They may have roofs made of a rock called slate.

Sculptors and stonemasons carve rocks into statues and monuments.

Trains, planes, and aircraft are made from metals and powered by fuel that comes from inside certain rocks.

COINS
Most coins are made of a mixture of metals called an alloy. Different kinds of alloys create different colors of coin.

POTS AND PANS
The pots and pans we use for cooking are made of various kinds of metals, including iron, aluminum, and copper.

Third Rock from the Sun

OUR PLANET is just one of many large rocks that travel around a star we call the Sun. Planets, moons, asteroids, meteoroids, and comets all share our part of the universe. Together, these rocks form a cosmic community called the solar system. Earth's address in the solar system is planet number 3, or third rock from the Sun.

Earth and the rest of the solar system formed about five billion years ago from a cloud of dust, rocks, and gas. These materials whirled around the Sun, continually crashing into each other. Some of the rock fragments stuck together, eventually forming a number of planets, including Earth. Earth's early history was like a demolition derby, with comets and asteroids constantly smashing into the new planet. All of these collisions plus decaying radioactive minerals created intense heat inside Earth and on its surface.

All of this heat had a profound effect on young Earth. Material inside began to melt. The heaviest parts sank to the core. The lighter substances floated up and formed the crust. Other matter settled in layers in between. We can't see these layers, but we can detect them. Scientists use instruments called geophones to listen to Earth's insides, just as a doctor uses a stethoscope to listen to your heart. This has allowed scientists to identify several layers. If we could slice the planet in half, these layers would look like the rings around a bull's-eye.

MOON WITH A VIEW
Earth looks like a gian blue marble when seen from its neighbor, the Moon. Many scientists believe that the Moon formed billions of year ago when a small plane smashed into Earth an pieces of debris from t collision stuck together

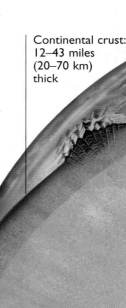

Upper mantle:
434 miles
(700 km) thick

Ocean crust:
3 miles (5 km)
thick

Continental crust:
12–43 miles
(20–70 km)
thick

Mantle	Outer core	Inner core
1,800 miles (2,900 km) thick	1,400 miles (2,250 km) thick	750 miles (1,200 km) thick

HANDS ON

Making Waves

To learn about Earth's interior, seismologists study seismic waves—waves from earthquakes or underground explosions that the scientists set off—as they travel through the planet. By measuring how fast and in which direction the waves move, the scientists can tell what kinds of rocks are present and how thick they are. In this project, the waves act like seismic waves, and the water and bottle act like rock layers.

❶ Fill a large bowl with water, then place a bottle in the middle of the bowl.

❷ Gently pour some drops of water into the side of the bowl. Ripples will move outward from the point where the drops hit the water. When the ripples hit the bottle, they are deflected. In the same way, seismic waves are deflected by certain kinds of rock.

Word Builders

• The word **gravity** comes from the Latin *gravitas,* meaning "heaviness."
• Waves from underground explosions are called **seismic waves**, and people who study these waves are called **seismologists**. The words come from the Greek *seismos,* meaning "earthquake."

That's Amazing!

• Digging at a rate of one foot (30 cm) per minute, it would take you 87 years to tunnel through Earth.
• The world's deepest drill hole, at Zapolyarnyy in eastern Russia, is nine miles (15 km) deep. However, this is barely a scratch on Earth's surface.

Pathfinder

• Hot rocks in the mantle rise as cooler rocks sink. This creates convection currents which in turn cause earthquakes and volcanoes. Find out how this happens on pages 76–77.
• Earth's rocky surface is shaped by forces called weathering and erosion. Turn to pages 78–79.
• When meteoroids crash to Earth, they are called meteorites. Take a look at a couple of meteorites on pages 88–89.

INSIDE STORY
Journey to the Center of the Earth

More than one hundred years ago, a French writer named Jules Verne took his readers to the center of our planet. In his book *A Journey to the Center of the Earth*, written in 1864 (and later made into a film), he described a route from one side of Earth to the other, through dark passages and past underground waterfalls, stony towers, and rivers of molten rock. We now know that this journey would be impossible, but explorations have shown that Verne's descriptions were like the extraordinary world of underground caves—a world he had never seen.

Asthenosphere

Lithosphere (crust plus upper mantle)

MAKING A SOLAR SYSTEM

The solar system is our cosmic home. Like all homes, it is made up of scraps of different materials. But the solar system wasn't built with lumber and nails. Instead, it came together from dust and gas.

About five billion years ago, a slowly spinning cloud of dust and hot gas—called a nebula—began to shrink. As it shrank, it spun faster and faster.

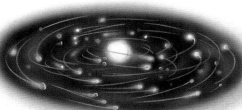

Hot gases at the center were pulled together, forming the Sun. Cooler gases and dust at the edges began to cluster, forming huge chunks of space rubble.

UPPER CRUST
Satellite photos allow us to study Earth's rocky surface. This picture shows the Himalaya Mountains in Asia.

WHAT'S INSIDE?
Earth is made up of several layers. The ground you stand on (the crust) and the rock beneath it (the upper mantle) form a layer called the lithosphere. The lithosphere rides on a layer of partially molten rock called the asthenosphere, which is in the upper part of a larger layer called the mantle. Beneath the mantle lie a liquid outer core and a solid inner core of iron and nickel.

After 100 million years or so, nine of these big chunks were left spinning around the Sun. These formed the planets we know today.

Uranus   *Neptune*   • *Pluto*

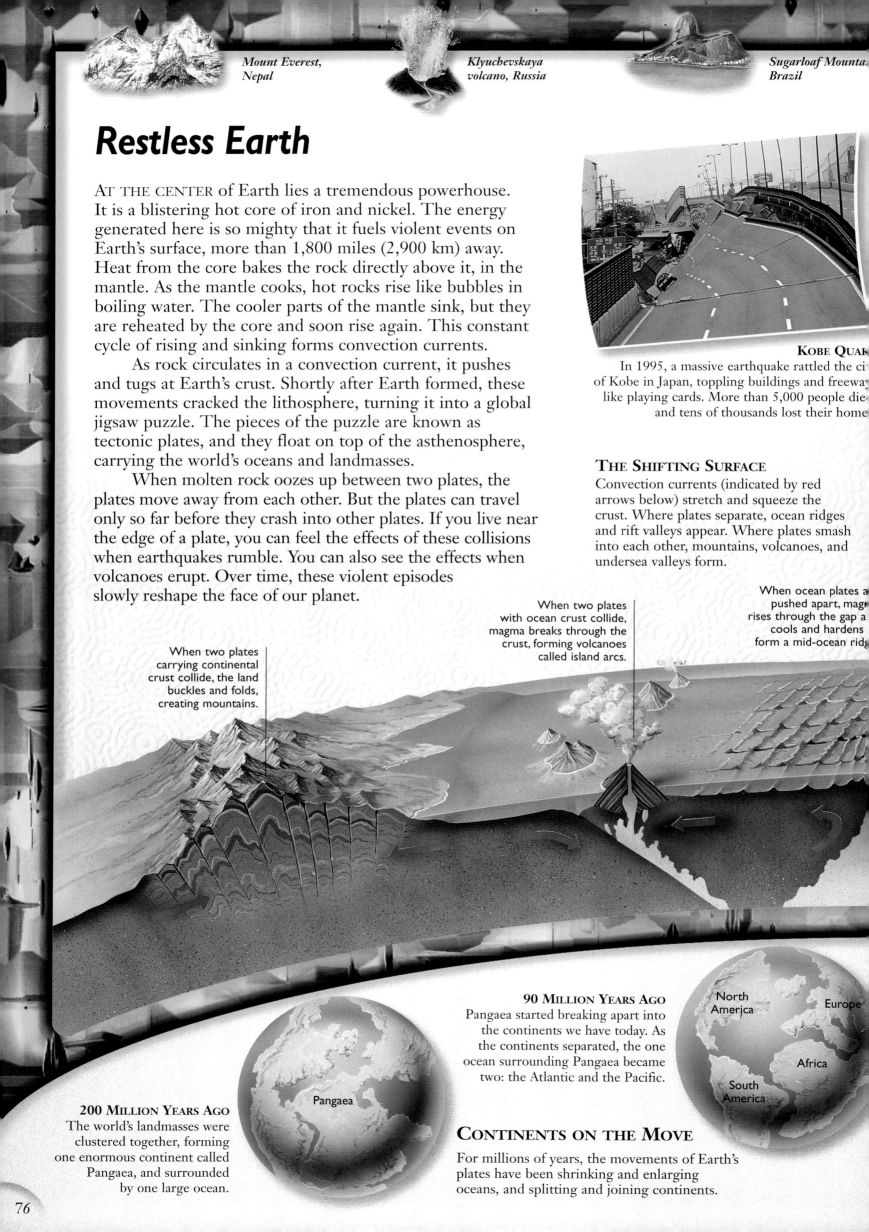

Mount Everest,
Nepal

Klyuchevskaya
volcano, Russia

Sugarloaf Mounta
Brazil

Restless Earth

AT THE CENTER of Earth lies a tremendous powerhouse. It is a blistering hot core of iron and nickel. The energy generated here is so mighty that it fuels violent events on Earth's surface, more than 1,800 miles (2,900 km) away. Heat from the core bakes the rock directly above it, in the mantle. As the mantle cooks, hot rocks rise like bubbles in boiling water. The cooler parts of the mantle sink, but they are reheated by the core and soon rise again. This constant cycle of rising and sinking forms convection currents.

As rock circulates in a convection current, it pushes and tugs at Earth's crust. Shortly after Earth formed, these movements cracked the lithosphere, turning it into a global jigsaw puzzle. The pieces of the puzzle are known as tectonic plates, and they float on top of the asthenosphere, carrying the world's oceans and landmasses.

When molten rock oozes up between two plates, the plates move away from each other. But the plates can travel only so far before they crash into other plates. If you live near the edge of a plate, you can feel the effects of these collisions when earthquakes rumble. You can also see the effects when volcanoes erupt. Over time, these violent episodes slowly reshape the face of our planet.

KOBE QUAK
In 1995, a massive earthquake rattled the ci of Kobe in Japan, toppling buildings and freeway like playing cards. More than 5,000 people die and tens of thousands lost their home

THE SHIFTING SURFACE
Convection currents (indicated by red arrows below) stretch and squeeze the crust. Where plates separate, ocean ridges and rift valleys appear. Where plates smash into each other, mountains, volcanoes, and undersea valleys form.

When two plates carrying continental crust collide, the land buckles and folds, creating mountains.

When two plates with ocean crust collide, magma breaks through the crust, forming volcanoes called island arcs.

When ocean plates a pushed apart, magm rises through the gap a cools and hardens form a mid-ocean rid

90 MILLION YEARS AGO
Pangaea started breaking apart into the continents we have today. As the continents separated, the one ocean surrounding Pangaea became two: the Atlantic and the Pacific.

North America
Europe
Africa
South America

Pangaea

200 MILLION YEARS AGO
The world's landmasses were clustered together, forming one enormous continent called Pangaea, and surrounded by one large ocean.

CONTINENTS ON THE MOVE

For millions of years, the movements of Earth's plates have been shrinking and enlarging oceans, and splitting and joining continents.

Word Builders

• The word **volcano** comes from the name of the Roman god of fire and metalworking, Vulcan. He was said to live beneath a volcano on the present-day island of Vulcano in Italy.
• **Pangaea** is the name of the single continent that existed 200 million years ago. Pangaea comes from the Greek words for "all of Earth."

That's Amazing!

• About 800 strong earthquakes shake the planet each year, but about 8,000 minor ones happen every day. Fortunately, these minor quakes are too weak to cause any damage.
• The plates surrounding the Pacific Ocean are colliding with ocean crust, forming an almost complete circle of volcanoes known as the Ring of Fire.

Pathfinder

• Lava cools and hardens to form various kinds of rocks. Learn about volcanic rocks on pages 82–83.
• When plate movements squeeze or heat Earth's crust, some rocks change into different rocks. Find out how this happens on pages 86–87.
• Discover how scientists study and map the ocean floor on pages 110–11.

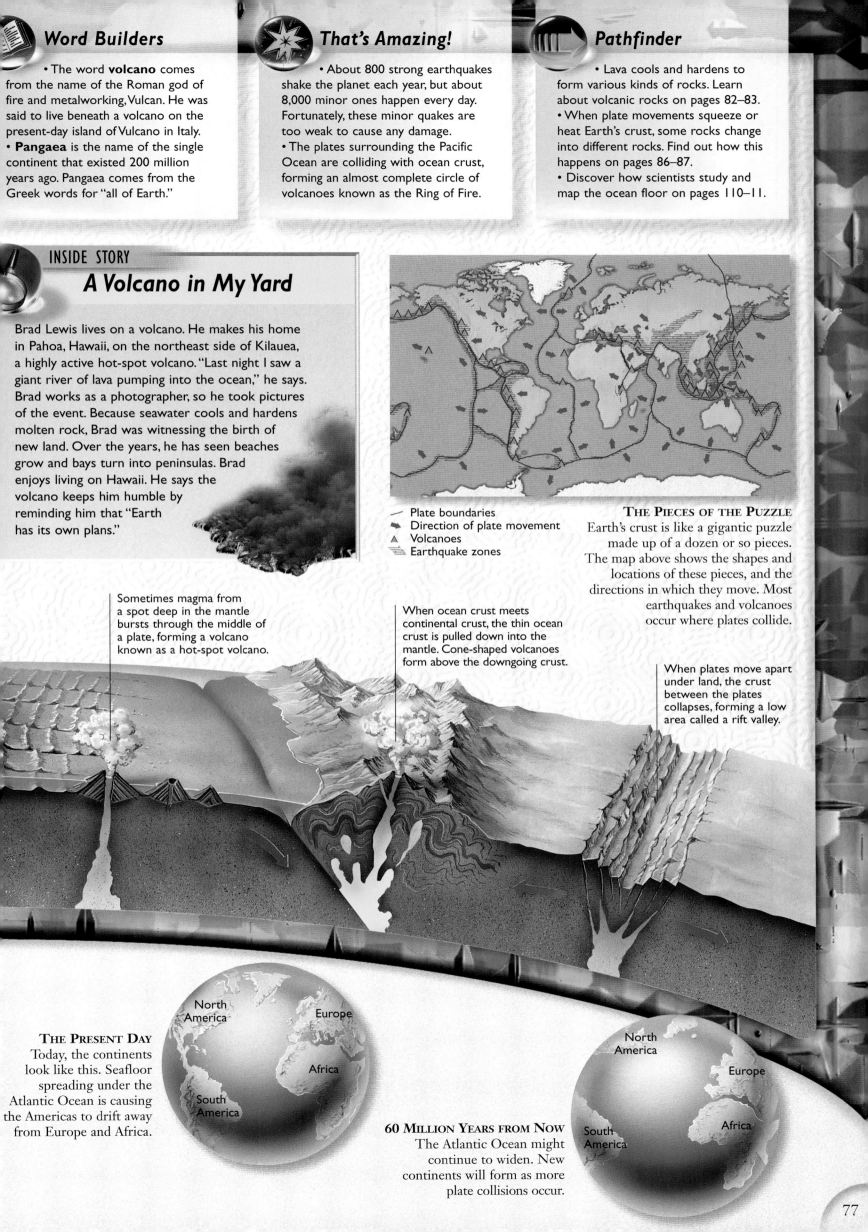

INSIDE STORY

A Volcano in My Yard

Brad Lewis lives on a volcano. He makes his home in Pahoa, Hawaii, on the northeast side of Kilauea, a highly active hot-spot volcano. "Last night I saw a giant river of lava pumping into the ocean," he says. Brad works as a photographer, so he took pictures of the event. Because seawater cools and hardens molten rock, Brad was witnessing the birth of new land. Over the years, he has seen beaches grow and bays turn into peninsulas. Brad enjoys living on Hawaii. He says the volcano keeps him humble by reminding him that "Earth has its own plans."

∕ Plate boundaries
➤ Direction of plate movement
▲ Volcanoes
≋ Earthquake zones

THE PIECES OF THE PUZZLE

Earth's crust is like a gigantic puzzle made up of a dozen or so pieces. The map above shows the shapes and locations of these pieces, and the directions in which they move. Most earthquakes and volcanoes occur where plates collide.

Sometimes magma from a spot deep in the mantle bursts through the middle of a plate, forming a volcano known as a hot-spot volcano.

When ocean crust meets continental crust, the thin ocean crust is pulled down into the mantle. Cone-shaped volcanoes form above the downgoing crust.

When plates move apart under land, the crust between the plates collapses, forming a low area called a rift valley.

THE PRESENT DAY

Today, the continents look like this. Seafloor spreading under the Atlantic Ocean is causing the Americas to drift away from Europe and Africa.

North America
Europe
Africa
South America

60 MILLION YEARS FROM NOW

The Atlantic Ocean might continue to widen. New continents will form as more plate collisions occur.

North America
Europe
Africa
South America

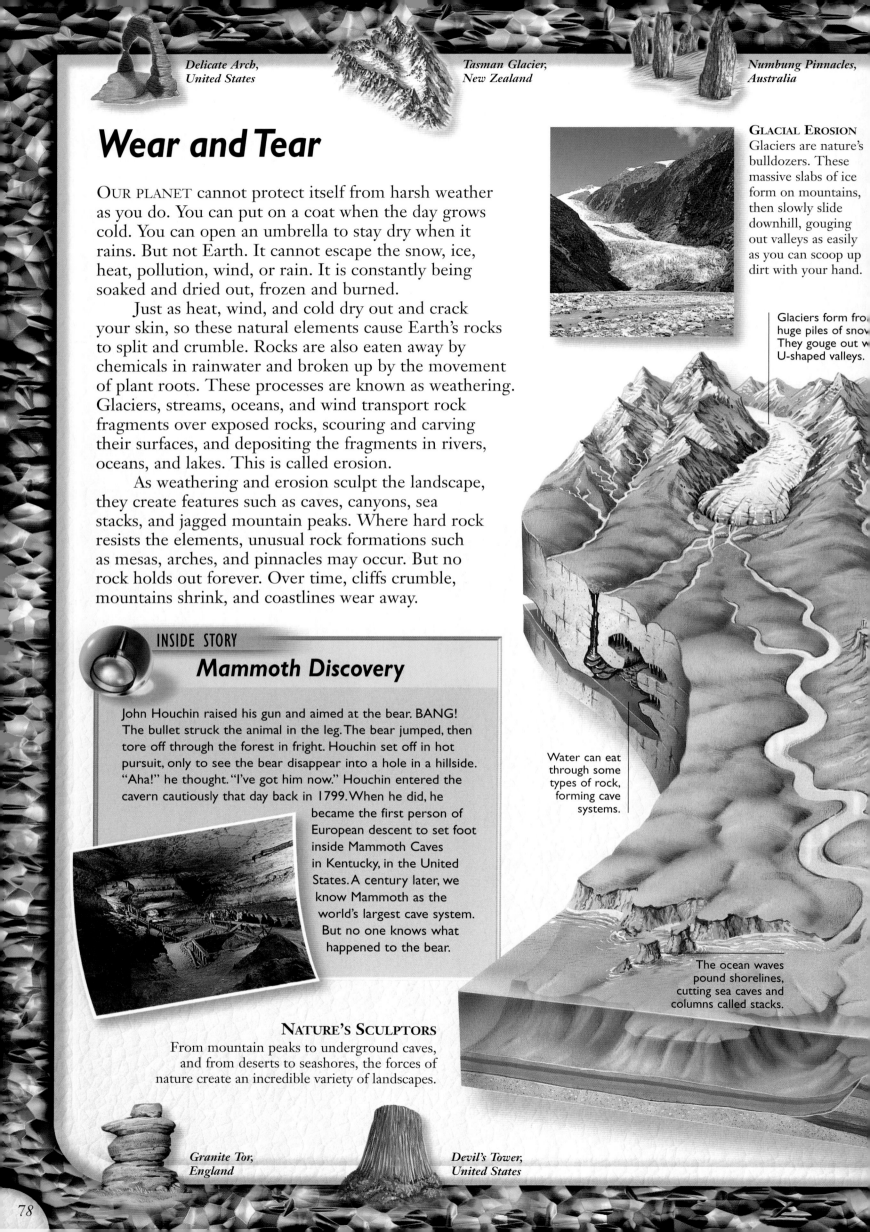

Delicate Arch,
United States

Tasman Glacier,
New Zealand

Numbung Pinnacles,
Australia

Wear and Tear

OUR PLANET cannot protect itself from harsh weather as you do. You can put on a coat when the day grows cold. You can open an umbrella to stay dry when it rains. But not Earth. It cannot escape the snow, ice, heat, pollution, wind, or rain. It is constantly being soaked and dried out, frozen and burned.

Just as heat, wind, and cold dry out and crack your skin, so these natural elements cause Earth's rocks to split and crumble. Rocks are also eaten away by chemicals in rainwater and broken up by the movement of plant roots. These processes are known as weathering. Glaciers, streams, oceans, and wind transport rock fragments over exposed rocks, scouring and carving their surfaces, and depositing the fragments in rivers, oceans, and lakes. This is called erosion.

As weathering and erosion sculpt the landscape, they create features such as caves, canyons, sea stacks, and jagged mountain peaks. Where hard rock resists the elements, unusual rock formations such as mesas, arches, and pinnacles may occur. But no rock holds out forever. Over time, cliffs crumble, mountains shrink, and coastlines wear away.

GLACIAL EROSION
Glaciers are nature's bulldozers. These massive slabs of ice form on mountains, then slowly slide downhill, gouging out valleys as easily as you can scoop up dirt with your hand.

Glaciers form fro
huge piles of snow
They gouge out w
U-shaped valleys.

INSIDE STORY

Mammoth Discovery

John Houchin raised his gun and aimed at the bear. BANG! The bullet struck the animal in the leg. The bear jumped, then tore off through the forest in fright. Houchin set off in hot pursuit, only to see the bear disappear into a hole in a hillside. "Aha!" he thought. "I've got him now." Houchin entered the cavern cautiously that day back in 1799. When he did, he became the first person of European descent to set foot inside Mammoth Caves in Kentucky, in the United States. A century later, we know Mammoth as the world's largest cave system. But no one knows what happened to the bear.

Water can eat through some types of rock, forming cave systems.

The ocean waves pound shorelines, cutting sea caves and columns called stacks.

NATURE'S SCULPTORS
From mountain peaks to underground caves, and from deserts to seashores, the forces of nature create an incredible variety of landscapes.

Granite Tor,
England

Devil's Tower,
United States

Word Builders

- The word **glacier** comes from the French word *glace,* meaning "ice."
- **Mesas** are flat-topped, steep-sided landforms. Mesa is a Spanish word that comes from the Latin *mensa,* meaning "table." Small mesas are called **buttes.** Butte comes from an old French word *bute,* meaning "mound" or "hill."

That's Amazing!

- The world's largest single cave is Sarawak Chamber in Borneo, Malaysia. It is big enough to hold eight jumbo jets.
- At any time, the world's rivers contain 302 cubic miles (1,260 cubic km) of water. If rain stopped falling and the rivers dried up, the sea would evaporate at a rate of 3 feet (1 m) each year.

Pathfinder

- Erosion is part of a process that continually recycles rocks. Read about this process on pages 80–81.
- Rock fragments deposited by rivers may eventually cement together to form new rock. Find out how on pages 84–85.
- Curious about canyons? Take a look inside the biggest canyon in the world on pages 110–11.
- Learn more about erosion at the seashore on pages 122–23.

HANDS ON

Cracking Up

❶ Roll a piece of modeling clay into a round ball. Wet it and then cover it with plastic wrap.

❷ Place the ball in the freezer and leave it overnight. Take it out the next day and examine it closely. What do you see?

❸ Cracks will have formed in the clay. This is because the water expands when it freezes, splitting the clay. The same thing happens to rock when it freezes.

Rivers carve canyons and mesas, and wash away rocks and dirt.

ONION-SKIN WEATHERING
A constant cycle of soaking, drying, freezing, and thawing has caused these huge boulders in central Australia to crack and peel. The rock comes off in layers—just like the skin of an onion.

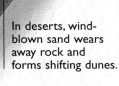

In deserts, windblown sand wears away rock and forms shifting dunes.

ROCK PINNACLES
At Bryce Canyon in the United States, weathering and erosion have shaped the stone into spires called hoodoos.

HOODOOS

The rocks of Bryce Canyon in Utah, U.S.A., formed at the bottom of a lake 50–60 million years ago. Since then, nature has been hard at work, sculpting strange stone columns known as hoodoos.

Small cracks crisscross the rock in the hillside. Water flowing down the hill cuts into the cracks, forming deep, narrow gullies. The water also seeps into cracks in the walls of the gullies.

In winter, the water freezes and expands, widening the cracks in the walls. Slowly, stone columns emerge. Because some types of rock erode more quickly than others, the columns form strange shapes.

Some of the columns topple or crumble to dust. Eventually, this set of hoodoos will disappear. But new ones will already be forming in the hillside.

The Rock Cycle

YOU WON'T NOTICE THIS, but the rocks around you are on a slow-motion roller coaster. Geological forces thrust them up as mountains, spew them into the air as molten rock, break them into bits and pieces, and plunge them deep under ground. Gradually, this rocky ride turns our planet almost completely inside out. Peaks become valleys, and ocean floors turn into mountains, leaving the remains of sea creatures on top of towering peaks such as the Himalayas in Asia.

During this turbulent ride, three different kinds of rock appear. When molten rock cools, igneous rocks form. When rocks on Earth's surface are pummeled to pieces by waves, broken up by ice, or scoured to bits by other rocks, the fragments settle in layers and become sedimentary rocks. Meanwhile, deep inside Earth, fierce temperatures and intense pressure cook and squeeze rocks, transforming them into metamorphic rocks.

It wasn't until this century that scientists figured out how long this roller coaster has been running. We now know it began when Earth formed, nearly five billion years ago. By our standards, the ride is a slow one. But for a rock, it's a journey that repeats over and over.

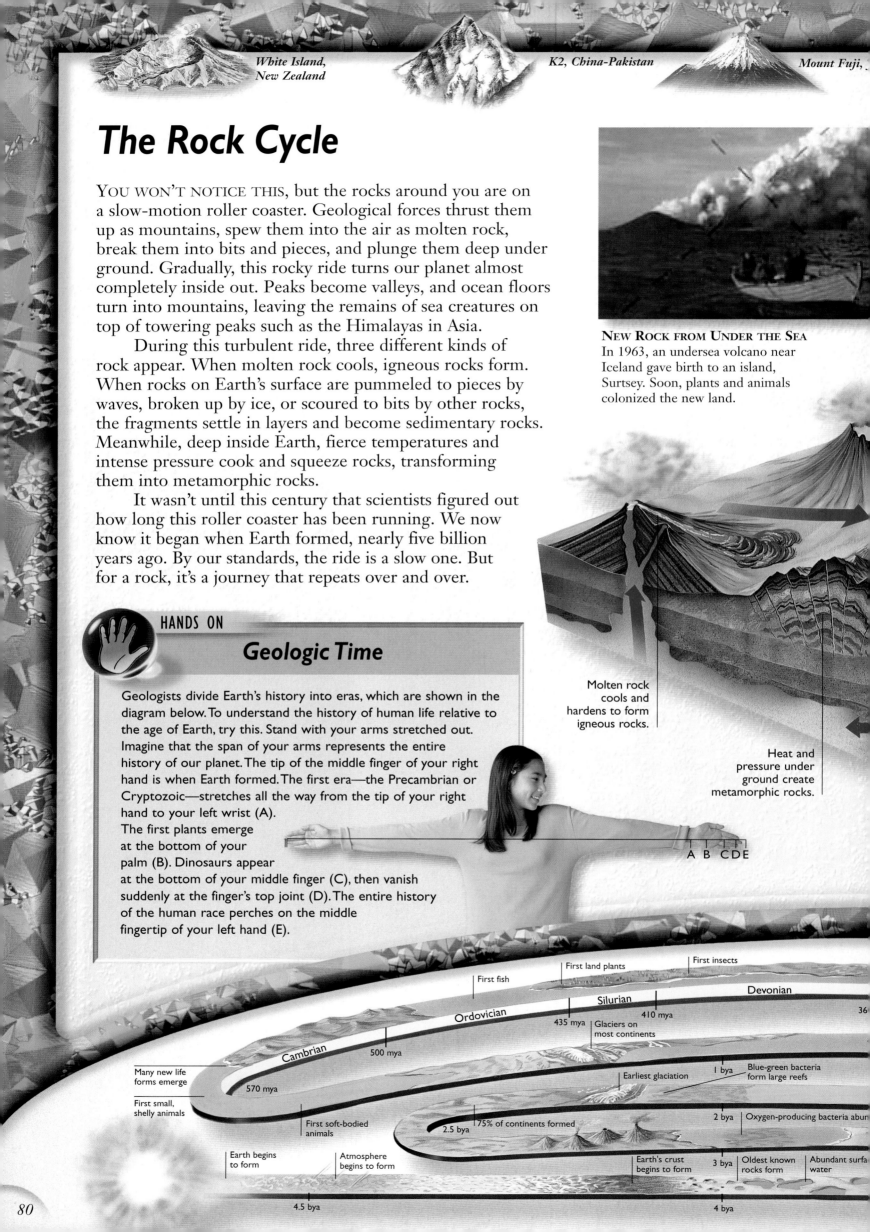

NEW ROCK FROM UNDER THE SEA
In 1963, an undersea volcano near Iceland gave birth to an island, Surtsey. Soon, plants and animals colonized the new land.

Molten rock cools and hardens to form igneous rocks.

Heat and pressure under ground create metamorphic rocks.

HANDS ON

Geologic Time

Geologists divide Earth's history into eras, which are shown in the diagram below. To understand the history of human life relative to the age of Earth, try this. Stand with your arms stretched out. Imagine that the span of your arms represents the entire history of our planet. The tip of the middle finger of your right hand is when Earth formed. The first era—the Precambrian or Cryptozoic—stretches all the way from the tip of your right hand to your left wrist (A).
The first plants emerge at the bottom of your palm (B). Dinosaurs appear at the bottom of your middle finger (C), then vanish suddenly at the finger's top joint (D). The entire history of the human race perches on the middle fingertip of your left hand (E).

A B C D E

First land plants

First insects

First fish

Devonian

Silurian

Ordovician

410 mya

435 mya | Glaciers on most continents

Cambrian

500 mya

36

Many new life forms emerge

570 mya

Earliest glaciation

1 bya | Blue-green bacteria form large reefs

First small, shelly animals

First soft-bodied animals

2.5 bya | 75% of continents formed

2 bya | Oxygen-producing bacteria abun

Earth begins to form

Atmosphere begins to form

Earth's crust begins to form

3 bya | Oldest known rocks form

Abundant surfa water

4.5 bya

4 bya

Word Builders

The names of Earth's eras are all made up of the Greek word **zoe**, which means "life," and another Greek word. **Cryptozoic** comes from *crypto*, meaning "hidden." **Paleozoic** includes *paleo*, meaning "ancient." *Meso*, in **Mesozoic**, means "middle." **Cenozoic** comes from *ceno*, meaning "recent."

That's Amazing!

• The oldest known rock lies in Canada's Northwest Territories. The Acasta gneiss, a metamorphic rock, is 3.96 billion years old.
• Lava emerges from Kilauea volcano on Hawaii, U.S.A., at a rate of 7 cubic yards (5 cubic m) per second.

Pathfinder

• Discover what causes plate movements on pages 76–77.
• Find out more about the formation of igneous, sedimentary, and metamorphic rocks on pages 82–87.
• Read about how scientists use fossils to date rock layers on pages 124–25.

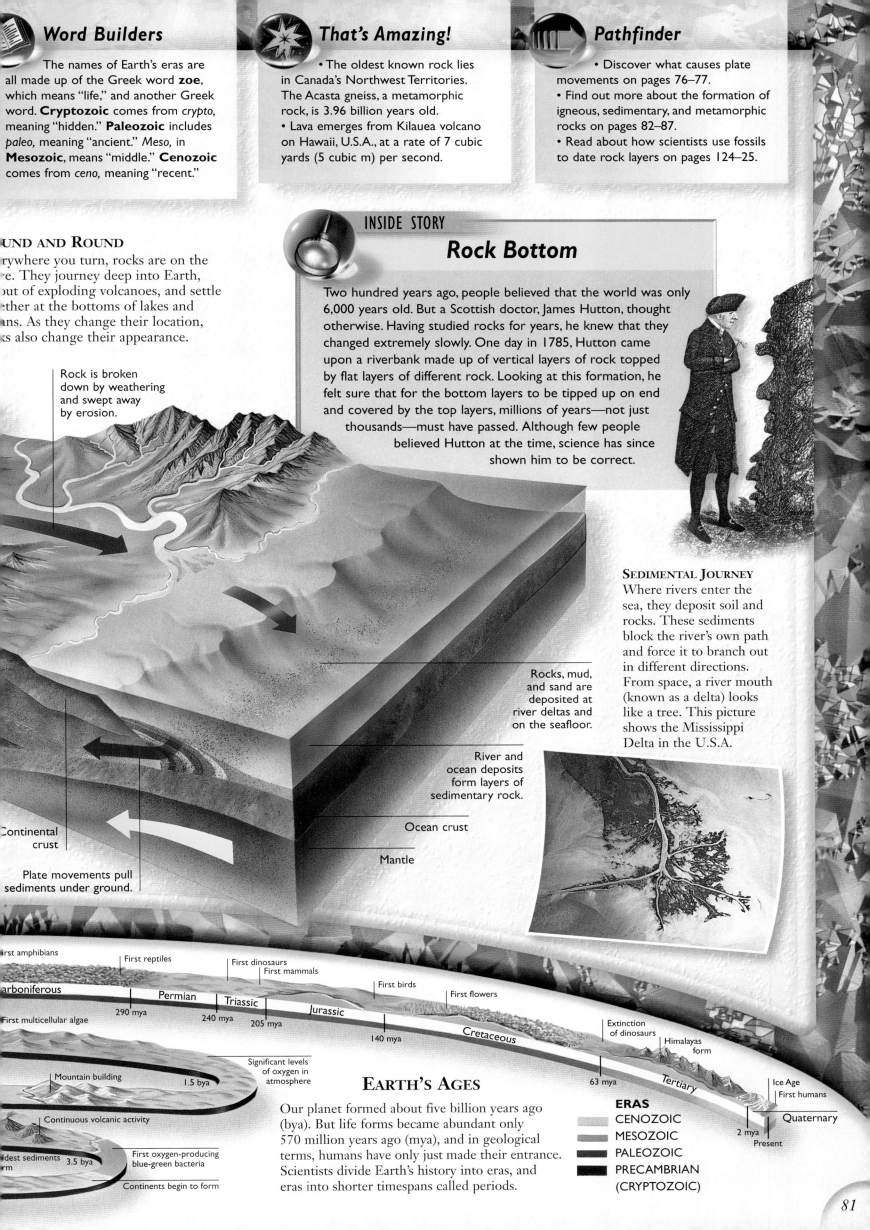

...UND AND ROUND

...rywhere you turn, rocks are on the ...e. They journey deep into Earth, ...ut of exploding volcanoes, and settle ...ther at the bottoms of lakes and ...ns. As they change their location, ...s also change their appearance.

Rock is broken down by weathering and swept away by erosion.

Continental crust

Plate movements pull sediments under ground.

INSIDE STORY

Rock Bottom

Two hundred years ago, people believed that the world was only 6,000 years old. But a Scottish doctor, James Hutton, thought otherwise. Having studied rocks for years, he knew that they changed extremely slowly. One day in 1785, Hutton came upon a riverbank made up of vertical layers of rock topped by flat layers of different rock. Looking at this formation, he felt sure that for the bottom layers to be tipped up on end and covered by the top layers, millions of years—not just thousands—must have passed. Although few people believed Hutton at the time, science has since shown him to be correct.

Rocks, mud, and sand are deposited at river deltas and on the seafloor.

River and ocean deposits form layers of sedimentary rock.

Ocean crust

Mantle

SEDIMENTAL JOURNEY

Where rivers enter the sea, they deposit soil and rocks. These sediments block the river's own path and force it to branch out in different directions. From space, a river mouth (known as a delta) looks like a tree. This picture shows the Mississippi Delta in the U.S.A.

Earth's Ages

Our planet formed about five billion years ago (bya). But life forms became abundant only 570 million years ago (mya), and in geological terms, humans have only just made their entrance. Scientists divide Earth's history into eras, and eras into shorter timespans called periods.

...irst amphibians
First reptiles
First dinosaurs
First mammals
First birds
First flowers

...arboniferous
Permian
Triassic
Jurassic
Cretaceous
Tertiary
Quaternary

290 mya
240 mya
205 mya
140 mya
63 mya
2 mya
Present

First multicellular algae

Extinction of dinosaurs
Himalayas form

Ice Age
First humans

Mountain building
1.5 bya

Significant levels of oxygen in atmosphere

Continuous volcanic activity

ERAS
CENOZOIC
MESOZOIC
PALEOZOIC
PRECAMBRIAN (CRYPTOZOIC)

...dest sediments 3.5 bya

First oxygen-producing blue-green bacteria

Continents begin to form

Obsidian
(extrusive)

Ropy lava
(extrusive)

Rivers of Fire

RIVERS OF FIRE flow through Earth's crust. They are made of a red-hot mixture of molten rock and crystals called magma, which rises from deep inside the planet. If magma breaks through Earth's surface, it emerges as lava. When magma and lava cool, they harden into a type of rock known as igneous rock. Most of Earth's crust is made of igneous rock, but much of this rock is buried under sediments, seawater, soil, or other rock.

Two kinds of igneous rock occur—intrusive igneous rock and extrusive igneous rock. Intrusive igneous rock forms when magma hardens below the surface. Magma rises through the crust, cramming itself through brittle rock, but it can't always break through. The cooled rock remains under ground until natural forces like erosion and tectonic uplift uncover it. Granite is an intrusive rock that is found when mountain ranges erode down to their cores. Extrusive or volcanic igneous rock forms when magma breaks through the crust as lava and cools on the surface. Basalt is an extrusive rock that makes up ocean crust. Since oceans cover much of Earth, most of Earth's crust is basalt.

Crystals in an igneous rock provide an important clue to how it formed. Intrusive rock cools slowly, producing big crystals you can see easily. Extrusive rock, on the other hand, cools quickly, forming tiny crystals that you can see only with a microscope.

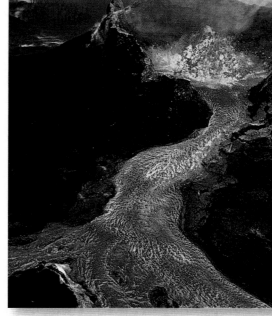

ISLAND BUILDING
Fiery lava frequently flows from Kilauea volcano on the Big Island of Hawaii, U.S.A. As the running lava cools, it hardens and creates new land. All of the Hawaiian Islands were formed in this way.

Regular, six-sided columns form when lava cools quickly.

INSIDE STORY
The Day the Sky Turned Black

One August afternoon in AD 79, a mountain blew its top. It was Mount Vesuvius, a volcano on the west coast of Italy. The writer Pliny the Younger lived nearby. As ashes rained down, Pliny and his mother fled their house. Above the volcano, "a black and dreadful cloud yawned open to reveal long, fantastic flames," Pliny later wrote. Darkness fell. "You could hear the shrieks of women, the crying of children, and the shouts of men," wrote Pliny. He and his mother had to keep shaking the ashes off themselves, "otherwise we should have been buried and crushed under their weight." But they were among the lucky ones. That day, two towns, Herculaneum and Pompeii, disappeared beneath surges of hot rock, clouds of gas, and mudflows. Centuries later, the towns were uncovered. Lava had hardened around the victims, leaving human-shaped spaces in the rocks after the bodies decayed. Scientists made casts from these molds.

Andesite
(extrusive)

Gabbro
(intrusive)

Word Builders

• **Igneous** comes from the Latin word *ignis*, which means "fire."
• Runny, fast-flowing lava hardens into ropelike coils of rock. In Hawaii, this kind of lava is called **pahoehoe**. Thick, slow-moving lava forms rough, bumpy rock called **aa**. This word is said to come from the sound you would make if you walked barefoot across the rock.

That's Amazing!

In 1815, Mount Tambora in Indonesia exploded in the largest eruption in recorded history. It coughed up 36–43 cubic miles (150–180 cubic km) of hot ash and gas, and killed more than 50,000 people. The ash cloud from the eruption blocked out the Sun for weeks, causing famines that resulted in at least 80,000 additional deaths.

Pathfinder

• Volcanoes occur at the edges of Earth's tectonic plates. Read about tectonic activity on pages 76–77.
• Volcanic plugs are revealed by weathering and erosion. Find out more about these processes on pages 78–79.
• Some igneous rocks contain large crystals. Learn more on pages 92–93.
• How do you identify igneous rocks? Find out on page 118–19.

A ROCK WITH WINGS
Ship Rock in New Mexico, U.S.A., is the remains of an ancient volcano. The local Navajo people call the 1,500-foot (457-m) structure *Tse Bida'hi*, which means "the winged rock."

VOLCANIC PLUGS

Ship Rock is an example of a volcanic plug. These massive stumps of igneous rock have fiery origins. They form when molten rock cools and hardens in the throat of a volcano.

SIX-SIDED STEPS

When lava cools quickly, it can crack and shrink, forming six-sided columns of basalt. These pillars in Northern Ireland are known as the Giant's Causeway. They formed when lava flooded a flat region about 30 million years ago.

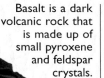

Basalt is a dark volcanic rock that is made up of small pyroxene and feldspar crystals.

TOUGH STUFF
Granite is a tough, light-colored rock that usually contains large crystals of feldspar, quartz, and mica.

During eruptions, large amounts of ash and lava pour out of the volcano. The lava-ash mixture cools into igneous rock and forms a cone-shaped mountain.

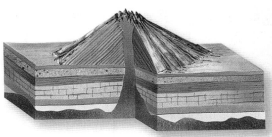

The eruptions end, and the magma cools and hardens inside the volcano. Weathering and erosion start to wear away the soft exterior of the mountain.

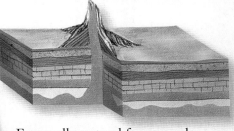

Eventually, natural forces erode the mountain completely. Only the more resistant plug stands as a reminder of the ancient volcano.

Conglomerate (rocky sediments)

Sandstone (sandy sediments)

Chert (che sediments)

Layer upon Layer

EARTH CHURNS UP rocks, spreads them out, and builds them in layers like a cake. This process starts when weathering and erosion break rocks into tiny pieces. Wind and flowing water then carry the pieces to river, lake, and sea beds, where they settle in layers. As the pieces, or sediments, build up over millions of years, they cement together to form sedimentary rock. Common sedimentary rocks include limestone, sandstone, and shale.

Weathering and erosion cut through soft sedimentary layers like a knife through a cake. But they have to work around tougher sedimentary rock. This creates unusual rock formations as different layers are exposed. Because each layer of rock formed in a separate environment, scientists can study these layers and reconstruct a landscape's history. Some limestone, for example, is made of seashell remains. Sandstone is what's left of a long-gone beach, riverbed, or desert.

Sedimentary rocks also contain useful substances. Coal forms between rock layers when plants from ancient swamps have decayed. Salt, which is sometimes found in layers of sedimentary rock, also forms when seawater evaporates. Did you realize that you were sprinkling your food with the remains of an ocean?

SALT FLATS

Rain and melting snow from distant mountains sometimes transform desert valleys into temporary lakes. When the water evaporates, it leaves behind a layer of salt crystals called a salt flat. This one is in Death Valley, in California, U.S.A.

The lower layers of dark red siltstone and mudstone formed from ancient lowland marshes.

The middle layers of sandstone, siltstone, and mudstone formed under rivers, swamps, and lakes.

HANDS ON

Making Sedimentary Layers

❶ Collect some gravel, coarse sand, fine sand, and a little dirt. Put a few tablespoonfuls of each into a jar and fill the jar halfway with water. With the lid on tight, shake the jar, making sure all the materials mix together.

❷ Leave the mixture to settle overnight. What do you see in the morning? The materials have settled into layers, with the fine sand on top and the heavy gravel at the bottom. This is how sedimentary layers form under water. If you bury the mixture, after a few million years it should turn into sedimentary rock.

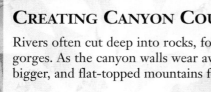

CREATING CANYON COUNTRY

Rivers often cut deep into rocks, forming canyons and gorges. As the canyon walls wear away, the valleys get bigger, and flat-topped mountains form.

Sedimentary rocks are exposed when the sea level falls or the land is uplifted. Rivers cut deep into rocks, forming narrow pathways in the land.

Word Builders

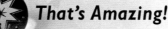

• The word **sedimentary** comes from the Latin *sedimentum*, which means "settling," and also from the Latin verb *sedere*, which means "to sink" or "to sit down."
• **Canyons** are steep-sided valleys. Canyon comes from the Spanish word *caña,* meaning "tube."

That's Amazing!

The sedimentary rocks dolomite and limestone usually contain pieces of shells that once belonged to tiny marine creatures called foraminifera. These single-celled animals are so small that one whole shell can fit inside the eye of a needle.

Pathfinder

• Discover more about weathering and erosion on pages 78–79.
• Sedimentary rocks often contain fossils. These are used by geologists to date rock layers. Go to pages 110–11.
• Learn how coal forms and take a look inside a coal mine on pages 112–13.

FROM THE DEEP
This odd-looking rock is a shelly limestone. It began to form when sea creatures died and their shells sank to the seafloor. Over time, the shells were cemented into a solid lump.

THE STUFF OF ANCIENT WATERS
Capitol Reef, in Utah, U.S.A., was named by a group of early settlers because the cliffs blocked their way just as a reef would at sea. Most of these sedimentary rocks formed about 200 million years ago under rivers and swamps.

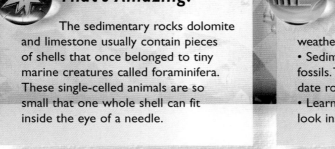

INSIDE STORY

Clinging to a Canyon

One-armed geologist and soldier General John Wesley Powell clings to a canyon wall high above the Colorado River. It is 1869, and he and his men are conducting the first survey of the river's sedimentary canyons. He climbed up here with his friend G. Y. Bradley to look for a safe route over the rapids. But now, with his foot wedged into a crack and his left hand grasping a rocky overhang, Powell is stuck. He calls for help. Bradley finds a way to the top of the rock but cannot reach the general. Suddenly he gets an idea. He takes off his pants and swings them down. Powell grasps them tightly, and Bradley hauls him up. Without Bradley's quick thinking, Powell's geological knowledge may have been lost forever.

The hard red sandstone cap resists erosion. It formed from ancient desert sand dunes.

This greenish gray shale contains volcanic ash.

THE WHITE CLIFFS OF DOVER
These cliffs at Dover in England are a type of powdery limestone called chalk. A thumb-sized chunk of this rock contains thousands of microscopic shell pieces that are about 70 million years old.

As the rivers cut deeper into the hard, resistant rock, they form steep-sided valleys. When they reach softer layers, the rivers start to dig under the hard rock.

The undercutting causes the upper layers to collapse, and the valley widens. This creates large, flat-topped rocks called mesas and small ones called buttes.

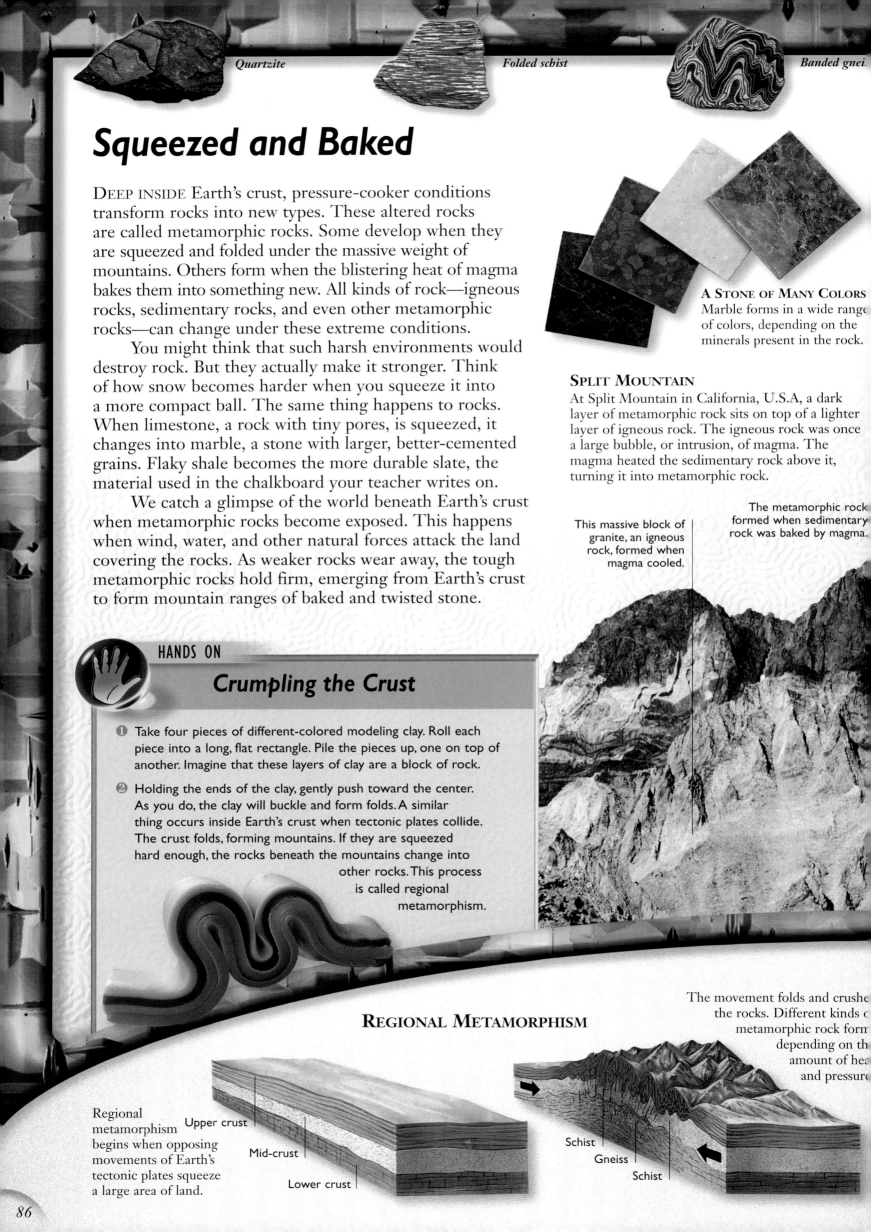

Quartzite

Folded schist

Banded gnei[ss]

Squeezed and Baked

DEEP INSIDE Earth's crust, pressure-cooker conditions transform rocks into new types. These altered rocks are called metamorphic rocks. Some develop when they are squeezed and folded under the massive weight of mountains. Others form when the blistering heat of magma bakes them into something new. All kinds of rock—igneous rocks, sedimentary rocks, and even other metamorphic rocks—can change under these extreme conditions.

You might think that such harsh environments would destroy rock. But they actually make it stronger. Think of how snow becomes harder when you squeeze it into a more compact ball. The same thing happens to rocks. When limestone, a rock with tiny pores, is squeezed, it changes into marble, a stone with larger, better-cemented grains. Flaky shale becomes the more durable slate, the material used in the chalkboard your teacher writes on.

We catch a glimpse of the world beneath Earth's crust when metamorphic rocks become exposed. This happens when wind, water, and other natural forces attack the land covering the rocks. As weaker rocks wear away, the tough metamorphic rocks hold firm, emerging from Earth's crust to form mountain ranges of baked and twisted stone.

A STONE OF MANY COLORS

Marble forms in a wide range of colors, depending on the minerals present in the rock.

SPLIT MOUNTAIN

At Split Mountain in California, U.S.A, a dark layer of metamorphic rock sits on top of a lighter layer of igneous rock. The igneous rock was once a large bubble, or intrusion, of magma. The magma heated the sedimentary rock above it, turning it into metamorphic rock.

This massive block of granite, an igneous rock, formed when magma cooled.

The metamorphic rock formed when sedimentary rock was baked by magma.

HANDS ON

Crumpling the Crust

1 Take four pieces of different-colored modeling clay. Roll each piece into a long, flat rectangle. Pile the pieces up, one on top of another. Imagine that these layers of clay are a block of rock.

2 Holding the ends of the clay, gently push toward the center. As you do, the clay will buckle and form folds. A similar thing occurs inside Earth's crust when tectonic plates collide. The crust folds, forming mountains. If they are squeezed hard enough, the rocks beneath the mountains change into other rocks. This process is called regional metamorphism.

REGIONAL METAMORPHISM

The movement folds and crushe[s] the rocks. Different kinds [of] metamorphic rock form[,] depending on th[e] amount of hea[t] and pressur[e]

Regional metamorphism begins when opposing movements of Earth's tectonic plates squeeze a large area of land.

Upper crust

Mid-crust

Lower crust

Schist

Gneiss

Schist

Word Builders

- **Metamorphic** and **metamorphism** are both made up of the Greek words *meta*, meaning "change," and *morphe*, meaning "form."
- **Gneiss** (pronounced "nice") comes from an Old Norse word *gneista*, meaning "to give off sparks."

That's Amazing!

Metamorphism can turn a rock into one of a number of other rocks, depending on the amount of heat and pressure involved. For example, shale can turn into slate (moderate heat and pressure), schist (high heat and pressure), or gneiss (extreme heat and pressure).

Pathfinder

- Find out how colliding tectonic plates cause Earth's crust to crumple on pages 76–77.
- Metamorphic rocks may contain gemstones. Turn to pages 98–99.
- Learn how to identify metamorphic rocks on pages 118–19.

METAMORPHIC MONUMENT
Emperor Shah Jahan built this tomb, known as the Taj Mahal, at Agra in India, as a monument to his wife, Mumtaz. It was constructed between 1632 and 1654 and is made entirely of white marble.

INSIDE STORY

Seeing Is Believing

Geologist Sir James Hall picked up his gun. He was determined to prove a point. His good friend, James Hutton, believed that heat and pressure could change chalky rocks like limestone and dolomite into marble. Other scientists laughed at this, but Sir James agreed with his friend. To prove it, he poured powdered chalk down the gun barrel, sealed the end, and roasted the weapon. Once it cooled, he tipped out a stony mass that looked like marble. Hutton was right! Not everyone was convinced. But Sir James went on to conduct 500 similar experiments between 1798 and 1805. Today, everyone agrees with him and Hutton.

UNDER PRESSURE
The rock in this cliff face used to be shale. Extreme pressure turned it into a new type of rock called slate.

CONTACT METAMORPHISM

Sandstone
Shale
Limestone
Magma

Quartzite
Hornfels
Marble
Magma

Contact metamorphism occurs when magma rises through rock. The magma chamber may be as big as a mountain or as small as a house.

The magma bakes the surrounding stone. Depending on the kind of rock present, different types of metamorphic rock form.

Dumbbell micrometeorite *Pyrite sand dollar* *Pumic*

Strange Rocks

JUST WHEN YOU THINK you have rocks figured out, a few odd ones pop up. Take meteoroids, for example. They rocket in from outer space, grazing the night sky in a streak of light. You might know them as shooting stars. But they aren't stars. They are chunks of black, heavy rock. When they zip through the atmosphere, friction causes them to burn brightly. In the past, enormous meteoroids have slammed into Earth, creating huge craters. Then the rocks are called meteorites. Fortunately for us, most of these flying rocks burn up in Earth's atmosphere.

Not all peculiar rocks come from space. For example, there is a type of sandstone called itacolumite that you can bend and twist with your bare hands, as easily as you can bend a piece of wire. This is possible because itacolumite contains flexible minerals linked together inside the rock. There is also a common type of volcanic rock that is so light that it floats in water. It is called pumice.

Other rocks just look strange. Pseudofossils are rocks that resemble fossils. People have often mistaken them for traces of prehistoric plants or animals. Some rocks look like live plants. You'd think a desert rose ought to be in a vase. But it's really a rock made of a mineral called gypsum.

RACING ROCKS
In Death Valley, in California, U.S.A., chunks of rock lie next to trails, as if they have been racing across the mud. Scientists believe that the rocks are lifted by sheets of ice that form on the lake when it fills in winter. As the ice drifts across the water, it trails the rocks along the lake bed.

CRYSTAL BALLS
Geodes are balls of rock that contain crystals. On the outside, they look plain and dull. But if you crack one open, you may get a surprise.

FLOWERS OF THE DESERT
Some "flowers" are made of rock. These gypsum roses form in deserts when groundwater containing calcium and sulfur evaporates. The gypsum that is left behind forms crystals. The crystals grow over the grains of sand, binding them into a roselike pattern.

BUBBLING UNDER
Geodes form in cavities inside igneous or sedimentary rocks. They emerge when the rock is worn away by erosion or weathering.

When igneous or sedimentary rock layers form, cavities may be created by gas bubbles. Water containing dissolved minerals sometimes seeps into the cavities.

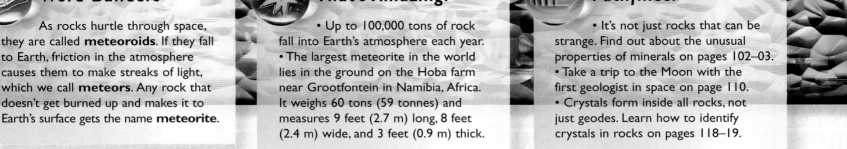

Word Builders

As rocks hurtle through space, they are called **meteoroids**. If they fall to Earth, friction in the atmosphere causes them to make streaks of light, which we call **meteors**. Any rock that doesn't get burned up and makes it to Earth's surface gets the name **meteorite**.

That's Amazing!

• Up to 100,000 tons of rock fall into Earth's atmosphere each year.
• The largest meteorite in the world lies in the ground on the Hoba farm near Grootfontein in Namibia, Africa. It weighs 60 tons (59 tonnes) and measures 9 feet (2.7 m) long, 8 feet (2.4 m) wide, and 3 feet (0.9 m) thick.

Pathfinder

• It's not just rocks that can be strange. Find out about the unusual properties of minerals on pages 102–03.
• Take a trip to the Moon with the first geologist in space on page 110.
• Crystals form inside all rocks, not just geodes. Learn how to identify crystals in rocks on pages 118–19.

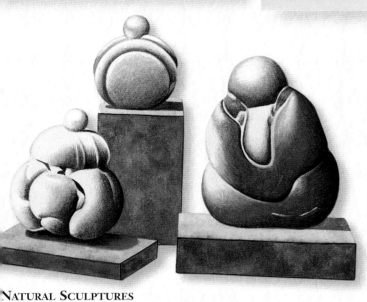

NATURAL SCULPTURES
Pseudofossils are oddly shaped rocks that look like the remains of ancient life forms. They may resemble plants, animals, or even humans.

INSIDE STORY

Strike It Rich

On October 9, 1992, Michelle Knapp sat at home in Peekskill, New York, U.S.A. Suddenly, she heard a loud bang. "It sounded like a three-car crash," she said later. She ran outside to investigate. The rear of her car looked like someone had punched a huge hole in it. Peeking under the trunk, she found a rock the size of a small watermelon, smelling like rotten eggs. It was a meteorite. The meteorite wasn't all bad news, however. Collectors paid Michelle's family $69,000 for the rock. They even bought the car, which was worth $300, for $10,000.

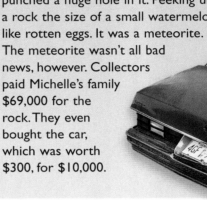

ROCKS FROM OUTER SPACE
Meteorites, like this one found in the Atacama Desert in Chile, are true space aliens. Most are chunks of rock that broke off asteroids or planets. By studying these extraterrestrials, scientists can learn about the history of the solar system.

IN A FLASH
Wiry stones called fulgurites form when lightning zaps soil, sand, or rock. The lightning heats a strip of the material, which melts and cools into a long, pipelike shape.

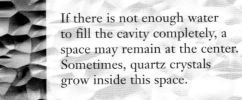

The mineral-rich water deposits concentric layers of tiny crystals on the walls of the rock cavity. Each layer may be a different color.

If there is not enough water to fill the cavity completely, a space may remain at the center. Sometimes, quartz crystals grow inside this space.

89

Minerals

page **92**

Are minerals habit forming?

Can you tell a crystal by its color?

Go to MEET THE MINERALS.

LOOK CLOSELY AT a rock and you may notice that it is made up of tiny pieces of one or more materials. These materials are called minerals. Minerals are the building blocks of rocks. They are solid chemical substances that form within Earth (as well as on other planets). There are thousands of different minerals, and they come in all colors, shapes, and sizes. They include metals such as gold and silver, as well as valuable gemstones such as diamonds. Minerals may form regular, flat-sided shapes called crystals. Often, crystals of different minerals grow together, forming rocks. When minerals have plenty of space to grow, they form large, beautiful crystals.

page **94**

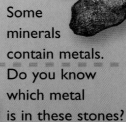

Some minerals contain metals. Do you know which metal is in these stones?

How do we extract metals from minerals?

Go to EARTH'S RICHES.

page **96**

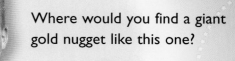

Gold, silver, and platinum are called precious metals. Which of these metals is the most valuable?

Where would you find a giant gold nugget like this one?

Go to BURIED TREASURE.

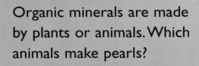

Copper: dendritic
(treelike) habit

Labradorite: massive
(rocklike) habit

Garnet: equant
(equal-sided) hab

Meet the Minerals

MINERALS ARE solid substances that occur naturally in Earth's crust. They are made up of chemicals called elements. Eight elements make up 99 percent of all minerals on Earth. They are oxygen, silicon, aluminum, iron, magnesium, calcium, potassium, and sodium. A mineral that contains only one element is called a native element. If more than one element makes up a mineral, it is called a compound.

Just like you, minerals contain tiny particles called atoms. If you could shrink yourself down to microscopic size, you would see that the atoms in most minerals form a repeating, three-dimensional pattern. This makes a mineral grow into a crystal with a regular shape and flat sides. Some crystals form cubes. Others grow into columns with three or more sides, which are called prisms. Often, minerals grow together with other minerals in irregular masses known as rocks. In these cases, the crystals may be so small that you cannot see them. But they still possess a regular internal structure.

Scientists have identified more than 2,500 different minerals. We can recognize minerals by examining their color, density, hardness, and habit. The habit of a mineral is the overall shape formed by its crystals. It depends on the internal structure of the crystals and the conditions in which they grow. Some habits are very unusual. There are minerals that look like piles of needles, bunches of grapes, and even tiny trees.

CRYSTAL STRANDS
Bundles of crystal strands make up this piece of amphibole asbestos, giving it a fibrous habit. Asbestos fibers won't burn, so asbestos was often used as fireproofing material before some varieties were proven to be a health hazard.

ROCK CANDY
Wulfenite usually forms flat tablet-like crystals. This is called a tabular habit. The shape of the crystals and their butterscotch color make them look like candy. Wulfenite crystals are often transparent. They sometimes contain wispy patterns, known as phantoms, that form when traces of other minerals are trapped in the crystals.

A VARIED WARDROBE
Many minerals come in a variety of colors. For example, fluorite shows up in several shades, including green, yellow, and purple. The colors are caused by impurities in the mineral.

Word Builders

• The word **mineral** comes from the Latin word *minera,* which means "mine" or "ore."
• **Crystal** comes from the Greek word *crystallos,* meaning "ice." The ancient Greeks believed that quartz was made of water that had frozen so hard it would never melt.
• **Rhodochrosite** gets its name from the Greek words *rhodon,* meaning "rose," and *chros,* meaning "color."

That's Amazing!

• The largest topaz crystal in the world was found in Brazil in 1940. It weighs 596 pounds (270 kg) and is on display in the American Museum of Natural History, New York, U.S.A.
• In South Dakota, U.S.A., miners found crystals of a mineral called spodumene that measure 47 feet (14.3 m) in length and weigh 80 tons (72.8 metric tons).

Pathfinder

• Find out how to identify rocks and minerals on pages 118–19.
• Azurite contains copper. Learn more about this metal on pages 94–95.
• Large crystals are common in igneous and metamorphic rocks. See pages 82–83, 86–87.
• Some people believe that minerals have magical powers. Turn to pages 102–03.

MAMMOTH MINERALS

Tiny crystals can grow into mammoth minerals. Crystals grow at different rates, but each one retains its internal structure. The topaz crystal below has a columnar shape called a prismatic habit. It developed this form while maturing into a 111-pound (50.3-kg) giant. People cut such crystals into huge gemstones. The cut gem shown below left is called the American Golden Topaz. It weighs 10 pounds (4.5 kg).

HANDS ON
Grow Your Own Crystals

You can grow your own crystals at home using salt and water.

❶ Stir salt into a jar of warm water until no more will dissolve. Attach a thread to a pencil and hang it above the solution.

❷ As the water evaporates, cubic salt crystals will form on the thread. Salt forms cubic crystals because its molecules are arranged in a cubic pattern that repeats itself as the salt grows.

❸ To encourage large crystals, break off the smallest crystals and throw them away. If your crystals stop growing, add more salt.

TRUE BLUE
Azurite shows up in different habits, but always in a deep blue color. Sometimes it grows in this botryoidal habit, making the mineral look like a bunch of grapes. People often polish azurite and use it to make jewelry.

NATURAL NEEDLES
Crocoite often grows with an acicular, or needlelike, habit. This rare and fragile mineral is a favorite with collectors. Some of the best specimens come from mines on the island of Tasmania in Australia.

THE SAME OLD CLOTHES
A number of minerals sport one color all of the time. For example, rhodochrosite is always a rosy pink. Malachite is usually rich green. And sulfur comes in nothing but bright yellow.

Bornite (copper ore)

Galena (lead ore)

Bauxite (aluminum or[e])

Earth's Riches

EARTH BOASTS a treasure trove of useful minerals. These include metals such as gold, silver, copper, and lead, and nonmetallic minerals such as sulfur and salt. Minerals that are useful to people and can be mined economically are called ores. These minerals have been valued and collected by humans for thousands of years.

One of the first ores to be mined was copper. It may form in the ground as a lump of pure metal, making it easy to recognize and collect. Other metals, such as gold, silver, and platinum also occur in this pure state. We call these minerals native metals. However, most metals mix with other elements to form minerals in rocks. Aluminum, for example, is combined with oxygen in a rock called bauxite. Lead, which rarely appears in a pure state, is found in minerals such as galena and cerussite. It took humans thousands of years to learn how to separate metals from rocks.

Metals are not the only useful materials obtained from rocks. People also gather a range of nonmetallic minerals. For example, we use graphite to make pencils. We heat gypsum to make plaster of paris. We even mine rocks to add to our food. Did you realize that you regularly eat a mineral called halite? It's more commonly known as salt.

LIQUID ROCK
These silvery beads are drops of mercury, the only metal that exists as a liquid at room temperature. It forms in cinnabar, a reddish ore. We use this metal in thermometers because it is sensitive to small changes in temperature and gives us accurate readings.

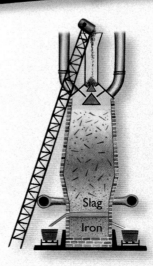

BEAUTIFUL BRIMSTONE
Sulfur is a bright yellow nonmetallic mineral. It forms near hot springs and volcanic vents. In ancient times, it was known as "brimstone" or "the fuel of Hell's fires." Sulfur looks beautiful, but it easily combines with hydrogen to form hydrogen sulfide, which stinks like rotten eggs. Despite this, people use sulfur to make fertilizers and chemicals that kill insects.

MAKING STEEL

Steel is a mixture of iron and carbon. We use it to make a wide range of objects, from cars and utensils to trains and tools. Producing steel involves many complicated processes. These illustrations show the main steps.

Iron ore

Coke

Limestone

Steel is made from iron, coke (a type of heated coal), and limestone. The iron must first be extracted from iron ore, which usually contains iron and oxygen.

The ingredients are put into a furnace that may stand 25 stories high. Workers then blast hot air into the furnace to raise the temperature. The coke combines with the oxygen in the ore to form carbon monoxide. The molten iron sinks to the bottom of the furnace. Adding limestone removes impurities, forming a waste material called sla[g].

Slag
Iron

Word Builders

- The word **copper** comes from the Greek name for the island of Cyprus, *Kyprios,* where copper was first mined five thousand years ago.
- **Hematite** is a major iron ore. When ground up, it forms a red powder. Its name comes from the Greek word *haimatites,* which means "bloodlike."
- **Bauxite** is named for the town of Les Baux in France, where this ore was first discovered in 1821.

That's Amazing!

- It takes four tons of bauxite to produce one ton of aluminum.
- A bucket filled with a gallon of water weighs 8.5 pounds (3.8 kg). The same bucket filled with liquid mercury would weigh 115 pounds (52 kg). Mercury is so dense that a piece of lead will float on its surface like a boat on the sea.

Pathfinder

- Which are the most valuable metals? Find out on pages 96–97.
- Most modern buildings are reinforced with steel. See pages 72–73 and 106–07.
- Strong, lightweight metals such as aluminum and titanium are used to build planes, helicopters, and even spacecraft. Turn to pages 114–15.

THE COLORS OF COPPER

Copper occurs both as a native metal and in a number of ores. The native form (below left) is reddish, and often looks like a clump of wires. But when copper combines with other elements, the resulting minerals are usually blue or green. Copper ores include this turquoise-colored rock called aurichalcite (far left) and this deep blue mineral, azurite (right).

SLENDER SPIKES OF STIBNITE
They may look like pins in a pincushion, but these are actually crystals of stibnite. Stibnite is the principal ore of a metal called antimony.

INSIDE STORY

Coppersmiths of Ancient Israel

My name is Solomon. I live in the valley of Timna in Israel. My people are coppersmiths. We mine copper for the Egyptian pharaoh. The copper we mine comes from a green mineral called malachite. I help my father and brother to separate the copper from the malachite, using a process called smelting. We fill a stone furnace with charcoal and then blow air through pipes to make the coals hotter. My brother and I keep blowing while my father sprinkles crushed malachite into the furnace and adds more charcoal. After a while, we let the furnace cool. Black lumps of waste called slag form at the bottom. We smash open the slag and retrieve pellets of copper. It's hard work, but our copper has made us famous throughout Egypt.

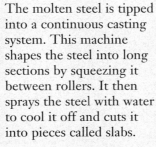

The iron is poured into another furnace that contains steel scraps. Heated oxygen is blasted into the iron to keep it hot and to combine with excess carbon. This reduces the amount of carbon in the iron, turning it into steel.

The molten steel is tipped into a continuous casting system. This machine shapes the steel into long sections by squeezing it between rollers. It then sprays the steel with water to cool it off and cuts it into pieces called slabs.

Sheet-metal workers bend, cut, and roll the slabs into a range of shapes, including wires, girders, sheets, and pipes. These items are then sold to manufacturers who use them to make a wide variety of products.

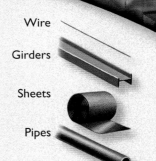

Wire

Girders

Sheets

Pipes

Buried Treasure

EARTH HOLDS a treasure trove of rare and precious metals. Gleaming pieces of gold, silver, and platinum lie in and on the ground, awaiting discovery. As far back as 6,000 years ago, people living near the Persian Gulf mined gold and silver. They hammered the soft metals into jewelry and other beautiful objects, just as we do today. Platinum, on the other hand, wasn't discovered until the early 1700s. But its extreme rarity makes it even more valuable than gold.

Precious metals often occur in their pure, or native, state. They turn up in veins—mineral deposits that fill cracks in Earth's crust. We also find them mixed with sand and gravel on riverbeds. These deposits, called placer ores, form when erosion separates the metal from rock and water washes it into a river, where it sinks to the bottom. This often happens to gold.

Gold frequently finds its way into beautiful jewelry. But it has properties that make it valuable in industry, too. For example, gold does not rust, so it is often used to make vital pieces of electronic equipment. The metal is also very shiny. When used as a coating on the outside of satellites and other space instruments, gold reflects cosmic radiation that would otherwise damage the equipment.

SILVER STRINGS
Treelike strands of native silver form where hot liquids deposit minerals. A small amount of mined silver is made into coins, jewelry, and utensils. But the most common use of this metal is in photographic film. When you take a photo, silver crystals are produced from the film emulsion. The crystals react to the light and capture the image.

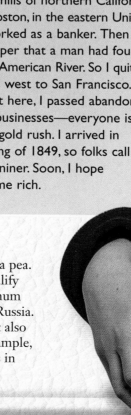

INSIDE STORY

The Gold Rush

My name is Pete. I'm a prospector panning for gold in the hills of northern California. I used to live in Boston, in the eastern United States, where I worked as a banker. Then I read in the newspaper that a man had found gold here in the American River. So I quit my job and headed west to San Francisco. On the way out here, I passed abandoned farms and businesses—everyone is joining the gold rush. I arrived in the beginning of 1849, so folks call me a forty-niner. Soon, I hope they'll call me rich.

PRIZE PLATINUM
Platinum nuggets are seldom larger than a pea. This one, shown at actual size, would qualify as a major find. The highest quality platinum comes from the Ural Mountains in Russia. We use platinum for jewelry, but it also plays less glamorous roles. For example, it is placed in antipollution devices in cars to trap dirt and toxic gases.

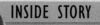

Word Builders

- **Platinum** comes from the Spanish word *plata,* meaning "silver." The name refers to the color of the metal.
- For centuries, people used **pyrite** to make fire. If you strike the mineral against flint or iron, it produces sparks. The word "pyrite" comes from the Greek word *pyr,* meaning "fire."
- The chemical symbol for silver is **Ag,** which comes from its Latin name *argentum,* meaning "white and shining."

That's Amazing!

- The biggest pure-gold nugget ever found was discovered at Moliagul, in Victoria, Australia, in 1869. Named the Welcome Stranger, it weighed in at 156 pounds (70.8 kg).
- Platinum is so rare that 2 million pounds (907,000 kg) of ore may contain only one pound (0.45 kg) of metal.
- Gold is so soft and easily worked that you could roll an ounce (28 g) of it into a hair-thin wire 50 miles (80 km) long.

Pathfinder

- Gold, silver, and platinum are all native elements. Find out more about native elements on pages 92–93.
- Precious metals are sometimes extracted from ores. Go to pages 94–95.
- Take a look at some beautiful gold objects on pages 108–09.
- To learn about tests used to identify minerals, go to page 119.

GOLD GROWTH

Some gold nuggets may grow in sediments like potatoes grow in soil. Scientists now think that these nuggets form when miniscule flecks of gold carried by water attach themselves to bacteria.

DON'T BE FOOLED

Prospectors often mistook this shiny, yellow mineral called pyrite for gold. This earned it the name "fool's gold." But you don't have to be tricked. You can tell the difference between gold and pyrite by scratching the minerals across a piece of unglazed white porcelain. Pyrite leaves a greenish-black mark, while gold streaks yellow.

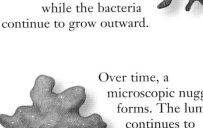

Microscopic strands of bacteria in sediments attract tiny, dissolved molecules of gold present in wet ground. Static electricity makes the gold stick to the bacteria, just as pieces of paper will stick to a rubber balloon that you have rubbed on your hair.

GOLD NUGGETS

Gold nuggets as large as these ones are rare finds. These are plaster casts of a pair of nuggets found at Rheola, in Victoria, Australia, in 1870. They are called the Viscount and Viscountess of Canterbury. If the nuggets were real, these children wouldn't be able to pick them up—gold is twice as heavy as lead.

More gold builds up and solidifies on the bacteria, coating it like a suit of armor. Gradually, the gold thickens, filling the gaps between the strands while the bacteria continue to grow outward.

Over time, a microscopic nugget forms. The lump continues to attract tiny pieces of dissolved gold. Eventually, it may grow as large as the nuggets on the left.

This photograph was taken through a microscope. It shows a thin layer of gold coating a tangled mass of bacteria. The top has been worn smooth by erosion.

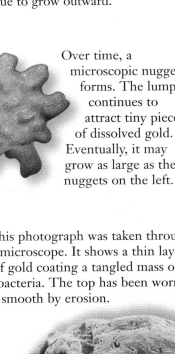

Rare Beauty

SOME MINERALS are in a class of their own. Known as gemstones, they are collected and treasured for their outstanding beauty. The most valuable gemstones, called precious gems, have two additional qualities. They are rare and durable. People seek rare stones because they like to own unique objects. They value hard gems because these minerals retain their beauty without scratching or breaking for a long time. Precious gems include diamonds, rubies, sapphires, and emeralds.

Some gemstones form during metamorphism—when rocks in the crust are buried, squeezed, and heated by plate movements. For example, rubies may form when sedimentary rock is transformed by mountain formation. On the other hand, diamonds grow deep under ground in Earth's upper mantle, and emeralds form when liquids crystallize in or around cooling granite. The hardness of a gemstone depends on the size, arrangement, and types of its atoms.

Gemstones may be carried to the surface by eruptions or plate movements and then exposed by erosion. Running water may dislodge gems from rock layers and leave them on riverbeds. These deposits are called placer deposits. Uncovering precious stones can be like hunting for a needle in a haystack. Miners often have to dig up 500 tons (454 tonnes) of ore to locate a single ounce (28 g) of diamond.

KING OF THE GEMS

Diamond is the hardest natural substance on Earth. It also possesses a fiery brilliance unmatched by any other gemstone. Many diamonds appear colorless, or clear, but most have a slight tinge of yellow. The famous 128-carat Tiffany Diamond, seen here, sparkles canary yellow. Other "fancy" colors include pink, green, blue, purple, and red—the rarest of all.

RUBY RED

Ruby (left) and sapphire are two types of a mineral called corundum. If a tiny amount of chromium mixes with corundum, the mineral is red and is called ruby. The red color of ruby varies from pale red to purple. Blood-red ruby is among the rarest and most valuable of gems. Rubies are also used to make certain lasers.

UNDER PRESSURE

Diamonds form about 90 miles (145 km) or more below the ground, in the upper mantle. The gems are carried to the surface during the formation of an igneous rock called kimberlite. Here are the basics of kimberlite formation.

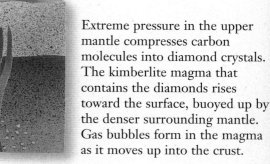

Extreme pressure in the upper mantle compresses carbon molecules into diamond crystals. The kimberlite magma that contains the diamonds rises toward the surface, buoyed up by the denser surrounding mantle. Gas bubbles form in the magma as it moves up into the crust.

Word Builders

- **Tourmaline** derives from the Sinhalese (Sri Lankan) word *touramalli,* meaning "stones of mixed colors."
- **Diamond** comes from the Greek word *adamas,* meaning "invincible."
- **Ruby** takes its name from the Latin word *rubeus,* meaning "red."
- **Corundum** comes from the Sanskrit word *kuruvinda,* meaning "ruby."

That's Amazing!

- The largest diamond ever found was the 3,106-carat Cullinan. Discovered in South Africa in 1905, it was cut into 9 large jewels and 96 smaller ones.
- Corundum is the second-hardest mineral after diamond. However, diamond is approximately 150 times harder than corundum.

Pathfinder

- More common gemstones are known as semiprecious stones. Find out about these minerals on pages 100–01.
- For centuries, people believed that gems had magical powers. Read about magical minerals on pages 102–03.
- A gem called topaz may form enormous crystals. Take a look at a giant topaz on pages 92–93.

INSIDE STORY

The Punch Diamond

In April 1928, 12-year-old William Jones—nicknamed Punch—made a remarkable discovery. Punch and his father, Grover, were pitching horseshoes in their backyard at Petertown, West Virginia, U.S.A. As one of the horseshoes landed, the father and son heard a loud "clang." When Punch brushed away the dirt, he saw a bluish-white crystal the size of a large marble gleaming in the sunlight. "See, I have found a diamond," he said to his father. They both laughed at this idea. Punch put the crystal into a cigar box, and it remained there for 15 years. In 1943, Grover took the stone to an expert. He confirmed that it was actually a 34.48 carat diamond—one of the largest ever found in the eastern United States. The Jones family put the Punch Diamond, as it was now known, on display in a museum. Then, in 1984, they sold it. The bluish stone, found in a dusty horseshoe pit, fetched $74,250.

SEARCHING FOR SAPPHIRES
This collector is searching for sapphires by using a pump to suck up river sediments. He will then pass the sediments through a sieve. As he swirls the sediments around on the sieve, centrifugal force pushes the lighter stones such as quartz to the outside, leaving the heavier red zircons and blue sapphires in the center (above right).

WATERMELON TOURMALINE
With its green "rind" and pink "flesh," this tourmaline crystal looks like a chunk of watermelon. Tourmaline displays a great variety of colors. It can be pink, red, blue, green, violet, yellow, orange, brown, black, or even crystal clear. The color depends on the metals present in the mineral. Pink is caused by manganese, while green may be due to iron or chromium.

RAW DIAMOND
Diamonds like the one on the left are commonly found in a rock called kimberlite. They usually form eight-sided crystals called octahedrons, which look like two pyramids glued together at the base.

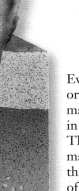

Every so often, a buildup of gas or a physical reaction between the magma and groundwater results in an explosive volcanic eruption. This blasts molten rock, rocky material, and diamonds up through the crust. The last event of this kind probably occurred about 60 million years ago.

After the explosion, the rock slowly cools, forming a carrot-shaped plug called a kimberlite pipe. Erosion may then wash some of the diamonds into streams. People hunt the gems by mining the kimberlite or searching for placer deposits on riverbeds.

When they were found, these stones looked rough and colorless. But polishing the stones completely transforms them, and we can now see their glorious colors.

Clockwise from top left: amazonite, jasper, tiger's eye, rhodonite, snowflake obsidian, hematite, lace agate, bloodstone

Nephrite

Colors and Shapes

SOME GEMSTONES are plentiful as well as beautiful. Because they are more common, these stones are less valuable than rare, precious gems. But we still collect and treasure them, usually for their rich colors or patterns. People sometimes refer to these gems as ornamental or semiprecious stones. For thousands of years, humans have used ornamental stones to enhance clothes, jewelry, and art. For example, people in France made jewelry out of polished pieces of a reddish stone called jasper as long as 20,000 years ago.

Ornamentals often occur as clumps of tiny, intergrown crystals. This is known as a massive habit, since no regular crystal shapes can be seen. Certain combinations of crystals create amazing patterns. Agate, for instance, contains wavy bands of color. They are formed by alternating layers of small chalcedony crystals containing slightly different chemicals and may occur with larger quartz crystals.

Other types of gemstones, called organic gems, are created by plants and animals. For example, pearls grow inside shellfish. The skeletons of sea creatures create coral. And jet, a black gemstone, is a variety of coal, a rock formed from animal or plant remains.

TWO IN ONE
Jade is the name given to either of two different minerals: nephrite and jadeite. Both are tough and come in a variety of colors. The people of New Zealand have been carving nephrite into artworks and tools like these knives since AD 1000.

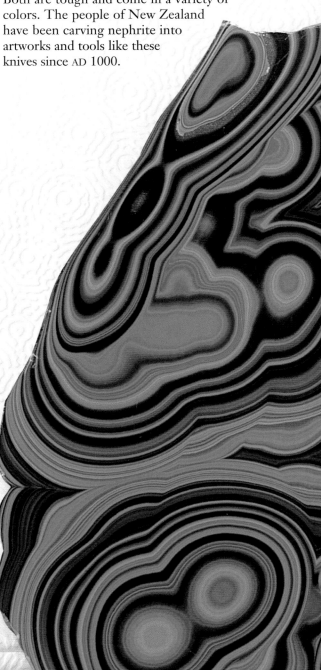

ULTRA BLUE
Lapis lazuli is treasured for its rich blue color and is often used in jewelry. The ancient Egyptians also used powdered lapis lazuli as eye shadow. In Renaissance Europe, artists used the same powder to make a highly prized paint called ultramarine. In this painting, "St. Francis Giving His Cloak to a Poor Soldier" (1437), the artist Sassetta used ultramarine to emphasize the value of the cloak.

Lapis lazuli

GEMS THAT GROW
A pearl begins to form when a piece of grit or a grain of sand lodges inside the shell of an oyster, clam, or mussel.

To protect itself from this irritant, the animal inside covers the grit with a substance called nacre. The nacre builds up in layers and, in seven years or so, forms a pearl.

Word Builders

- Merchants from Venice used to purchase **turquoise** in Turkish markets and then sell it to Europeans. As a result, the French people who bought the gemstone referred to it as *pierre turquoise,* or "Turkish stone."
- **Lapis lazuli** comes from the Latin word for "stone," *lapis,* and the Arabic *lazaward,* meaning "heaven" or "sky."

That's Amazing!

- The Pueblo people of North America used to place turquoise beads in their tombs. One burial site known as Pueblo Bonito, in New Mexico, U.S.A., contains about 24,900 of these beads.
- The highest-quality lapis lazuli comes from the mountains of Badakhshan in Afghanistan. People have been mining this source for more than 6,000 years.

Pathfinder

- Most ornamental stones form in massive habits. Find out about mineral habits on pages 92–93.
- Colorful stones called agates often line geode cavities. See pages 88–89.
- Ornamental stones have been used in jewelry for centuries. See pages 108–09.
- Amber is an organic gem. It looks like a mineral but is actually fossilized tree sap. Sometimes it contains ancient life forms. Take a look at one on page 124.

HANDS ON

Rock and Roll

In their natural state, most ornamental stones are rough and dull. To bring out their colors and patterns, collectors polish the stones using a tumbling machine. This consists of a hollow drum that is rotated by motor-driven rollers. You can buy tumbling machines, but the best way to learn how to use one is to join a lapidary club. These groups collect and polish ornamental stones, and use them to make jewelry.

To tumble stones, you place the rocks into the drum with water and coarse grit. Then you turn on the machine and leave it running for a week or so. Next, you replace the grit with a finer grit and leave the machine on for another week. The grits grind away the hard edges of the stones until they are smooth. Finally, you remove the grit, add a fine polishing powder, and run the machine again. The powder gives the stones a shiny finish.

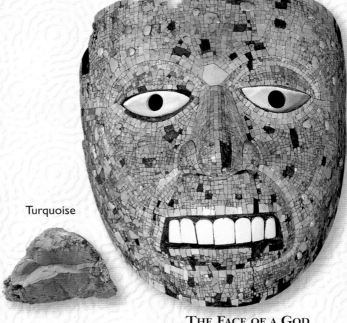

Turquoise

THE FACE OF A GOD

The first recorded use of turquoise dates back to 5000 BC in Mesopotamia (now Iraq), where people used the gemstone to make beads. The Aztec people of North America used turquoise in pendants and ceremonial masks. This mask, made about AD 1500, represents the Aztec god of the wind, Quetzalcoatl.

SHAPES IN THE STONE

Swirling shades of green give malachite a unique beauty. The light green bands are clusters of extremely small crystals. The dark green stripes contain larger crystals. Malachite rarely occurs as big, individual crystals, but it does take on many different shapes. This malachite has a massive habit. Other habits include fibrous, radial (spokelike), and botryoidal (like a bunch of grapes).

Malachite

JEWELS FROM THE DEEP

Pearls usually grow as small, round stones that are often strung together to make necklaces (above). But people have been known to change the shape of pearls. These Buddha pearls (right) were made by implanting small lead Buddhas into a living mussel. Over several years, the shellfish covered the figures with layers of nacre. This practice began in China in the 12th century.

People create cultured pearls by placing a small bead inside a shellfish. The nacre grows around the bead just as it grows around a sand grain.

Sliced in half, a natural pearl would reveal many concentric layers of nacre around a tiny piece of grit. A cultured pearl would contain only a few layers around the bead.

Natural pearl   Cultured pearl

Quartz crystal ball for seeing the future

Eye agate for protecting against the evil eye

Magical Minerals

THE EXTRAORDINARY shapes, colors, and properties of minerals created amazement among early peoples. Our ancestors marveled at smooth, clear quartz crystals that looked like ice but didn't melt, and at stones shaped like needles, grapes, and crosses. They were puzzled by the properties of certain minerals, such as magnetite, which can act like a magnet, and amber, which may contain insects.

Their bewilderment gave rise to many beliefs about minerals, some of which had a basis in fact. For example, quartz was often placed on a person's forehead to cure a fever. This mineral is a good thermal insulator—it retains heat and cold. So, if kept in a cold place, it would feel cool and soothing, just like a cold towel. Native Americans rubbed quartz crystals together during ceremonies to simulate lightning. Quartz does glow when struck or squeezed—a property known as triboluminescence.

Other superstitions relating to minerals have no scientific basis. Some children in Greece wear garnets to keep them safe from drowning. Some farmers in the Middle East tie turquoise to their horses' tails to protect the animals from accidents. And people in many societies still believe that crystals can promote healing and even predict the future.

HOLY CRYSTALS
When the volcano Mount Vesuvius erupted in 1666, crosses rained down on the city of Naples. People called the event a miracle. But the crosses were really crystals of pyroxene that had intergrown at right angles. This process is known as twinning.

Fluorite

HANDS ON

Sweetness and Light

Take a sugar cube into a dark room and squeeze it with a pair of pliers. The cube will glow faintly. Then squeeze harder until the cube shatters. As it breaks, you should see a blue flash.

When you crush the sugar crystals, they break into positively and negatively charged fragments. Energy jumps between the opposite charges, producing sparks. The sparks react with nitrogen in the air to create a bluish flash. This effect—the creation of light by friction—is called triboluminescence. Some minerals, such as quartz and fluorite, are also triboluminescent. Certain materials create a brighter flash because the chemicals they contain also emit light.

FLUORESCENT MINERALS
Fluorescent minerals glow in vibrant colors under ultraviolet light. Other minerals, such as diamond, may continue to glow for a short time after a light is turned off—a trait called phosphorescence. These changes occur because the minerals absorb the light rays and then reradiate them at a different wavelength, producing a visible color.

CAT'S-EYE GEMS
This gemstone seems to stare right back at you. Its color and stripe of reflected light make it look like the eye of a cat—an effect known as chatoyancy. Several minerals display this effect when cut into round, smooth gems called cabochons. But chatoyant chrysoberyl, shown here, is the truest cat's-eye. The bright yellow line is caused by a row of parallel fibers made of a mineral called rutile, which reflects the light.

Word Builders

• People once believed that **jade** could cure kidney pains if applied to the side of the body. The word "jade" comes from the Spanish *piedra de ijada,* which means "stone of the side."
• Ancient Greeks thought that if you put an **amethyst** in your wine, you wouldn't get drunk. Amethyst comes from the Greek word, *amethystos,* which means "not drunken."

That's Amazing!

• The Ancient Egyptians placed emeralds in the throats of mummies to keep them strong in the underworld.
• In the Middle Ages, some doctors believed that if people rubbed themselves with bloodstone and herbs, they could become invisible.
• In the 17th century, an eminent English doctor, William Rowland, claimed that taking crushed garnets would cure heart problems.

Pathfinder

• Rocks display some strange characteristics, too. Turn to pages 88–89.
• Learn more about the odd shapes of minerals on pages 92–93.
• Many unusual gems are used to make jewelry. See pages 108–09.
• Certain minerals have extraordinary properties that we have only recently learned to use. Go to pages 114–15.

Strontianite

Willemite (green) and calcite (red)

BIRTHSTONES

Birthstones can be traced back to ancient times. They may be linked to the twelve gems set in the breastplate of Aaron, a Hebrew priest and brother of the prophet Moses, which represented the 12 tribes of Israel. Later, people began to associate the stones with signs of the zodiac and then with birth months. Today it is still said that your birthstone will bring you good fortune.

JANUARY Garnet

FEBRUARY Amethyst

MARCH Aquamarine

APRIL Diamond

MAY Emerald

JUNE Pearl

JULY Ruby

AUGUST Peridot

SEPTEMBER Sapphire

OCTOBER Opal

NOVEMBER Topaz

DECEMBER Turquoise

RUBY IN MARBLE
Rubies, seen here embedded in marble, are associated with many myths. Burmese warriors believed that if they sewed rubies into their flesh, the gems would protect them in battle. Other peoples claimed that if a ruby turned dark, something bad would happen to its owner.

PIECES OF THE MOON
Certain kinds of feldspar have a pearly white sheen. People thought this looked like the reflection of the moon, so they called these minerals moonstones. The sheen is actually caused by layers of tiny crystals that reflect light. The Roman naturalist Pliny believed that if you held a moonstone up to the stars, it would collect the starlight.

103

Collecting Rocks and Minerals

THROUGHOUT HISTORY, people have collected rocks and minerals to make useful materials and objects. They have turned them into handy tools. They have gathered them to make homes and other buildings, as well as fuels, ornaments, and jewelry. But some people also collect and study rocks and minerals to learn about our planet. These people are called geologists. You can become a geologist, too. All you need are a few simple tools and a basic knowledge of rocks and minerals. You can study the geology of your area, visit unusual landforms, and gather interesting samples. Eventually, you may create your very own rock and mineral collection.

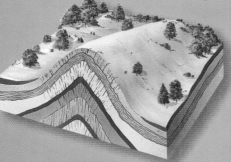

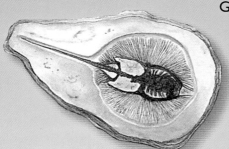

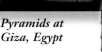

Building Blocks

FOR MILLIONS of years, humans have used rocks to make homes and other buildings. Early humans found shelter in natural caves and soon learned how to carve out their own. Then they began to build shelters using wood, thatch, or mud bricks. But gradually they realized that the strongest, longest-lasting buildings were those made of stone.

As people's skills and knowledge of rocks improved, so did their buildings. The ancient Egyptians learned how to cut limestone from quarries and build enormous pyramids. They also discovered how to use giant slabs of granite to make pavements and walls. The Romans built elegant temples and enormous stadiums using stone such as travertine, a cream-colored porous limestone. In the second century BC, the Chinese began to construct the world's longest wall out of bricks made of granite and other rocks. Many of these ancient structures still stand today.

As time went on, people discovered new materials and techniques. They learned how to make glass out of sand and cut slate tiles for roof shingles. More recently, they began to use steel and concrete (a mixture of water, crushed rock, and cement) to build skyscrapers. Today, you don't need to look far to see rocks being put to good use.

INSIDE STORY
Walled In

The Ch'in ruler Shih Huang Ti, emperor of China, banged his fist on the table. His advisors had just brought him bad news. Mongol horsemen from the north had invaded another village. "We must keep the barbarians out!" he yelled. He then commanded his citizens to reinforce existing village walls and build many new ones. By 210 BC—11 years after the emperor's order—these walls had been joined to form one long wall. Later emperors extended this wall until it encircled the entire kingdom. Today, the Great Wall stretches 2,150 miles (3,461 km) around northern China, and stands 30 feet (9 m) tall in some places.

HANDS ON
Build a Book Bridge

Many early peoples, including the Maya, built bridges, arches, and doorways by stacking stones like steps until the top ones were almost touching. Then they placed another stone on top to form an arch. You can do the same using a pile of books and two chairs.

Place the chairs opposite each other, about 18 inches (46 cm) apart. Build a pile of books on each chair. Place each book so that it is closer to the other chair than the book underneath. When the two piles almost meet, place one last book on top to create an arch or bridge.

SHORE TO SHORE
Different kinds of rocks and minerals were used to build Sydney Harbor Bridge in New South Wales, Australia. The bridge was completed in 1932 and contains 38,000 tons of steel (a mixture of iron and carbon). The pylons are made of granite and the foundations are yellow sandstone.

FROM CAVE TO HIGH-RISE
Through the ages, people have used different types of rocks and minerals to make a wide variety of homes.

TUFF STUFF
Four thousand years ago, people in Cappadocia, Turkey, carved homes in stone pinnacles made of a volcanic rock called tuff. Some of these homes are still in use today.

BRICK BY BRICK
For centuries, some native peoples in the Americas have built homes from adobe bricks. These bricks are made of a mixture of clay (broken-down rock), straw, and water.

Word Builders

- The word **build** comes from the old English term, *byldan,* which comes from another old English word, *bold,* meaning "house" or "dwelling."
- The word **cement** comes from the Latin *caementum,* which means "tough stone."
- The Romans referred to their stadiums as **coliseums**. This name comes from the Latin word *colosseus,* meaning "gigantic."

That's Amazing!

- The Incas, who ruled western South America between 1400 and 1532, constructed huge buildings without mortar. Instead, they cut the stones to fit together perfectly.
- Scientists think that it may have taken prehistoric people a total of 30 million hours to build Stonehenge in southern England. That's equal to spending 24 hours a day in school for 3,424 years!

Pathfinder

- The Mayan and Egyptian pyramids are made of limestone, a sedimentary rock. Find out more about sedimentary rocks on pages 84–85.
- The steel used to build Sydney Harbor Bridge was made from iron ore. Find out how this is done on pages 94–95.

First, the Maya built rough stone walls and filled the cavities behind them with rubble.

Then they built an exterior wall with fine-cut limestone blocks.

PYRAMIDS OF THE WEST

About 2,000 years ago in Mexico and Central America, a people called the Maya used the techniques shown here to create enormous stone temples, some of which contain the tombs of their rulers. Many of these pyramids still stand today.

The exterior wall was covered with fine plaster.

Completed temple.

Workers painted bright colors and designs on the plaster.

Laborers broke rocks into rubble.

Laborers cut the limestone into rectangular blocks.

Stonemasons carved decorative stones to place on the outside of the building.

COUNTRY COTTAGE
In southwest England, people used to build cottages like this one out of a sedimentary stone called oolite. They cut flat pieces of the same rock to make roof tiles.

HIGH-RISE LIVING
Modern apartment buildings house many people on a small area of land. These buildings usually have steel frameworks, concrete floors, and large, steel-framed windows.

Rock Art

PEOPLE HAVE created art from rocks and minerals since ancient times. Twenty-five thousand years ago, prehistoric humans used colorful dyes made from rocks and minerals to paint scenes on cave walls. Five thousand years ago, the ancient Egyptians carved jewelry from a variety of minerals, including quartz, obsidian, lapis lazuli, and gold. Later, the ancient Romans and Greeks sculpted magnificent works of art from blocks of marble. Today, people flock to museums to admire this art.

But rock art is not just about beauty. Ancient artworks that have survived for centuries tell us about our ancestors' lifestyles. Cave paintings show us which animals the first humans hunted. Metal tools and weapons reveal how people worked and fought. Ancient jewelry tells us which minerals a people valued most. Sculptures preserve artistic perceptions for new generations.

Today, we continue to use rocks and minerals in art. We fashion jewelry from precious metals and gems. We create sculptures from stones and metals. Modern technology makes it simpler for us to create rock art than it was for our ancestors. For example, advanced techniques make it easier to extract stone, gems, and metals from Earth's crust. We know how to mix metals together to make them stronger and how to cut a gemstone to make it shine brighter. Thousands of years from now, our rock art may well help future societies understand how we lived.

CROWN JEWELS
This spectacular crown was made in 1605 for the coronation of Prince Stephen Bocksay of Transylvania, in eastern Europe. It is made of gold and inset with rubies, emeralds, turquoise, and pearls.

MODERN ROCK ART
Many artists use metals to make modern sculptures. This artist is polishing a sculpture made of bronze, a mixture of the metals copper and tin.

PAINTING WITH ROCKS
The Navajo people of North America use powdered rocks to create pictures. First, they color sand using dyes obtained from rocks, minerals, plants, and ashes. Then they gently pour the sand onto the ground to create traditional designs. Originally, the Navajo made these paintings for healing ceremonies. After the ceremony, they destroyed the painting.

The mask is made of solid gold.

MASK OF TUTANKHAMEN
This spectacular death mask was made for Tutankhamen, an Egyptian king, or pharaoh. He began his reign in 1361 BC at age nine, and died mysteriously at age 18. His subjects mummified his body and put this mask over his head and shoulders. Then they placed the body inside a pyramid. This tomb remained sealed until 1922, when it was discovered by archeologist Howard Carter.

The Egyptians didn't have enough lapis lazu to make these stripes on the hood, so they used blue glass instead

The collar is encrusted with lapis lazuli, quartz, and green feldspar.

Word Builders

Gems are measured in **carats**. The word "carat" comes from the Greek word *keration*, which means "carob bean." At one time, gems were weighed against piles of carob beans. One carat is roughly the weight of a carob bean—0.007 ounce (0.2 g).

That's Amazing!

• Cave paintings found in Namibia in Africa may be the world's oldest rock art. They are about 27,500 years old.
• In ancient Egypt, there were hundreds of royal tombs like that of Tutankhamen. But almost every one was robbed within 10 years of being sealed.

Pathfinder

• Before they can be used for jewelry, stones have to be polished. Find out how to do this on page 101.
• Gems are crystals of minerals. Learn more about crystals on pages 92–93.
• Gold is a precious native metal. Take a look at two giant gold nuggets and find out how they formed on pages 96–97.

INSIDE STORY

All in a Day's Work

Gem cutter Lazare Kaplan held what looked like a glass egg. But this was no egg. It was the Jonker diamond, a 726-carat gem discovered in 1934 by Jacobus Jonker in South Africa. Two years later, the owners hired Kaplan to cut the diamond into smaller ones. Lazare etched a groove into the gem. Sweat ran down his brow. If he split the stone in the wrong place, it could shatter into tiny bits. Holding his breath, he placed a steel rule in the groove and gave it a sharp tap. CRACK! The diamond split perfectly in half. Lazare breathed a sigh of relief. Eventually, he cut the halves into 12 diamonds, one of which was sold for one million dollars.

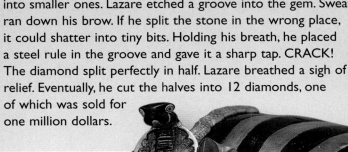

e eyes contain
artz and
sidian,
d the
ebrows
d eyelids
e lapis
uli.

THE PLAY OF LIGHT

Gem cutters make gems sparkle. They grind angled cuts, or facets, on the surface of a stone. Light enters each facet and bounces around inside before shooting back out. Different cuts create a different dance of light. Here are some diagrams of common gem cuts (left) with examples of cut gems (right).

Table cut

Emerald cut

Round brilliant cut

Pear-shaped brilliant cut

Heart-shaped brilliant cut

Cabochon (smoothly polished—no cuts)

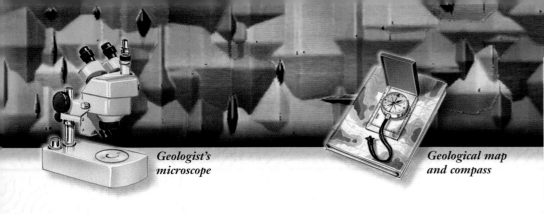

Geologist's microscope

Geological map and compass

The Keys to the Rocks

ONCE HUMANS became aware of the value of rocks, they started to ask questions. Where do rocks come from? Do rocks grow? To find answers to these questions, people began to study rocks. But their answers weren't always correct. The Greek philosopher Aristotle taught that minerals rose from vapors inside Earth. And only 200 years ago, most scientists believed that the world was just 6,000 years old.

Today, people who study rocks are called geologists, and they know a little more. Geologists are like detectives. They search the world for clues to Earth's past. Because rocks are gradually yet continually changing, much of the evidence has disappeared. But geologists use a range of modern techniques and devices to retrieve what is left. They drill into seafloors to look at ancient sediments. They monitor earthquakes to learn what happens under ground. And they use microscopes to examine minerals and fossils. They can even create computer models that simulate geological processes on Earth.

Their detective work has paid off. Today we know that Earth is about 4.8 billion years old. We have a good idea of how it formed and why it continues to change. And, thanks to one intrepid geologist, we have even learned about the geology of our nearest neighbor, the Moon.

THE BIG PICTURE
By adjusting the color range of a satellite image, scientists can map the locations of different rocks. This satellite image shows part of the Himalaya Mountains in Tibet, China. Most of the rocks are granites, which appear as an orangey brown color. The bluish patches are sedimentary rocks.

INSIDE STORY

The First Geologist on the Moon

On December 11, 1972, geologist Harrison "Jack" Schmitt stepped onto the Moon's rough surface. As part of the *Apollo 17* mission, Jack was the first geologist on the Moon. He would also be the last, so he knew his job had special meaning. As Jack said later, the Moon was "a geologist's paradise." He collected many rock samples, including breccia and other igneous rocks. Scientists were able to learn a great deal about the Moon from these rocks. They found out that it had experienced lava eruptions, earthquakes, and many asteroid impacts. Jack's lunar rock hunt had paid off.

GEOLOGISTS AT WORK
Wherever there's a geological puzzle, you'll find scientists searching for the answers. Their curiosity can take them to the tops of high mountains and deep into caves. These geologists are braving intense heat to study a fiery lava tube in Hawaii, U.S.A.

MAPPING THE OCEAN FLOOR

Vast mountain ranges, deep canyons, and immense plains lie deep beneath the ocean. Scientists use a variety of instruments and techniques to study these formations.

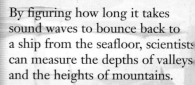

By figuring how long it takes sound waves to bounce back to a ship from the seafloor, scientists can measure the depths of valleys and the heights of mountains.

Word Builders

- The study of the history and structure of Earth is known as **geology.** The word "geology" comes from the Greek words *geo,* meaning "earth," and *logos,* meaning "study of."
- **Microscope** comes from two Greek words: *mikros,* meaning "small," and *skopein,* meaning "to look at."

That's Amazing!

- Ocean ridges cover 23 percent of Earth's surface. That's almost as much as all the continents combined.
- If you were to dig 10 miles (16 km) down under the southern Rocky Mountains in the U.S.A., you would find the same rock that lies at the bottom of the Grand Canyon—Vishnu Schist.

Pathfinder

- How do geologists study Earth's interior? Learn more on pages 74–75.
- Earth may be nearly five billion years old, but in geological terms, humans have just arrived. Turn to pages 80–81.
- Interested in becoming a geologist? Get a head start on pages 116–17.
- Fascinated by fossils? See pages 124–25.

HANDS ON

Making a Core Sample

To study rock layers, scientists take core samples from Earth's crust. They do this by drilling into the ground with a hollow drill. You can make your own core sample using modeling clay and a straw.

1. Roll several pieces of different-colored clay into flat pieces. Place them one on top of the other to form colorful layers.

2. Take a strong, wide drinking straw and slowly push it through the layers of clay.

3. Pull the straw out, then ask an adult to cut it open. Inside you'll find your clay core sample.

RECREATING THE PAST

By studying fossils and rocks in the walls of the Grand Canyon, geologists can paint a picture of the canyon's history. This history dates back more than two billion years. To follow the history, read the labels from the bottom of the canyon up. The numbers on the right show when each part of the canyon formed.

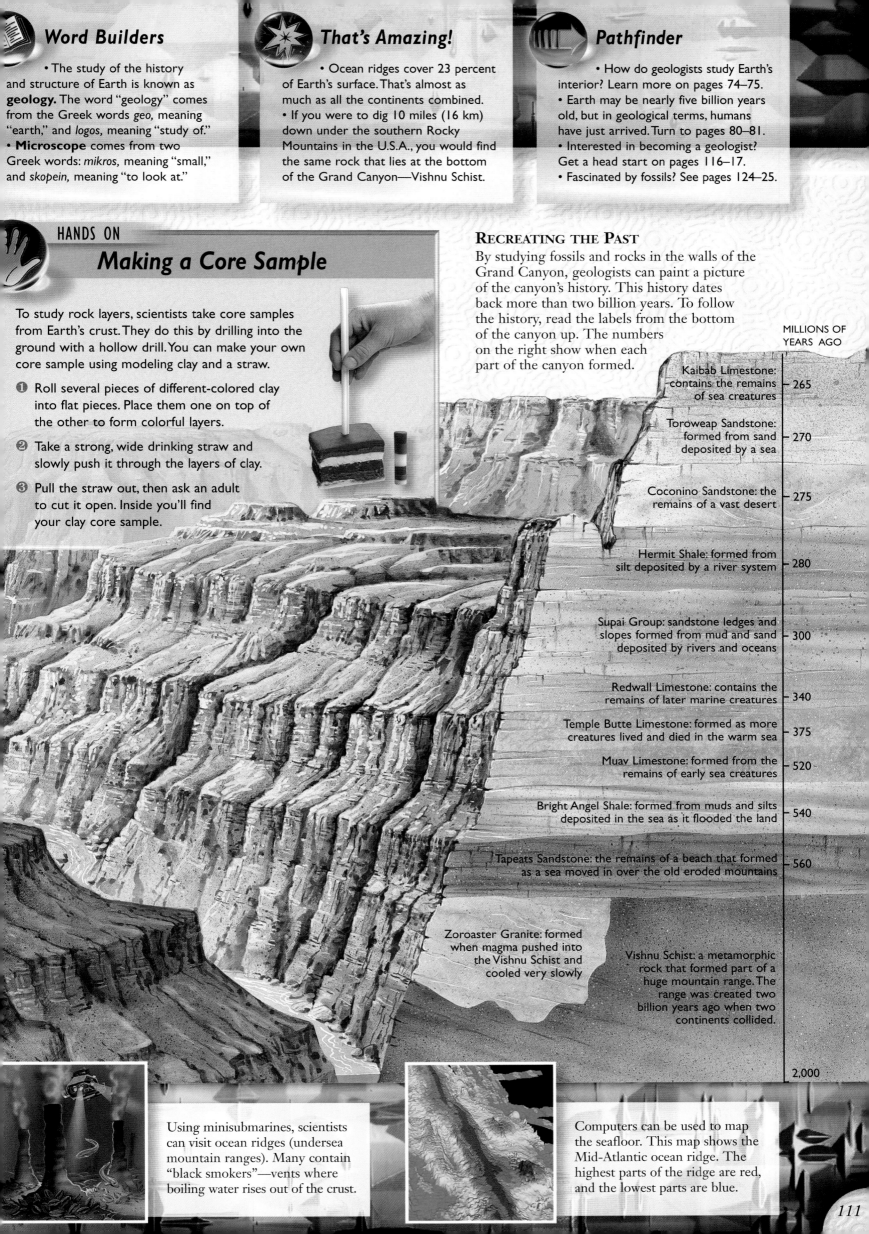

MILLIONS OF YEARS AGO

Kaibab Limestone: contains the remains of sea creatures — 265

Toroweap Sandstone: formed from sand deposited by a sea — 270

Coconino Sandstone: the remains of a vast desert — 275

Hermit Shale: formed from silt deposited by a river system — 280

Supai Group: sandstone ledges and slopes formed from mud and sand deposited by rivers and oceans — 300

Redwall Limestone: contains the remains of later marine creatures — 340

Temple Butte Limestone: formed as more creatures lived and died in the warm sea — 375

Muav Limestone: formed from the remains of early sea creatures — 520

Bright Angel Shale: formed from muds and silts deposited in the sea as it flooded the land — 540

Tapeats Sandstone: the remains of a beach that formed as a sea moved in over the old eroded mountains — 560

Zoroaster Granite: formed when magma pushed into the Vishnu Schist and cooled very slowly

Vishnu Schist: a metamorphic rock that formed part of a huge mountain range. The range was created two billion years ago when two continents collided.

2,000

Using minisubmarines, scientists can visit ocean ridges (undersea mountain ranges). Many contain "black smokers"—vents where boiling water rises out of the crust.

Computers can be used to map the seafloor. This map shows the Mid-Atlantic ocean ridge. The highest parts of the ridge are red, and the lowest parts are blue.

Rocks to Burn

ROCKS HOLD the power to fuel the world. Coal, oil, gas and other energy resources lie buried in layers of sedimentary rocks. If it weren't for these fuels, you couldn't ride in a car, fly in a plane, or stay warm in the winter.

One of the most widely used fuels is coal. We burn it to produce heat and energy. Coal consists of the remains of ancient swamp plants. As the plants decay in mud, they turn into peat, a substance that looks like moist tobacco. Sometimes, sedimentary rocks form on top of the peat, crushing it with their weight. The squashed peat then turns into a dark brown rock called lignite. As more layers of rock press down on it, lignite becomes bituminous coal. Under extreme pressure, bituminous coal changes into anthracite, a hard, shiny, black coal. The more coal is squeezed, the harder it becomes and the more energy it releases when burned.

Unfortunately, our supplies of coal, oil, and gas are running out. Because of this, people have tried to find other sources of energy. One type—called nuclear energy—comes from uranium-rich rocks. Uranium is a heavy element with big atoms. When the atoms are split apart, energy is released. This energy is turned into power at nuclear power stations.

SOMETHING IN THE AIR
When people burn oil, coal, or gas, it creates a type of pollution called smog. Smog is a mix of dust, smoke, and gases that makes it hard for some people to breathe.

MODERN MINING
For centuries, people have descended f... below Earth's surface to dig coal out of... sedimentary rocks. Today, machines do... most of the digging. The method show... here is now used in most coal mines. It is known as continuous mining.

To reach the coal face, miners take the downcast shaft. Fans at the top of the shaft supply them with air.

The miners dig tunnels through the rock. They use metal pillars to support the roof.

The miners descend to the coal face in a metal elevator known as a cage.

UNDER THE SEA
Oil and gas form when the decayed remains of ocean animals are crushed between layers of rock.

Microscopic sea creatures die and fall to the ocean floor. Over millions of years, layers of mud and silt slowly cover the sea creatures and turn into sedimentary rocks.

The rock layers continue to pile up on top of the dead sea creatures. As the pressure from the rocks increases, the sea creatures slowly turn into oil and gas.

Word Builders

- Oil and gas are **petroleum** products. The word "petroleum" comes from the Latin words *petro,* meaning "stone," and *oleum,* meaning "oil."
- **Uranium** is named after the Greek god of the heavens, Uranus.

That's Amazing!

An underground coal seam on Mount Wingen in southeastern Australia has been on fire for 5,000 years. Smoke continually seeps out of the mountain, which is too hot to walk on. The name "Wingen" comes from an Aboriginal word meaning "fire."

Pathfinder

- Coal is a type of sedimentary rock. To find out more about these rocks, turn to pages 84–85.
- Did you know that coal and diamonds are made of the same material—an element called carbon? To learn more about diamonds, turn to pages 98–99.

The upcast shaft is used to bring coal to the surface. A fan at the top of the shaft sucks stale air out of the mine.

Coal is loaded onto rail cars for transportation.

INSIDE STORY

The Breaker Boy

My name is Paul. I work in a coal mine in Scranton, Pennsylvania. That's in the United States. My job is to split the slate apart from the coal using a hammer. That's why I'm called a "breaker boy." I work long days and often don't get home until after dark. The coal is dirty. Black dust covers my skin and gets inside my nose and mouth. My boss told me that the coal we find helps power new steam locomotives. I guess that makes my job important. But I can't wait to be a miner. Miners get to buy explosives from the company store and blow up rock to search for more coal. Maybe I'll get promoted after my birthday. I'll be 11 on May 6, 1894.

The coal is taken to the surface in a large metal container called a skip.

The broken coal falls onto a conveyor belt that takes it to the upcast shaft.

A machine called a cutting head tears into the coal with its sharp-toothed wheel.

OFFSHORE OIL
Geologists use offshore oil platforms to explore ocean sediments for oil and gas. From a single platform like this one, workers can drill as many as 50 different wells and collect millions of barrels of oil each day. Most oil platforms remain at sea for about 25 years, though one was in use for 60 years.

The oil and gas rise through the rock layers. They pass through porous rocks, such as sandstone, but are blocked by impermeable (nonporous) rocks, such as shale.

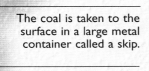

Under the right conditions, the oil and gas collect in a reservoir under the impermeable rocks, with the gas on top of the oil. Humans drill into reservoirs to remove the fuels.

Chips Off the Old Block

IN RECENT YEARS, information from geologists and advances in technology have helped us to find new uses for rocks and minerals. For example, in the early 1880s, two scientist brothers found that a common mineral called quartz produces an electric current when squeezed. Today, quartz clocks and watches use this property to keep time. Quartz is also the raw material for silicon, a substance that helps energy flow through electronic instruments. Without silicon, you wouldn't be able to play electronic games or use a computer, telephone, television, or stereo.

Modern technology has also created super-strong materials from substances extracted from rocks and minerals. By combining carbon fibers obtained from petroleum with a plastic resin, scientists can make a strong, flexible material that is commonly referred to as graphite. Manufacturers use this substance in everything from tennis rackets to skis and fishing rods. Scientists have also learned how to use oil extracted from rocks to make other synthetic fibers, plastics, paint, and fuels.

Rocks and minerals have even helped humans travel to outer space. The metal titanium, for example, can be mixed with other metals to produce a strong, lightweight material that doesn't rust. This makes it ideal for building spacecraft.

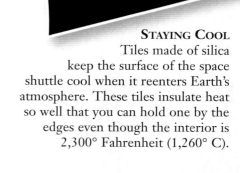

STAYING COOL
Tiles made of silica keep the surface of the space shuttle cool when it reenters Earth's atmosphere. These tiles insulate heat so well that you can hold one by the edges even though the interior is 2,300° Fahrenheit (1,260° C).

The payload doors are made of a mixture of carbon, graphite, and fiberglass that is 23 percent lighter than aluminum.

INSIDE STORY

A Tight Squeeze

In 1880, two chemist brothers, Jacques and Pierre Curie, decided to perform an experiment. With a special saw, they cut a thin slice of quartz. Then they attached a sheet of tin to either side of the slice of quartz. Next, they used a machine to squeeze the tin tightly against the mineral. This pressure created a small flow of electric charges in the quartz. The brothers were delighted with this result. But it was only later, in the 1920s, that scientists realized that this phenomenon—known as piezoelectricity—could be used to keep time. Today, almost all clocks and watches are operated by tiny, pulsing quartz crystals.

Kevlar window shades covered with silver tape protect astronauts from sun glare.

The nose cone is reinforced with carbon to resist intense heat.

The windows hav a scratch-resistar diamond coating.

COUNTING THE HOURS
Charged by a battery, the quartz crystal in a watch vibrates 32,786 times per second. A circuit counts the vibrations and sorts them into seconds, minutes, and hours.

DIAMOND HARD
A scratch-resistant coating made of diamonds protect these ordinary sunglasses. This lens coating was originally developed to protect the windows on the space shuttle.

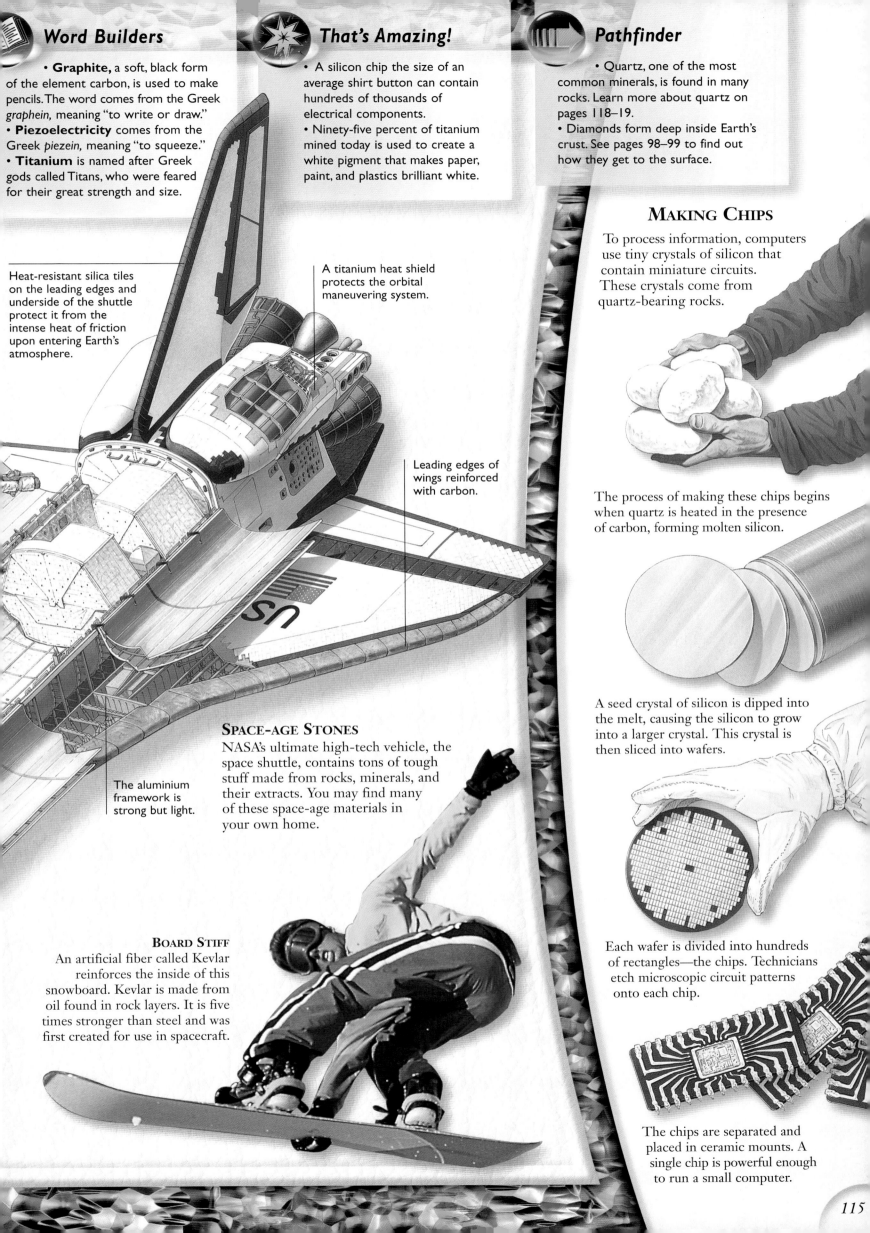

Word Builders

- **Graphite,** a soft, black form of the element carbon, is used to make pencils. The word comes from the Greek *graphein,* meaning "to write or draw."
- **Piezoelectricity** comes from the Greek *piezein,* meaning "to squeeze."
- **Titanium** is named after Greek gods called Titans, who were feared for their great strength and size.

That's Amazing!

- A silicon chip the size of an average shirt button can contain hundreds of thousands of electrical components.
- Ninety-five percent of titanium mined today is used to create a white pigment that makes paper, paint, and plastics brilliant white.

Pathfinder

- Quartz, one of the most common minerals, is found in many rocks. Learn more about quartz on pages 118–19.
- Diamonds form deep inside Earth's crust. See pages 98–99 to find out how they get to the surface.

Heat-resistant silica tiles on the leading edges and underside of the shuttle protect it from the intense heat of friction upon entering Earth's atmosphere.

A titanium heat shield protects the orbital maneuvering system.

Leading edges of wings reinforced with carbon.

The aluminium framework is strong but light.

SPACE-AGE STONES

NASA's ultimate high-tech vehicle, the space shuttle, contains tons of tough stuff made from rocks, minerals, and their extracts. You may find many of these space-age materials in your own home.

BOARD STIFF

An artificial fiber called Kevlar reinforces the inside of this snowboard. Kevlar is made from oil found in rock layers. It is five times stronger than steel and was first created for use in spacecraft.

MAKING CHIPS

To process information, computers use tiny crystals of silicon that contain miniature circuits. These crystals come from quartz-bearing rocks.

The process of making these chips begins when quartz is heated in the presence of carbon, forming molten silicon.

A seed crystal of silicon is dipped into the melt, causing the silicon to grow into a larger crystal. This crystal is then sliced into wafers.

Each wafer is divided into hundreds of rectangles—the chips. Technicians etch microscopic circuit patterns onto each chip.

The chips are separated and placed in ceramic mounts. A single chip is powerful enough to run a small computer.

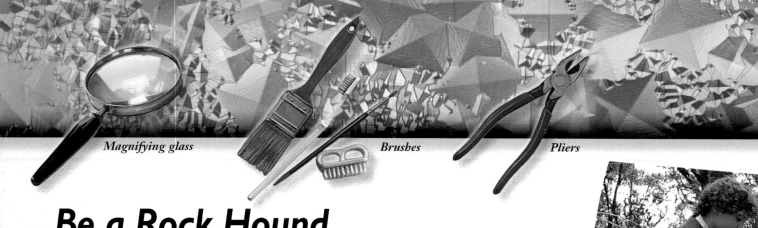

Magnifying glass   Brushes   Pliers

Be a Rock Hound

YOU CAN COLLECT and study rocks just like the experts. It's easy to get started, and you don't need much equipment. Gather together a rock hammer, a sample-collecting bag, a notebook, a pen, safety glasses, pliers, some newspaper, and a field guide to rocks and minerals. Now you're ready to go. Don't forget to pack a snack before you head off.

You can search for rocks and minerals almost anywhere. Try your backyard first. If you don't have one or don't find much there, look along the banks of streams or near rocky outcrops. Always use caution. Watch for falling rocks and stay out of dangerous places such as quarries. It's safer, and usually more fun, to hunt for rocks with a friend. Ask permission before you look for rocks on private property. When you're there, act like a guest. Only pick up rocks that will enhance your collection. Be a rock hound, not a rock hog.

When you find a rock you like, note the location, the date, and who found it. You can trim off the parts of the rock you don't want with a hammer or pliers, but make sure you protect your eyes with safety glasses. Wrap the rock in newspaper and put it in your bag. Once you get home, clean and number the rock. Then transfer the information about your find to an index card. Now your rock is ready for display.

A CLOSER LOOK
You can use a magnifying glass to take a close look at rocks. Is the rock bumpy or smooth? Can you identify the minerals in the rock?

Write the details of your find on an index card. Note where and when you found it.

A small set of shelves can make an excellent display case for rock and mineral samples.

HANDS ON
Make a Display Case

You can make a simple rock and mineral display case out of an egg carton. Simply place wads of cotton or tissue paper in each compartment. This kind of box is ideal for displaying small specimens. It's also handy for carrying your rocks around.

For a larger display box, find a big, low-sided cardboard box. You can make compartments with smaller boxes, or with strips of heavy card. Simply cut the strips of card to fit the length and width of the box. Then cut slits in the strips so that you can slot them together.

PREPARING SPECIMENS

When you bring your specimens home, carefully unpack them from their newspaper wrapping. Then prepare them as follows.

First, clean your rock using a toothbrush or other soft brush, and soap and water. If your specimen is delicate, you should skip this step.

Word Builders

• People who search for rocks and minerals are known as **rock hounds** because they hunt rocks just as a hunter's hounds pursue animals.
• The rocks and minerals you collect in the field are known as **specimens**. The word "specimen" comes from the Latin *specere*, which means "to look at."
• **Museum** comes from the Greek *mouseion*, which means "place of study."

That's Amazing!

• People started collecting rocks at least 2.3 million years ago. That's when ancestors of humans first began to use rocks as tools.
• The Natural History Museum in London, England, has one of the largest rock collections in the world. It contains 350,000 minerals and 100,000 rocks.

Pathfinder

• Learn how to identify rocks and minerals on pages 118–19.
• What's the difference between a rock and a mineral? Find out on pages 92–93.
• For more tips on where to go rock hunting, turn to pages 120–21.
• Keen on beachcombing? Go to pages 122–23 for advice on seashore collecting.

Putting on a Show

You can arrange your collection just as museums do. First, use a field guide to identify and label your rocks. Then organize them into groups. You can sort them according to where you found them, or into igneous, sedimentary, and metamorphic types. Keep fragile specimens in boxes or drawers. But don't hide your rocks. You worked hard to find them, so display them with pride.

Study your rock carefully with a magnifying glass. Compare your specimen to the photos in a field guide of rocks and minerals.

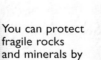

INSIDE STORY

Collector Extraordinaire

Australian amateur rock hound Albert Chapman created one of the world's best private mineral collections. As a child, Albert started picking up rocks at the harbor near his home. Later he traveled the country in search of unique specimens. Albert liked to visit mines, where he sometimes bought rocks from miners. He traded the rocks with geologists, museums, and other collectors. But the rocks he found himself were his favorites. "Anything you collect for yourself is a thrill," he would say. Albert couldn't get enough of rocks and minerals. "I like the way they come out of the ground," he explained. "I like their colors and forms." Albert died in 1996. But his magnificent collection is now on display in the Australian Museum in Sydney for all to see.

Learning from the Experts

You can learn more about the geology of your area by visiting your local museum. Museums usually have big glass cases filled with interesting rocks and minerals. You might recognize some that are in your collection. Others may be unique specimens or come from other countries.

You can protect fragile rocks and minerals by keeping them in a drawer.

Divide the drawer into compartments using strips of cardboard, or put each sample into its own box.

Next, carefully paint a small white spot on the bottom of your rock or mineral using white model paint or correction fluid. Leave it to dry.

Write a number on the white spot. Put the same number on an index card. Use the card to note important details about the rock and where you found it.

Name That Rock

JUST LIKE PEOPLE, rocks and minerals possess certain traits that make them stand out from the crowd. For example, you can identify minerals by examining how shiny, dense, and hard they are. The colors, textures, and types of minerals in a rock may tell you how it formed. By learning to recognize these characteristics, you can become a top rock spotter.

When you find an interesting rock, look at it carefully. Is it made up of a single mineral or many minerals? More than 600 basic rock types exist, so if it's a rock, you should start by narrowing the field. Try to work out which kind of rock you have—sedimentary, igneous, or metamorphic. Certain clues, such as the shape, size, alignment, and distribution of the crystals, will tip you off. For instance, most intrusive igneous rocks have large- to medium-sized mineral grains that you can see without a magnifying glass.

If the rock contains large crystals, the minerals can sometimes be identified. A number of simple tests can help. For example, quartz and calcite crystals may look similar. But quartz is harder and will scratch the calcite when the two are rubbed together. Compare your observations and test results to the information in a field guide. With a little practice, you'll soon learn to put names to rock faces.

IDENTIFYING ROCKS
When you find an unidentified rock, pick it up and study it closely. How heavy is it for its size? What color is it? Can you make out details such as large crystals, bands of differen colored stone, or clumps of pebbles? All of these features will help you make the first step in rock identification—deciding whether the rock is sedimentary, igneous, or metamorphic.

Conglomerate

This sedimentary rock is called conglomerate. It consists of pebbles of milky quartz surrounded by smaller fragments of sand, clay, and iron oxide.

Milky quartz

SEDIMENTARY ROCK
Sedimentary rocks may have distinct layers made up of grains of different sizes, or look like a mixture of different rocks. They are seldom shiny and seldom contain well-defined crystals. If you can see fossils in a rock, it is probably sedimentary.

IGNEOUS ROCK
Igneous rocks can cont large, well-defined crys appear smooth and gla or fall somewhere in between. But, in gener they all have a uniform texture and even distribution of colors.

Granite

Feldspar

Quartz

INSIDE STORY

He Wrote the Book on Minerals

People have collected rocks for thousands of years. But a practical book about minerals didn't appear until 1546. It was called *De Natura Fossilium* and was written by a German scientist named Georgius Agricola. Agricola wrote the book while working as a doctor near a major mining center in Germany. Agricola visited the mines every day and gained a wide knowledge of rocks. He was the first scientist to describe minerals by their form, color, hardness, and luster—the very properties we use to identify minerals today.

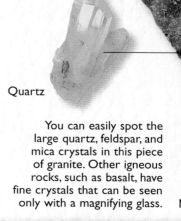

You can easily spot the large quartz, feldspar, and mica crystals in this piece of granite. Other igneous rocks, such as basalt, have fine crystals that can be seen only with a magnifying glass.

Mica

Word Builders

• The **Mohs scale** of hardness is named for its inventor, an Austrian mineralogist called Friedrich Mohs. He devised the scale in 1822.
• Rock hounds are often confused by a mineral called **apatite**. It often looks like other minerals, such as aquamarine, olivine, and fluorite. Apatite takes its name from the Greek word *apate*, which means "deceit."

That's Amazing!

• Although diamond is the hardest mineral on Earth, it is still brittle. If you strike it with a metal hammer, you can shatter it into tiny pieces. Many a good diamond has been accidentally destroyed in this way.
• A common mineral called calcite is a master of disguise. It is found in over 300 different crystal forms—more than any other mineral.

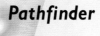

Pathfinder

• Learn about the fiery origins of igneous rocks on pages 82–83.
• You can make your own sedimentary layers. Turn to page 84.
• Find out how heat and pressure create metamorphic rocks on pages 86–87.
• The habit of a mineral may be a clue to its identity. See pages 92–93.

Banded gneiss

This gneiss (pronounced "nice") has a coarse texture and folded layers of light and dark minerals. Gneiss can look similar to granite, but it commonly contains layers of crystals rather than scattered pieces.

Feldspar

Biotite

Quartz

METAMORPHIC ROCK
Many metamorphic rocks contain bands of light and dark minerals or layers of flaky minerals. This is called foliation. Other metamorphic rocks, such as marble, have a more even color and are made up of small, interlocking crystals.

HANDS ON

Test Cases

If you find a piece of a mineral, you can identify it using these steps.

1 Make notes on the mineral's appearance. What color is it? Is it transparent (you can see through it) or opaque (you can't)? Is it shiny or dull? What habit (shape) does it have?

2 Rub your mineral against an unglazed white porcelain tile (the back of a ceramic tile will do). This is called a streak test. What color streak does the mineral leave? You can take a look at some examples at the top of the opposite page.

3 Hold the mineral in your hand or weigh it on scales. Some minerals are much heavier than others of the same size. For example, sulfur is light, but a piece of pyrite the same size is much heavier.

4 Use the information on the right to conduct a hardness test. (Be careful not to damage the specimen.) What is the hardness of your mineral?

To determine the type of mineral, compare your test results to the measurements for color and luster, weight, streak-test color, and hardness in a good field guide.

Sulfur

Pyrite

MOHS SCALE

The Mohs scale of hardness uses 10 minerals that range from the softest to the hardest to help determine the hardness of other minerals. If you scratch quartz against an unknown mineral and it leaves a mark, you know that the mystery mineral is softer than quartz. You can also use the items on the right-hand side to test for hardness in the same way.

1. TALC

2. GYPSUM

2.5. Fingernail

3. CALCITE

3.5. Copper coin

4. FLUORITE

5. APATITE

5.5. Glass

6. ORTHOCLASE
(A TYPE OF FELDSPAR)

6.5. Steel knife

7. QUARTZ

8. TOPAZ

8.5. Emery board

9. CORUNDUM

10. DIAMOND

Hard hat and safety goggles

Bag for carrying samples

Hammer and chisels

Take to the Hills

ROCKS ABOUND in hills, mountains, and other upland areas. Here you'll find natural landforms such as jagged mountain peaks, craggy outcrops, and deep river valleys. You'll also come across human-made features, such as road and rail cuts, that reveal interesting rocks and minerals.

Road cuts are great places for studying rocks. They appear whenever a construction crew blasts through a hillside to make room for a new road. A fresh road cut lets you look at rocks that aren't covered by plants or altered by exposure to the elements. You might be able to take a close look at layers of sedimentary rock, for instance. Each layer will have its own color and minerals. A road cut in igneous or metamorphic rocks may have mineral veins cutting through it or nice, large crystals. If you want to get a close look at a road cut, be sure you obey the road rules and keep away from traffic.

Certain higher-ground features provide happy hunting for rock hounds. For example, rivers and streams cut through the land, carrying off rocks and minerals. You can then find excellent specimens washed up on their banks. Erosion and uplift can expose rocks that are still rooted in the ground. These are called outcrops. Usually, the rock is made from strong minerals—a fine addition to any collection.

WINDOWS ON THE PAST
Road cuts expose rock layers and allow us to study the landscape's past. This one in Australia shows two faults in sedimentary rock layers. The faults were created by movement in Earth's crust.

Rivers create V-shaped valleys. With renewed uplift or along faults and joints, gorges may form.

Mountain peaks often have little vegetation, so yo can take a close look at the rock

Road cuts reveal rock layers and interesting formations.

HANDS ON
Field Notes

When you go out into the field, always take a notebook so you can record your observations and discoveries. Choose a notebook with a hard cover—preferably one that's waterproof.

Each time you find an interesting geological feature (like the ones shown below), draw a rough map to record its location. Then try to sketch the feature. For example, if you are studying a road cut, draw any rock layers, faults, or joints. If you can identify the layers, label the rock types. You may also want to take photographs of particularly interesting or unusual landforms. Eventually your notebook will provide you with a fascinating record of the geology of your area.

WRINKLES IN THE ROCKS

Look out for these landforms when rock hunting in the hills. They are signs of major events in the history of any landscape. The illustrations show you how to recognize each feature and what to look for when you find it.

Folded rock layers

A fold is a bend in rock layers formed when the rock was crumpled by plate movements. You can often see folds in road and rail cuts. If the layers fold upward, it's called an anticline. If the layers crumple downward, it's a syncline. A crack in the rock is called a joint.

Joints

Word Builders

- Mountains, valleys, and plains make up a landscape's **topography**. The word topography comes from the Greek words *topos,* meaning "place," and *graphein,* meaning "to write."
- A **drumlin** is an oval hill created by a glacier. The name comes from the Irish word *druim,* meaning "back" or "ridge."
- An **esker** is a long, narrow hill formed by a glacier. The name comes from the Irish word *escir,* meaning "ridge."

That's Amazing!

- During the last ice age, a glacier cut a valley 2,000 feet (610 m) deep into the Rocky Mountains in the U.S.A.
- The tiny country of San Marino in Italy is upside down! Scientists have worked out that millions of years ago the rock layers under the country were overturned by plate movements.

Pathfinder

- Glaciers are giant rivers of ice. Find out more on pages 78–79.
- Road and rail cuts can reveal rock layers that may contain fossils. Find out about fossils on pages 124–25.
- People have often found precious metals such as gold and silver in rivers. Learn more on pages 96–97.

GEOLOGICAL SURVEY

From a hilltop, you can survey the countryside for prime rock-hunting locations. Look for road or railway cuts that expose layers of rock. Search mountainsides for rivers that carry rocks and pebbles. Scan the horizon for U-shaped valleys carved by glaciers. And don't forget to inspect other, more obvious features such as cliffs and outcrops.

INSIDE STORY

Layers of History

By studying the rocks along slices and holes that people had cut into the land, William Smith became the first scientist to understand the significance of rock layers. Smith worked as a surveyor in England during the 1790s. While examining coal mines and canal banks in different parts of the country, he noticed that they contained similar rock layers. By comparing fossils in the layers, Smith worked out that the rocks always appeared in the same order. From this, he correctly concluded that they had built up on top of each other, so that the oldest rocks were at the bottom and the youngest at the top. Smith's discoveries allowed him to create the first geological map of England. They also provided other geologists with a whole new way of looking at landscapes.

Valleys gouged by glaciers have a distinctive U shape.

Resistant rocks protrude from softer ground that has been worn down.

Cliff faces may contain layers, folds, and faults. They are also good spots for finding fossils.

Rail cuts and quarries reveal rock that may have been hidden for centuries.

ROUND THE BEND

As a river rounds a corner, it leaves pebbles and stones on the shore. A river bend is therefore a great spot to find rock and mineral samples. Use caution when hunting near rivers. Better yet, ask an adult to come along.

Glaciers literally sculpt the landscape. They may leave mounds of debris called moraines or eskers, or create new features called drumlins or hanging valleys. A hanging valley indicates the presence of a smaller glacier next to the main one.

Hanging valley

Esker

Drumlin

Moraine

A fault is a special kind of crack in the land. It forms when the crust is stretched or compressed by plate movements, causing land to collapse or rise. Signs of faults include layers that don't line up and clifflike structures called scarps.

Scarp

Joint

Fault

Large, flat mica
beach pebbles

Flat slate
beach pebbles

Rounded
granite pebbles

Fine quartzite
beach pebbles

Coast Watch

THE COAST is a great place for geology watchers. Water and wind constantly sculpt the coastline into fantastic landforms. Pounding waves carve arches, caves, platforms, and sea stacks out of cliff faces. Heavily laden rivers dump silt, gravel, and mud on the shore. Gusting winds pile sand into massive dunes. All this happens bit by bit, although you can sometimes see huge changes after a big storm.

These natural forces also polish pebbles, stones, and shells into ready-made samples for your collections. They may also bring you specimens from other locations. For example, rivers transport pebbles and stones from far upstream. And large waves and strong ocean currents may deposit rocks and sand from other beaches.

Because the coastline is constantly changing, geologists who study these environments must stay on their toes. Rivers carry heavy loads of sediment that can pile up and alter a current's course. This can put boats in danger. Erosion can sweep away fragile cliffs. And when cliffs crumble, nearby houses may collapse, too. But these changes can also be fascinating, and not just for geologists. They are continually revealing new mineral samples, rock formations, and ancient fossils—evidence of Earth's most powerful forces.

A WHALE OF A ROCK
In Western Australia, water spurts from this blowhole as if the rock were a whale. The hole formed when pounding surf cut through weak rock at the bottom of the cliff and tunneled up to the surface. Now when a big wave crashes against the cliff, its weight forces water up through the hole.

Erosion causes cliffs to collapse, forming piles of rock.

Sea cliffs may contain interesting rock layers and fossils.

Sea stacks are the remains of headlands.

Blowholes for when the sea tunnels throu a headland.

Waves gnaw at cliffs, creating sea caves and arches.

WORN BY THE WAVES
Huge mounds of rock and pillars called sea stacks form where waves claw at the shore. The process may take thousands of years.

Erosion often creates formations called headlands, which jut out into the water. Waves pound the headlands, scooping out caves from areas of softer rock.

Word Builders

- **Coast** comes from the Latin word *costa,* meaning "side."
- **Shore** comes from the old German word *schor,* meaning "foreland."
- **Spit** comes from the old English word *spitu,* which in turn comes from the old German word *spizzi,* meaning "pointed."

That's Amazing!

At Cape Cod in Massachusetts, U.S.A., about 10,000 waves batter the coast each day, and the cliff retreats landward by 3 feet (1 m) a year. In 1996, the Cape Cod lighthouse, built in 1857, had to be moved 450 feet (137 m) back from the cliff edge to prevent it from falling into the sea.

Pathfinder

- Erosion can change landforms dramatically. Read how on pages 78–79.
- Pebbles and shells that settle on the seafloor may turn into sedimentary rock. Learn how this happens on pages 84–85.
- Beaches provide a wide range of rock samples. Find out how to identify rocks and minerals on pages 118–19.

INSIDE STORY
London Bridge Has Fallen Down

On January 17, 1990, 18-year-old Kelli Harrison and her cousin David Darrington paid a visit to London Bridge, a spectacular double sea arch on the southeast coast of Australia. The cousins had just crossed the bridge when they heard "a huge splash." Looking back, they saw that the ground they had just walked across had vanished. "If we were another 30 seconds later, there is no way in the world we could have survived it," said Kelli. For thousands of years, the waves had been gnawing at the limestone and sandstone cliffs. The arches had stood for centuries, but finally, on this day, one gave way. Thankful to be alive, Kelli and David waited patiently on the new sea stack until a police helicopter carried them to safety.

ON THE BEACH

You'll find rocks of all shapes, colors, and sizes on the seashore. As waves crash into the coast, they grind rocks and pebbles against each other, cracking, smoothing, and polishing them. Over hundreds of years, the water wears the rocks down to sand. If you look at sand under a magnifying glass, you'll see tiny grains of minerals.

Beaches are great places for finding a wide variety of polished pebbles.

Sand dunes form when the wind blows loose, fine sand into large mounds.

At a river mouth, you may find rocks carried from far inland by the river.

Sediments deposited by rivers and waves may trap water, forming a coastal lagoon.

Waves may sculpt rocky terraces at the base of cliffs.

Sand deposited by currents may form a long beach that sticks out into the sea. This is called a spit.

SCANNING THE SHORELINE

As you walk the shore, look for the geological features shown here. At each of these places, you will find different rocks and minerals. Always keep an eye out for big waves and changing tides that may strand you on rocks or beaches.

The nonstop action of the waves digs deeper into the headland. The caves get bigger until they join up. This creates a formation called a sea arch.

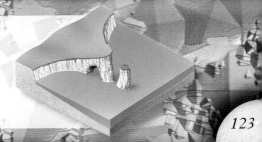

Eventually, the top of the arch collapses into the surf, leaving a sea stack. Further stacks may form as the waves continue to pound and pummel the cliffs.

123

Rhacopteris
plant fossil

Heliobatus
ray fossil

Eucalyptus
plant fossil

Fossil Hunting

ROCKS OFTEN CONTAIN traces of ancient life. These are called fossils. They can be bones, footprints, impressions, or other signs of prehistoric plants or animals. Fossils form when living things walk on or die in swamp, lake, river, or ocean sediments. When the sediments become rock, they may retain the impression of the life form. Sometimes, minerals replace parts of dead animals or plants and turn them into rock.

Hundreds of years ago, people didn't know what to make of fossils. Some thought they were the remains of animals that lived underground. Others believed that fossils grew inside rocks. Today, scientists search for fossils to learn about ancient life forms and environments. The presence of certain fossils can tell us what the climate was like millions of years ago. For example, fossils of coral reefs in the eastern United States suggest that the area was once a tropical sea. Scientists can also use fossils to date rock layers. We know that certain plants and creatures lived at specific times. Their presence or absence can therefore help us work out how old a rock is.

You can be a fossil hunter, too. Look in layers of sedimentary rock, such as sandstone and shale. Limestone often contains fossils of sea creatures. Once you have collected a few fossils, sort them into categories such as vertebrates (animals with backbones), invertebrates (animals with no backbones), and plants. You can put your best samples on display, alongside your rocks and minerals.

PETRIFIED TRE
These stone tree trunks are the remains ancient trees. They turned to stone when wat laden with silica replaced the living tissue wi minerals. This process is called petrificatio

A GEM OF A FOSSIL
This multicolored shell is a fossil. It formed when water containing silica filled a rock cavity formed by a seashell, or slowly replaced the shell. The silica solution then hardened into opal, a type of gemstone.

INSIDE STORY

She Sells Fossil Shells

At the beginning of the 19th century, scientists had just become aware that fossils were important records of the history of life. Museums and universities began to hunt for and collect fossilized remains of all kinds. In Dorset, England, a girl called Mary Anning helped her father to gather and sell fossilized shells from the local seashore. (It is said that Mary inspired the tongue twister "She sells sea shells by the seashore.") One day in 1811, when Mary was 12, she spotted an unusual, whitish object sticking out of some rocks. When she carefully chipped away the rock with her hammer, she saw that it was a skeleton. It turned out to be the first complete fossil of an ichthyosaur, a dolphinlike creature that lived between 245 and 65 million years ago. Mary went on to find many other important fossils, some of which are displayed in the British Museum.

PRESERVED IN AMBER
Millions of years ago, this insect was smothered by a glob of sticky tree sap. Slowly, the sap hardened into a substance called amber, which has perfectly preserved this sample of ancient life.

Frozen woolly mammoth

Stegosaurus
skeleton

Word Builders

• **Fossil** comes from the Latin word *fodere*, which means "to dig."
• Scientists who study fossils are called **paleontologists**. This word comes from the Greek *palaios*, meaning "ancient," *onta*, meaning "existing things," and *logos*, meaning "study of."
• **Trilobite** comes from the Greek words *tri*, meaning "three," and *lobos*, meaning "lobe." The name refers to the three parts of the animal's midsection.

That's Amazing!

• The longest complete dinosaur skeleton comes from remains found in Wyoming, U.S.A., in 1899. *Diplodocus carnegii* measures 87.5 feet (26.6 m) long. That's longer than a tennis court.
• Scientists believe that 99 percent of all the life forms that ever existed on Earth died without leaving any fossil records. Fossilization is truly a special event!

Pathfinder

• You are most likely to find fossils in sedimentary rocks. Learn about these rocks on pages 84–85.
• By identifying and dating fossils in rock layers, geologists can reconstruct the history of a landscape. See pages 110–11.
• Coastal cliffs often contain marine fossils. Find out more on pages 120–21.

DIGGING FOR DINOSAURS

These dinosaur bones turned to stone millions of years ago. It happened after the dinosaurs died and their bodies were buried in sediments. Mineral-rich water seeped into the bones, filling the pores with minerals. Today, scientists carefully chisel away the surrounding rock to remove the fossils.

COMMON CRUSTACEANS

Trilobites are among the most common fossils. These crablike sea creatures thrived between 550 and 250 million years ago.

FROM BONE TO STONE

The formation of an animal fossil begins when the creature dies. Its soft body parts decay, leaving the hard parts, such as teeth, bones, or shell.

Gradually, layers of sediments cover the remains. Sometimes, mineral-rich water can seep into the hard body parts and may replace them with minerals.

As the sediments are compacted, they press around the remains. When the sediments turn into rock, the rock retains the imprint of the body parts.

Plate movements bring the fossil to the surface. Erosion may then wear away the rock, revealing more of the fossil.

Geologist's microscope

Labradorite: massive habit

Glossary

anticline A fold in layers of sedimentary rock that bulges upward.

asthenosphere A weak layer inside Earth. It is part of the upper mantle and consists of partially molten rock.

atom The smallest unit that can be called a chemical element. All things on Earth are made up of atoms.

bacteria Single-celled, microscopic life-forms found in air, water, plants, animals, and Earth's crust.

butte An obvious, flat-topped, steep-sided hill sometimes found in desert areas. Some form by erosion of a large mesa.

canyon A deep, steep-sided valley formed by river erosion.

clay A fine-grained sediment formed by the chemical breakdown of rocks. It is moldable when wet and hard when dry. It can be baked to make china, pottery, tile, and brick.

coal A sedimentary rock formed by the compression of plant remains and sediment layers. It can be burned for fuel.

compound A chemical substance made up of more than one element. Most minerals are compounds.

concretion A usually rounded, hard mass of mineral matter that typically has a fossil at its core.

contact metamorphism The transformation of one type of rock into another, mostly as a result of heating.

continent One of Earth's seven main landmasses: Africa, Antarctica, Asia, Australia, Europe, North America, and South America. The landmasses include edges beneath the ocean as well as dry land area.

convection currents (mantle) Movement within the mantle caused by heat transfer from Earth's core. Hot rock rises and cooler rock sinks. This movement is most likely responsible for the motion of Earth's tectonic plates.

core The center of Earth. It consists of a solid inner core and a molten outer core, both of which are made of an iron-nickel alloy.

core sample A long column of rock that has been extracted from the ground by drilling with a hollow drill. Geologists use core samples to study rocks, ice, or soil beneath the surface.

crust The outer layer of Earth. There are two types of crust: continental crust, which forms the major landmasses, and oceanic crust, which is thinner and forms the seafloor.

crystal One grain of a mineral. Some crystals have a regular shape with smooth sides.

earthquake A sudden, violent vibration in Earth's crust that generally occurs at the edges of tectonic plates.

element A chemical substance that contains only one kind of atom.

era A division of time in Earth's history. Geologists divide eras into periods.

erosion The gradual wearing away of rock by water, ice, or wind.

evaporation The process by which a liquid turns into a gas without necessarily boiling.

fault A crack in Earth's crust along which motion has occurred.

fluorescent mineral A mineral that glows under ultraviolet light.

fold A bend in layers of rock typically produced when plate movements compress the crust.

fossil Any evidence of pre-existing life. It may be the remains of a plant or animal tha have turned to stone or have left their impression in rock.

fossil fuel A fuel that formed when plant remains were compressed under sedimentar rock layers. The most common fossil fuels are coal, oil, and natural gas.

gemstone Any mineral or other natural material that can be cut and polished into a jewel.

geode A rounded, hollow rock that is coate with layers of chalcedony and larger crystals

geology The study of Earth. Rocks, minera and fossils give some of the clues to Earth's history. A person who studies geology is called a geologist.

glacier A large mass of ice formed by the buildup of snow on a mountain or a continent. The ice moves slowly downhill, gouging out rocks and carrying debris.

habit The exterior shape of a single crystal or a group of crystals of the same mineral.

hoodoo A tall column of rock formed by erosion.

hotspot volcano A volcano that forms from a deep plume of magma. It commonly occur in the middle of a tectonic plate.

igneous rock Rock that forms when magm cools and hardens. Intrusive igneous rock solidifies under ground, and extrusive igneous rock solidifies above ground.

impermeable rock Rock through which liquids cannot pass.

intrusion A large mass of rock that forms under ground when magma is injected into other rocks and then cools and hardens.

Glacier

Hoodoos

kimberlite A type of rock formed from magma in the mantle. It is often associated with diamonds and other minerals from the deep Earth.

lava Magma that has erupted onto Earth's surface.

lithosphere The rigid outer layer of Earth, made up of the crust and the upper mantle.

magma Hot, liquid rock or a mush of liquid rock and crystals found beneath the surface of Earth. When magma erupts onto Earth's surface, it is called lava.

mantle The layer of Earth between the crust and the outer core. It includes the solid lower mantle, the weak asthenosphere, and the solid upper mantle.

massive A manner of occurrence of some minerals in which many mineral grains are intergrown to form a solid mass rather than single crystals with geometric shapes.

mesa A wide, flat-topped hill with steep sides. Small mesas may erode to form buttes.

metal Any of a number of elements that are shiny, moldable, and will conduct electricity. Many metals are found in minerals as compounds.

metamorphic rock Rock formed by the transformation of a pre-existing rock as a result of heat and/or pressure.

meteor A streak of light in the night sky caused by a lump of rock entering Earth's atmosphere from space. Before the rock enters the atmosphere it is known as a meteoroid. If it lands on Earth's surface, it is called a meteorite.

mid-ocean ridge An undersea mountain range formed by magma erupting through the gap between tectonic plates that are moving apart.

mineral A naturally formed solid with an ordered arrangement of atoms found in Earth's crust that is neither plant nor animal.

molecule A cluster of atoms formed when one or more types of atoms join (bond).

native element An element that exists alone and not in combination with another element. Examples include sulfur and gold.

ocean trench A deep and narrow undersea valley formed when the oceanic crust of one tectonic plate collides with the crust of another.

ore A rock or mineral from which it is possible to extract a useful material such as a metal.

ornamental stone A gemstone that is not considered precious but can be used for jewelry or other types of ornamentation.

outcrop The part of a rock formation that is exposed at Earth's surface.

period A standard division of time in Earth's history that is shorter than an era.

petrification The cell-by-cell replacement of organic matter such as bone or wood with minerals from surrounding solutions.

phosphorescent mineral A mineral that continues to glow for a short time after exposure to ultraviolet light.

placer deposits Pieces of heavy minerals found in river or beach sediments. They have been washed away from rocks by flowing water.

plate movement The movement of Earth's tectonic plates, probably caused by convection currents in the mantle.

regional metamorphism Large-scale transformation of one rock type into another as a result of heat and pressure due to plate collisions and the formation of mountains.

rift valley A wide valley formed as a result of the stretching of Earth's crust.

rock A solid mass usually made up of minerals and/or rock fragments.

sedimentary rock Rock formed near Earth's surface from pieces of other rocks or plant or animal remains, or by the buildup of chemical solids.

sediments Weathered pieces of rocks or plant or animal remains that are deposited at the bottom of rivers and lakes by water, wind, or ice.

seismic waves Sound waves that travel through Earth after an earthquake.

solution A mixture of two or more chemical substances. It may be a liquid, a solid, or a gas.

streak test A test that involves rubbing a mineral across an unglazed porcelain tile to produce a powder. The color of the powder left by the mineral can help identify it.

syncline A fold in layers of sedimentary rock that bulges downward.

tectonic plates Rigid pieces of Earth's lithosphere that move over the asthenosphere.

tectonic uplift The raising up of rock as a result of plate movements.

volcanic plug A stump of hard igneous rock that remains after a volcano has been worn away by erosion.

volcano An opening in Earth's crust through which lava erupts. It may form a cone-shaped mountain.

weathering The disintegration of rocks as a result of the freezing and thawing of ice, the action of chemicals in rainwater, or the growth of plant roots.

Index

Space

Contents

Exploring Space   132

Our Solar System   146

Our Universe   172

Pick Your Path!

YOU ARE ABOUT to blast off on an incredible journey into *Space*. No other book offers so many paths to explore the universe. You can start out in your own cosmic neighborhood, zoom through outer space, and end in the far reaches of the universe. Or you can follow your own interests. If you're especially interested in supernovas, nature's most powerful explosions, head straight to "Changing Stars," and move through the book from there.

You'll find plenty of other discovery paths to choose from in the special features sections. Read about real-life space heroes in "Inside Story," or get creative with "Hands On" activities. Delve into words with "Word Builders," or amaze your friends with fascinating facts from "That's Amazing!" You can choose a new path with every reading—READER'S DIGEST PATHFINDERS will take you wherever *you* want to go.

INSIDE STORY

Space Heroes

Peer at the Milky Way with Galileo and be the first person to see the stars through a telescope. Hear the noise and feel the cockpit shake with commander Eileen Collins as the space shuttle blasts off. Study an amazing photograph with Clyde Tombaugh and discover Planet X—mysterious Pluto. INSIDE STORY introduces you to the men and women who are exploring the frontiers of space. Imagine you are there with them, and you will understand how it feels to unravel the mysteries of the universe.

HANDS ON

Create and Make

Use Popsicle sticks to prove Earth spins. Track the movements of Jupiter's four largest moons with binoculars. Find out when to see meteor showers. Prove for yourself why stars twinkle. Create an "alien" that might live on one of Saturn's moons. The HANDS ON features suggest experiments, projects, and activities that make astronomy—and the night sky—come alive!

Word Builders

What a strange word! What does it mean? Where did it come from? Find out by reading *Word Builders*.

That's Amazing!

Awesome facts, amazing records, fascinating figures—you'll find them all in *That's Amazing!*

Pathfinder

Use the *Pathfinder* section to find your way from one subject to another. It's all up to you.

Ready! Set!
Start exploring!

Exploring Space

GET READY TO explore the mysteries of space. Your journey begins with Earth and its place in the vast universe. You then share the vision of all the people who have investigated the night sky— from early astronomers with their simple telescopes to modern scientists who capture magnificent images with the Hubble Space Telescope. Leave Earth behind and join the astronauts as they travel to the Moon aboard Apollo or orbit our planet in the space shuttle. Go where no human can go, by tracking the progress of robot probes. And ponder one of the greatest mysteries—is there other life in the universe?

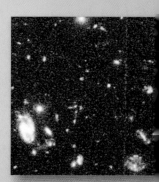

Our Planet and Its Moon
Light-travel time to Moon =
1.3 seconds

*People have traveled only
as far as the Moon.*

Our Place in Space

IF YOU WALK outside at night and look up at the stars, it might seem as if you are the center of the universe—surrounded by planets and stars that are moving around Earth. For thousands of years, people did think that the universe revolved around Earth.

In 1543, astronomer Nicolaus Copernicus realized that the best way to explain the motions of the planets was to say that all the planets, including Earth, moved around the Sun. Over the next century or so, the picture of the universe changed from an Earth-centered model to one with the Sun at its center. Since then, this model of the universe has grown many times. Astronomers have discovered that the Sun is just one of many stars, that it orbits far from the center of the Milky Way galaxy, and that the Milky Way is one of billions of galaxies.

The universe is so big that beams of light from the most distant regions of space take billions of years to reach us. This means we see faraway galaxies as they appeared billions of years ago, when the universe was young. The farther we look out into space, the farther we look back in time.

*Nine planets revolve
around our star, the S[...]*

**Our Solar
System**
Light-travel time
to Pluto = 6 hours

**Our Galaxy,
the Milky Way**
Light-travel time
across our galaxy =
100,000 years

IN A GALAXY LONG AGO AND FAR AWAY
For 10 days in December 1995, astronomers aimed the Hubble Space Telescope at a tiny patch of sky near the Big Dipper (far right). The Hubble photo (near right) revealed almost 2,000 galaxies. Many of these galaxies are so far away, and the light from them takes so long to reach us, that we see them as they looked just after they formed 14 billion years ago—only a billion years after the universe itself began.

THE VIEW BACK HOME

LOOK CLOSELY AT EARTH...
Satellites orbiting above Earth's atmosphere can look down and see objects on Earth as small as cars. This view shows the streets, bridges, and piers of San Francisco and Oakland in California, U.S.A. The green rectangles are city parks. Dots in the harbor are ships. The shades of blue in the water show currents and silt in the harbor.

Word Builders

The word **universe** comes from Latin words *uni-* and *versus,* meaning "one turn." The universe is everything that exists. People once thought that the Sun and the planets made up most of the universe, but by 1600 they began to understand that there were other stars like the Sun. When astronomers discovered other galaxies in the 1920s, our picture of the universe grew again.

That's Amazing!

• If you were driving in a car at highway speeds, it would take you 340 billion years to reach the center of the Milky Way galaxy—that's more than 25 times the age of the universe.
• Earth, the Sun, and the rest of the solar system are whirling around the Milky Way galaxy at 560,000 miles per hour (900,000 km/h).

Pathfinder

• Where does space start? Go to page 141.
• Why was Nicolaus Copernicus worried about saying Earth moved around the Sun? Go to page 148.
• What can astronomers do with variable stars? Go to page 178.
• How did the universe begin? Go to pages 186–87.

COSMIC ZOOM

The fastest thing in the universe is a beam of light. In one second, it travels 186,000 miles (300,000 km). In one hour, it zips across 670 million miles (1,078 million km). In one year, light travels 5.9 million million miles (9.5 million million km), a distance that astronomers call one light-year. Using the speed of light as our cosmic yardstick, we can zoom to the edge of the universe in five big jumps.

Our spiral galaxy contains about 200 billion stars.

The Local Group contains about 30 galaxies.

Our Galactic Cluster, the Local Group
Light-travel time to Andromeda galaxy = 2.8 million years

The Whole Universe
Light-travel time to edge of universe = 15 billion years

The universe contains as many as 50 billion galaxies.

INSIDE STORY

Expanding the Universe

"You will be interested to hear that I have found a Cepheid variable in the Andromeda Nebula." With those words, Edwin Hubble announced to the world that the universe was larger than anyone had thought. The year was 1924. Hubble had found a winking variable star that allowed him to prove Andromeda is not a nebula (a cloud of dust and gas) in our galaxy, but another galaxy far away. This meant that the Milky Way is just one of many galaxies. Hubble went on to discover that the other galaxies are moving away from ours and that the universe is expanding. Today's Hubble Space Telescope is named after Edwin Hubble. Both have investigated the edge of space.

THEN ZOOM AWAY...

A view from a space shuttle reveals part of the coastline of Mozambique in Africa. The red areas in this infrared image are forests and fields, and the blue and black areas are the Indian Ocean. The white streaks are plumes from forest fires that people have set deliberately to clear land for farming.

...AND AWAY AGAIN...
From the Moon's surface, 240,000 miles (386,000 km) away, Apollo astronauts looked back at their home planet. They saw a beautiful blue globe rising above the barren lunar surface.

...AND EVEN FARTHER
From 3.9 million miles (6.2 million km) away, the Galileo spacecraft showed Earth and the Moon floating in the blackness of space.

Scoping Out Space

SPACE IS SO enormous that today's fastest rocket would take almost 100,000 years to reach the nearest star beyond the Sun. So to learn about the universe, astronomers use telescopes. Telescopes collect the light coming from distant objects and magnify it, allowing us to see the planets, stars, and galaxies as if they were much closer to us—almost as good as hopping in a starship.

The first telescopes, known as refractors, used a lens to collect light. Then in 1671, Sir Isaac Newton invented the reflecting telescope, which used a mirror to collect light. Today, most observatory telescopes are reflectors. The bigger the mirror, the more light it can collect, so bigger telescopes can show us objects that are fainter and farther away. Many observatories are now building monster scopes that will use mirrors as wide as houses.

Not all telescopes collect the kind of light that our eyes can see. Planets, stars, and galaxies also send out invisible waves, such as radio beams and X-rays. In the past 50 years, astronomers have invented telescopes that can detect this invisible radiation. The air above us blocks some of the waves, so astronomers place infrared, ultraviolet, and X-ray telescopes in orbit high above our atmosphere. These space telescopes have revealed strange objects, such as exploding galaxies and black holes, that no one knew existed.

INSIDE STORY
The First Observer

"Upon whatever part of the Milky Way the spyglass is directed, a crowd of stars is presented that is quite beyond calculation." These words were written by Galileo Galilei, the first person to see the sky through a telescope. He announced his sensational discoveries in 1610. "The greatest astonishment is this—I have observed four planets which have their orbits around Jupiter." These were moons of Jupiter, and they proved that not everything revolves around Earth. Galileo added, "I give infinite thanks that I alone have been the first observer of amazing things."

HANDS ON
Looking Up

You don't need the Hubble Space Telescope to explore space. With nothing but your eyes, you can gaze at the stars and find ancient constellations, such as Orion the Hunter, or Leo the Lion. You can also see five of the planets, watch the Moon go from crescent to full, or spot a streaking meteor.

Binoculars show as much detail as Galileo saw through his simple telescope. They let you follow the moons of Jupiter, admire the many stars of the Milky Way, or find the fuzzy Orion Nebula.

A telescope reveals even more—from Saturn's rings and Jupiter's clouds to the spiral arms of the Andromeda galaxy. If you want to look through a telescope or just ask questions about the night sky, contact your local observatory, planetarium, or science center.

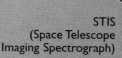

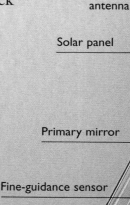

Secondary mirror

High-gain antenna

Solar panel

Primary mirror

Fine-guidance sensor

Light reaches focus.

STIS (Space Telescope Imaging Spectrograph)

NICMOS (Near-Infrared Camera and Multi-Object Spectrometer)

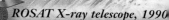

Word Builders

Galileo was the first person ever to use a telescope for astronomy, but he called his instrument a spyglass. In 1611, at a banquet that was held in Galileo's honor, a Greek poet named John Demisiani suggested the name **telescope,** from two Greek words, *tele* and *skopein,* meaning "to view far off."

That's Amazing!

• With four 27-foot (8.2-m) mirrors, the Very Large Telescope, when it is first used in 2001, will become the largest optical telescope on Earth.
• When launched into orbit past the Moon after 2007, the Next Generation Space Telescope may use a mirror 26 feet (8 m) across that will unfold like the petals of a flower.

Pathfinder

• What amazing photos has the Hubble Space Telescope taken? Go to pages 134, 178–79, and 180–81.
• Are radio telescopes listening for extraterrestrial broadcasts? Go to page 145.
• For more skywatching tips, go to pages 156, 170, 174–75, 181, and 183.

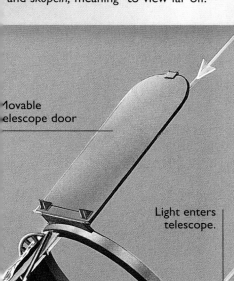

Movable telescope door

Light enters telescope.

High-gain antenna

EAGLE EYE IN THE SKY

Our atmosphere blurs the view seen through telescopes on the ground, so astronomers placed the Hubble Space Telescope above the atmosphere. Hubble is about as big as a school bus, orbits Earth every 90 minutes, and provides the sharpest pictures of stars and galaxies ever taken. It uses electronic cameras with tongue-twisting names like Near-Infrared Camera and Multi-Object Spectrometer to take digital pictures. The telescope then transmits the pictures by radio to mission control on Earth. Every three years, astronauts visit Hubble in a space shuttle to repair or replace old parts.

WIDE EYES ON THE MOUNTAINS

Astronomers build telescopes where the sky is clear—on mountaintops far from city lights. The summit of Mauna Kea in Hawaii, U.S.A., is home to many optical telescopes (the kind that collect visible light). Each of the two Keck Telescopes uses a mirror 33 feet (10 m) across, making them the biggest optical telescopes in the world. They are housed in two large domes.

BIG EARS ON THE COSMOS

The Very Large Array (VLA) in New Mexico, U.S.A., is one of the world's largest radio telescopes. Its 27 dish-shaped antennas can tune in to crackling radio signals coming from planets, stars, and galaxies. Astronomers have used radio telescopes like the VLA to map the shape of our Milky Way galaxy.

SEEING THE INVISIBLE

Like a single note on a piano, light is just one type of radiation coming from space. Objects in the universe send out an entire keyboard of radiation. If our eyes could detect these invisible waves, we would see a very different universe.

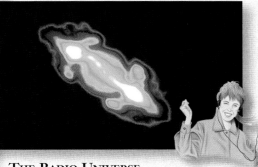

THE RADIO UNIVERSE

We use radio waves to broadcast music and TV. Objects in space with strong magnetism also send out radio waves. In this radio picture of Jupiter, we see the planet's giant magnetic field.

THE INFRARED UNIVERSE

Warm objects, like just-popped toast, send out infrared radiation, or heat. Infrared pictures, such as this one of Saturn, tell us the temperature of objects and allow us to peer through thick clouds of dust in space.

THE X-RAY UNIVERSE

Doctors and dentists use X-rays to examine our bodies and teeth. Astronomers use X-ray telescopes to watch superhot gas falling into black holes, as in the star Cygnus X-1, shown in this X-ray photo.

Vostok, 1961

Gemini, 1965

Soyuz, 1967

Future space plane

Blast Off!

WHILE TELESCOPES LET astronomers look at distant galaxies, rockets allow people to explore nearby space. The first person to travel into space was the Soviet Union's Yuri Gagarin, in 1961. The United States and the Soviet Union then raced to put a human on the Moon. The space race ended in 1969, when an American, Neil Armstrong, stepped onto the lunar surface.

To soar high enough to start orbiting Earth, a spacecraft needs speed. If it goes any slower than 17,000 miles per hour (28,000 km/h), the spacecraft will fall back to the ground. Only rocket-powered spacecraft travel fast enough to reach space. Most are made of several stages that drop off, leaving a light upper stage to reach orbit. In the future, rocket-powered space planes will reach orbit with just a single stage.

The National Aeronautics and Space Administration (NASA) now has four space shuttles. The shuttles can orbit Earth but they cannot travel any farther. The Saturn V rocket propelled people to the Moon on Apollo missions, but the last Saturn V was launched in 1973. Future rockets will allow people to travel back to the Moon and past it to Mars.

A FAR-OUT GOLF COURSE
From 1968 to 1972, 27 astronauts visited the Moon in the Apollo spacecraft. During most missions, two astronauts landed using the lunar module while one astronaut orbited overhead in the command module. In 1971, during the Apollo 14 mission, Alan Shepard played golf on the Moon. He made a golf club from a rock-collecting tool and hit a ball "miles and miles."

 HANDS ON

Launch a Rocket

It's easy to show how a rocket launch works.

❶ Blow up a party balloon and squeeze the neck of the balloon between your fingers so the air can't get out.

❷ Point the balloon toward the ceiling and let go. As the air escapes, it pushes the balloon forward.

Instead of air, a rocket uses hot gases for propulsion. Its engines burn fuel to make the gases, which spew out the exhaust. These gases push against the rocket and force it to lift off.

SPLASHDOWN!
During the American space missions of the 1960s and 1970s, astronauts returned to Earth in capsules that splashed down into the ocean. The astronauts then had to be fished out by helicopters. Today's shuttles land at runways, a will future space planes. Astronauts walk off lik passengers disembarking from a jet airliner.

FLYING THE SPACE SHUTTLE

LIFTOFF
You are about to blast off on the shuttle. Hold on! At Takeoff Time (T) minus 6.6 seconds, the three main engines fire. At T equals 0, the two solid rocket boosters (SRBs) ignite, and the space shuttle takes off.

SRB SEPARATION
With a bang at T plus 2 minutes, the SRBs burn out and shoot away from the shuttle. They parachute back to Earth, where they will be collected. The ride becomes smooth and quiet.

TANK FALLS AWAY
The main engines are powered by liquid hydrogen and oxygen from the external tank. At T plus 8.5 minutes, the engines shut off. Its fuel gone, th external tank falls into the Pacific Ocean.

Word Builders

People who fly on American space missions are called **astronauts,** from two Greek words, *astron* and *nautes,* meaning "star voyagers." Russians, and others from the former Soviet Union, who fly into space are called **cosmonauts,** meaning "voyagers into the cosmos." Now the two kinds of voyagers fly together on joint missions.

That's Amazing!

• The last two Saturn Vs, the only rockets able to send people to the Moon, are now museum displays at NASA in Houston and Cape Canaveral.
• During launch, a space shuttle burns up to 10 tons of fuel every second.
• Nearly 28,000 ceramic tiles protect the shuttle from the intense heat of reentry.

Pathfinder

• What does it feel like to be in zero gravity? Go to page 141.
• What other machines can explore space? Go to pages 142–43.
• What was it like to walk on the Moon? Go to page 152.
• Will people ever travel to Mars? Go to page 158.

Dogs in Space
Belka and Strelka, two Russian dogs, were the first creatures to return to Earth after orbiting it. They flew aboard Korabl-Sputnik 2 in August 1960, eight months before cosmonaut Yuri Gagarin boarded the Vostok 1 spacecraft and became the first person in space.

INSIDE STORY
Wild Ride into Space

"A shuttle launch is unlike anything I've ever experienced on Earth," explains commander Eileen Collins. "You *see* smoke around the shuttle on liftoff, then bright flashes of light, like a lightning storm, for the next eight and a half minutes. You *hear* fire. You *smell* electrical components and dry air. You *feel* your back aching after spending four hours lying vertical during countdown. Then, during the ascent, you are hurled into space faster and faster. Breathing is difficult. Reaching and moving is difficult. But suddenly the acceleration cuts off, and you are in zero gravity."

In Orbit
Once in orbit, the payload-bay doors open, and you're ready to begin work. Traveling at about 17,500 miles per hour (28,000 km/h), the shuttle orbits Earth every 90 minutes.

Reentry
Time to come home. As you descend at 25 times the speed of sound, the shuttle surface and the air around it glow red hot. The thickening atmosphere slows the shuttle to aircraft speed.

Touchdown
The shuttle uses its wings to glide down through the atmosphere. Just above the landing strip, the shuttle's wheels extend. Moments later, you touch down. Welcome home!

Working in Space

SHUTTLE ASTRONAUTS HAVE only a little time to enjoy the view of Earth below while they're in space. There's always work to do! They conduct long, complicated experiments, testing how zero gravity affects people or how to make new materials such as ultrapure crystals or medicines. On some missions, astronauts release satellites for observing Earth, the Sun, or the stars. Space work can also involve an extravehicular activity (EVA)—in other words, a spacewalk—to repair satellites or assemble space station parts.

Flights on a space shuttle last only a week or two, but cosmonauts and astronauts can spend months on a space station. Here they conduct much longer experiments. Life on a space station can be draining—the lack of gravity affects the flow of blood, wastes away muscles, and weakens bones. Space station residents must exercise for hours every day to keep their bodies strong.

Along with space shuttles and space stations, hundreds of satellites are working in space. Some were put into orbit by space shuttles, but most were lofted into space by rockets. Satellites make it possible to send TV pictures around the world instantly, to navigate ships across the ocean, or to predict the weather days in advance. We now depend on these eyes and ears in the sky.

FLYING FOOD
Some food on the shuttle is ready to eat, and some is like dehydrated camping food—you just need to add water. A typical day's menu includes a breakfast of orange drink, scrambled eggs, and a sweet roll; a lunch of soup, sandwich, banana, and cookies; and a dinner of beefsteak, broccoli, pudding, and cocoa. Here Michael Baker grabs a bite of lunch—a free-floating peanut butter and jelly sandwich.

DRESSED FOR SPACE
A spacesuit is like a miniature spaceship. Tanks in the backpack supply oxygen for breathing. Layers of Kevlar, Teflon, and Dacron insulate the astronaut from the extreme temperatures—250°F (120°C) in sunlight and –250°F (–156°C) in shadow. The suit blocks the Sun's radiation and keeps out tiny bits of space dust. Water pumped through tubes in the underwear keeps the hard-working astronaut cool. The astronaut can sip water from a drink container, munch on a snack bar, and talk to the other astronauts through a headset called a Snoopy cap. On Earth, the entire suit weighs more than an astronaut, but in orbit, it weighs nothing.

Spandex mesh underwear

Water-cooling tube

Spacesuit made of several layer[s]

Urin[e] coll[ection] devi[ce]

Tool kit

Visor and helmet

Primary life-support-system backpack

Cordless electric screwdriver

Lights on helmet

Word Builders

Astronauts feel weightless because they are always in **free fall** around Earth. Anything falling from a great height feels weightless—for a few seconds—until it hits the ground! But objects in orbit are so high and traveling so fast that they never hit Earth. They experience **zero G**, or zero gravity, more correctly called **microgravity**.

That's Amazing!

• During weightlessness, the vertebrae of the spine spread apart. Astronauts grow 1–2 inches (2.5–5 cm) taller during a space flight. When they return to Earth, astronauts shrink back to preflight size.
• Space toilets can't use water to flush, so they use air. They are like vacuum cleaners that you sit on.

Pathfinder

• Why do astronauts visit the Hubble Space Telescope? Go to page 137.
• How do astronauts get into space? Go to pages 138–39.
• What would it be like to be the first astronaut on Mars? Go to page 158.
• How can an astronomy satellite help to explain how the universe formed? Go to page 186.

LABORATORY IN THE SKY

The International Space Station will replace the Russian Mir space station. This new station will be gradually assembled in space during 45 visits from United States space shuttles and Russian Proton rockets. When completed in 2004, the station will be as big as a football field and home to astronauts and scientists from around the world.

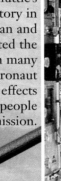

Display and control module

Metal airtight collars

Gloves

Snoopy cap for communication

SPACE WORK NEVER ENDS

On the space shuttle's Microgravity Laboratory in 1995, Catherine Coleman and six other astronauts tested the effects of zero gravity on many different materials. Astronaut John Glenn tested the effects of zero gravity on older people during a 1998 shuttle mission.

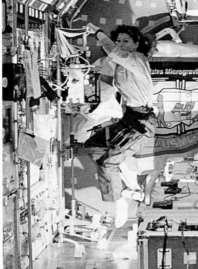

INSIDE STORY

A Day in Space

In 1998, Australian-born Andrew Thomas spent five months on Mir, the Russian space station. "Although we see the Sun rise sixteen times a day," explained Thomas, "we get up at 8:30 AM Moscow Time. To wash, we can't splash water because it would float everywhere. So we use a damp washcloth. After breakfast we work on our experiments. By 7:00 PM it's time for dinner. Then I watch the world go by out the window. We are in bed by 11:00 PM, in bags we tie to a wall."

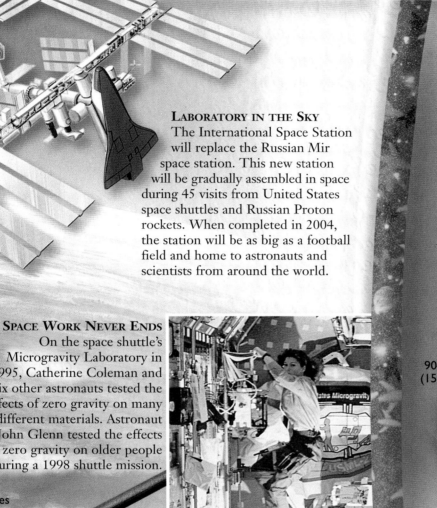

Last traces of atmosphere
600 miles
(1,000 km)

Hubble Space Telescope
370 miles
(600 km)

Space shuttle
120–370 miles
(200–600 km)

International Space Station
220 miles (350 km)

Aurora
90–300 miles
(150–500 km)

Low Earth-orbiting satellite
185 miles (300 km)

Meteor shower
50 miles
(80 km)

Concorde
9 miles (15 km)

Clouds
4–6 miles
(6–10 km)

Jumbo jet
6 miles
(10 km)

Mount Everest
5.5 miles
(8.8 km)

WHERE DOES SPACE START?

No sharp line divides air and space. The atmosphere just gets thinner as you go up. On Mount Everest, the air is so thin that climbers use bottled oxygen. But even 200 miles (320 km) up, there are still a few oxygen and nitrogen molecules. The drag from these molecules would make a space station fall to Earth, so the station needs a boost from its rockets every few months. Above 600 miles (1,000 km), satellites circle beyond the last bits of air and can orbit for many years.

Robot Probes

MOST PLANETS, COMETS, and asteroids are too far away to visit in person, but we still want to learn more about them. Because it would be too dangerous and expensive to send astronauts, we send remote-controlled robot probes instead.

Most of our knowledge about the planets has come from these robots, which first visited Venus and Mars in the 1960s. Some probes orbit a planet—Magellan orbited Venus. A few, such as the Galileo Probe at Jupiter, enter the planet's atmosphere, while probes like Mars Pathfinder actually land on the planet. Others fly past the planet—Voyager studied Jupiter, Saturn, Uranus, and Neptune on a flyby. While probes are zooming past a planet, they get a boost in speed from its gravity and can then fly on toward a more distant planet. Using this slingshot method, we have now sent probes to every planet in the solar system except tiny Pluto.

Robot probes can also explore other objects in the solar system. Future probes are expected to land on comets, hop across an asteroid, and zoom through the hot atmosphere of the Sun. So far, no robot probe has returned to Earth. Instead, probes send their digital pictures and data to Earth as radio waves, and the signals are picked up by giant radio telescopes. In the future, though, some probes will carry samples from Mars, comets, and asteroids back to Earth.

HANDS ON
Probe the Web

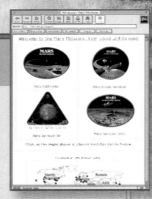

The best way to keep up to date on planet missions is to explore the World Wide Web, where you can find the very latest information, along with loads of pictures of robot probes and the planets they have visited. A good place to start is the web site of NASA's Jet Propulsion Laboratory—*www.jpl.nasa.gov*. From here, links take you to prior missions such as Magellan (Venus) and Mars Pathfinder; current missions such as Cassini (Saturn) and Galileo (Jupiter); and future missions such as Pluto-Kuiper Express and Stardust (comets). When the Sojourner rover visited Mars in 1997, its pictures were immediately displayed on the Web. The busiest day saw the NASA web site deluged with 47 million hits—more than any other web site has ever received.

ROVING AROUND MARS
In July 1997, the first rover to visit another planet rolled off the Pathfinder lander and ont the surface of Mars. Called Sojourner, the rove used cameras and a cuplike detector to look at rocks up close and found evidence that wate had gushed across Mars billions of years ago. Sojourner's mission ended three months later when the Pathfinder lander, which commande the rover, became too cold and stopped workin

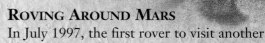

Word Builders

Space probes are named in a variety of ways. **Galileo, Cassini,** and **Huygens** are named for astronomers. Some probe names, such as **Ulysses,** come from mythology. **Magellan** is named for an explorer; **Giotto** for a painter who depicted Comet Halley. The **Clementine** probe was named for a song character in "Darling Clementine."

That's Amazing!

• Pioneer 10, the first probe to reach Jupiter, is now heading for the star Aldebaran, which is 65 light-years from Earth. The probe will take more than two million years to reach the star.
• The billion-dollar Mars Observer probe blew up just as it approached Mars in 1993. It had taken only one picture.

Pathfinder

• How did Magellan see through the clouds of Venus? Go to pages 156–57.
• What is a nanorover and where is it going? Go to pages 160–61.
• What messages are the two Voyager probes carrying? Go to page 167.
• When will a probe visit Pluto? Go to pages 168–69.
• How will a probe collect comet dust? Go to pages 170–71.

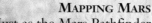

MAPPING MARS
Just as the Mars Pathfinder lander mission was ending in 1997, Global Surveyor arrived to orbit Mars. Its four-year mission is to map the entire planet with cameras that can see objects on Mars as small as a house.

GETTING DOWN TO TITAN

Cassini, a spacecraft the size of a truck, began its trip to Saturn in 1997. It is scheduled to arrive on July 1, 2004. Attached to Cassini's side is a probe called Huygens. Here's what Huygens will do.

PROBE AWAY!
On November 6, 2004, Cassini releases the Huygens probe. Its destination is Titan, Saturn's largest moon.

Cassini | Huygens

HOT FLIGHT
Three weeks later, Huygens plows into Titan's thick atmosphere at 12,000 miles per hour (20,000 km/h). Huygens's heat shield becomes twice as hot as the Sun.

Heat shield

BUILDING A PROBE
Hundreds of people work together to build a space probe. Once it is flying toward its target, the robot probe is beyond the reach of astronauts, so all its parts must work for many years without repair. The European Ulysses probe, shown here, was launched in 1990 and should keep exploring the polar regions of the Sun until 2001.

PUTTING ON THE BRAKES
With Huygens slowed to 900 miles per hour (1,400 km/h), a small parachute opens.

MAIN CHUTE POPS
A large parachute further slows Huygens. Fifteen minutes later, it is discarded.

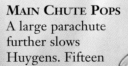

INSIDE STORY

Explorer of the Planets

"In our time we've crossed the Solar System," wrote Carl Sagan. Best known for explaining space to millions of people through his books and TV shows, Carl Sagan also helped plan many missions to the planets. He eloquently described the significance of robot probes: "These spacecraft have taught us about the wonders of other worlds, about the uniqueness and fragility of our own, about beginnings and ends. They have given us access to most of the Solar System.... They are the ships that first explored what may be the homelands of our remote descendants." After Carl Sagan died in 1996, NASA honored him by giving the Mars Pathfinder lander a new name—it is now called the Sagan Memorial Station.

BELOW THE CLOUDS
The last descent on a small chute takes two hours. Huygens's cameras snap pictures of the surface below.

Heat shield is released.

TOUCHDOWN!
Huygens lands on ice or splashes into a lake of liquid methane. It sends back a few pictures, but survives no more than 30 minutes.

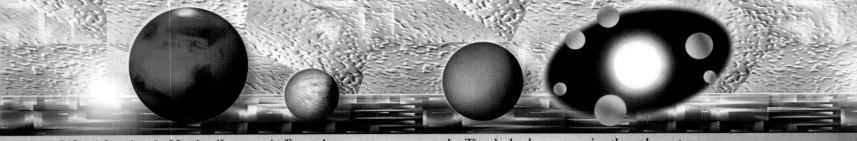

Looking for Life

WHEN YOU GAZE at the stars, you might find yourself asking the big question—are we alone? We find life everywhere on Earth, even in unlikely places such as deep oil wells, pools of boiling water, and inside Antarctic rocks. Has life also adapted to the extreme conditions on other planets? It seems possible, but where do we look?

All life that we know requires water. Mars had oceans of water billions of years ago. Perhaps life started there but died out. One of Jupiter's moons, Europa, might have an ocean under its icy crust. And Titan, a smoggy moon of Saturn, is rich in the carbon compounds that started life on Earth. It may also be made partly of water ice.

In recent years, astronomers have found dozens of planets orbiting other stars. These planets are not places like Earth. They are all giant worlds, like Jupiter, where life is unlikely to exist. But perhaps astronomers will find Earth-like planets, too. Future space telescopes will be able to take pictures of these smaller planets, if they exist.

Some astronomers suggest that our galaxy could contain as many as one million other civilizations. Are aliens visiting Earth now in UFOs? Most scientists think that UFOs can be explained in other ways. But perhaps in your lifetime, we will find proof that aliens exist.

INSIDE STORY

Seeing Signs of Martians

One hundred years ago, Percival Lowell was sure that Martians were real. "The telescope presents us with perhaps the most startling discovery of modern times—the canals of Mars," he wrote. Lowell saw lines crisscrossing Mars. He thought they must be canals built by intelligent beings. "What we see hints at the existence of beings who are in advance of, not behind us, in the journey of life." But the canals were not real—they were optical illusions. Although Lowell was wrong, his ideas sparked interest in Mars that continues to this day.

ALIEN IDEAS
Here are some guesses of what aliens might look like. Of course, they could be unlike any life we know, or might not exist at all.

SMART REPTILES
Perhaps advanced dinosaurs would dominate on Earth-like planets. Some scientists think that if Earth's dinosaurs had not become extinct, they might have evolved into intelligent, upright creatures.

GAS GIANT FLOATERS
On gas giant planets, perhaps there would be creatures that float in the dense atmosphere, like fish that swim in our seas.

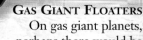

Word Builders

Space exploration uses many acronyms—short words that stand for a longer phrase.
• The acronym **SETI** (which is pronounced *set-tee*) stands for "Search for Extra Terrestrial Intelligence."
• Extra Terrestrial, as in **ET,** means "from beyond Earth."
• The acronym **UFO** stands for "Unidentified Flying Object."

That's Amazing!

• In 1974, astronomers used the Arecibo radio telescope to beam a message to M13, a star cluster so far away that if aliens get our message and respond, we won't receive their reply until the year AD 44,000.
• As late as 1965, people thought that some kind of canals might exist on Mars. It took the first Mars probe, Mariner 4, to prove that water-filled Martian canals don't exist.

Pathfinder

• What else do we use radio telescopes for? Go to pages 136–37.
• When will we investigate Titan? Go to page 143.
• How did a Martian meteorite get to Earth? Go to page 159.
• Which probes have investigated Jupiter's moon Europa? Go to page 163.
• Who discovered planets around other stars? Go to page 177.

LISTENING FOR LIFE

Scientists with Project Phoenix and other SETI programs use radio telescopes around the world to search for signals from alien civilizations. If such a signal was detected, it would be the greatest discovery of all time—but would we be able to decode it?

BUGS ON MARS?

Is this a Martian life form? In 1996, a team of scientists announced that they had discovered fossilized bacteria in a meteorite from Mars. Other scientists doubt the results and think that the evidence has other explanations. The debate may continue until we get more rocks from Mars to study.

HANDS ON

Recipe for a Titanite

Create an alien that might live on Titan, one of Saturn's moons. You can use modeling clay or common household items such as old boxes, foil, and straws. Think about what the Titanite eats, how it moves around, how it avoids predators, how it copes with the temperature, and how it breathes, sees, and hears. Keep in mind what Titan is like as you create your Titanite:
• Titan is extremely cold—about −289°F (−178°C).
• Titan is covered in thick smog, and the nitrogen atmosphere does not contain any oxygen.
• The surface is probably rocky, icy, and cratered.
• Almost all water on Titan is frozen, but there may be seas of sticky red-brown liquid methane, as well as methane clouds, rain, and snow.

UNDER THE ICE OF EUROPA

A crust of cracked ice covers Europa, one of Jupiter's moons. Underneath the ice, there may be an ocean of liquid water, heated from below by volcanic vents. In Earth's deepest oceans, strange worms, blind fish, and heat-loving bacteria thrive in the darkness around volcanic vents. Could Europa harbor life in its dark ocean? A submarinelike probe now being planned could find out.

LOW-G LIFE

On low-density planets with weak gravity, life forms might resemble giraffes, with tall, spindly bodies. Like us, intelligent aliens would probably have two arms and two legs, because it is a simple but efficient body design.

HIGH-G ALIENS

The gravity on large, dense planets is strong. Aliens there might be squat, slow-moving creatures, with elephantlike legs and a strong tail to support their weight.

Our Solar System

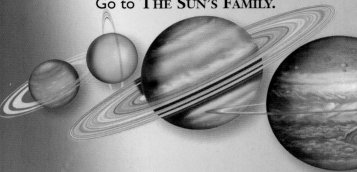

You are about to travel through your cosmic neighborhood. Here you will find Earth's neighbors—the other planets, their moons, and the asteroids and comets—all circling our nearest star, the Sun. Your tour begins with something very familiar—our own planet Earth and the Moon. You then shoot to the center of our solar system with a visit to the scorching Sun. Hold on tight. The journey continues to the nearby rocky planets, the asteroid belt, and the distant gas giant planets. Your tour ends with Pluto and the comets at the cold, dark edges of the solar system.

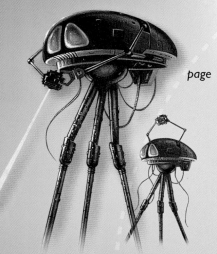

The Sun's Family

YOU BELONG TO a cosmic family called the solar system. The Sun heads this collection of nine planets, dozens of moons, and countless asteroids and comets. The biggest and best-known family members are the planets, and the planet we know best is Earth itself. You can see five of the planets with the naked eye because they shine brightly in our sky. These are Mercury, Venus, Mars, Jupiter, and Saturn. The other three—Uranus, Neptune, and Pluto—lie so far from the Sun that you need binoculars, or even a telescope, to see them.

Most planets aren't alone in space. Seven of the planets have companions called moons. Earth has one moon. Saturn has the most—18 in total. Only Mercury and Venus travel around the Sun without any moons.

Many other worlds belong to the Sun's family. Thousands of rocky minor planets called asteroids move in a belt between Mars and Jupiter. Some small asteroids travel close to the Sun. At the edge of the solar system, past Pluto, there are millions of ice balls. When one of these shoots toward the Sun, we may see it as a comet with a glowing tail of gas and dust.

The Man Who Moved Earth

The year is 1543. Everyone believes Earth is the center of the solar system, but you have a different theory. "It is in the very center of all the planets," you write, "that the Sun finds its place." You suggest that Earth and the other planets move around the Sun. Your theory shifts Earth from the center of the universe. You know people won't like your ideas. They might even arrest you. What do you do? Astronomer Nicolaus Copernicus faced that question more than 450 years ago. To avoid trouble, he waited until he was dying to publish his theory. Nearly 100 years passed before people accepted his ideas.

ET DES ARTS. LIV. II.

NICOLAS COPERNI

GOING AROUND AND AROUND

Gravity, a powerful pull from the Sun, holds the planets, comets, and asteroids in paths called orbits. These orbits are ellipses, like squashed circles. As planets orbit the Sun, they spin like tops. One trip around the Sun is a planet's year. A planet's day is the time it takes to spin around once. Earth's year is about 365 days. Pluto pokes along, taking 248 Earth years to complete its year, but Sun-hugging Mercury whips around the Sun in 88 days.

Uranus
Distance from Sun:
1,787 million miles
(2,875 million km)
One day: 17.2 Earth hours
One year: 83.8 Earth years

Pluto
Distance from Sun:
3,676 million miles
(5,916 million km)
One day: 6.4 Earth days
One year: 248 Earth years

Neptune
Distance from Sun:
2,799 million miles
(4,504 million km)
One day: 16.1 Earth hours
One year: 163.7 Earth years

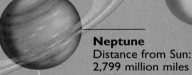

HANDS ON

Pacing Out the Solar System

You can make your own model of the solar system with a peppercorn, two peas, two small marbles, two limes, an orange, a grapefruit, and a blow-up beachball.

Put the beachball on a long pavement. The ball stands for the Sun. Take one step and put down a pea for Mercury. Take another step and put down a marble for Venus, then a half step and another marble for Earth, our home.

Just one and one-half steps on from Earth, put down a pea for Mars. Then take nine steps before plunking down the grapefruit for Jupiter. Eleven steps after Jupiter, place the orange for Saturn. After 24 more steps, add a lime for Uranus, and 27 steps later, put down the other lime for Neptune. Finally, add a peppercorn for tiny Pluto, 24 steps after Neptune—and 99 steps from the beachball Sun.

The solar system is big! If Pluto were really just 99 steps from the Sun, the Sun would be no bigger than a marble and all the planets would be tiny specks.

PLANETS BIG AND SM

There are two kinds of planets. G Jupiter, Saturn, Uranus, and Neptune balls of gas far from the Sun. Merc Venus, Mars, and our own planet, Ea are small rocky planets close to the Pluto, the smallest planet, doesn't fit in a tiny ice world at the edge of the s system. The size comparison at right each planet's diameter (the distance ac the planet). You can see that even Jup the biggest planet, is small next to the S

Word Builders

Everyone calls it the Sun, but our star's proper name is **Sol.** It was named for the ancient Roman god of the Sun. From this name we get the word **solar,** as in the solar system.

That's Amazing!

• Hold on tight! You are shooting through space at more than 64,000 miles per hour (103,000 km/h) right now. That's the speed that Earth travels as it orbits the Sun.
• You could pack 1,400 Earths inside Jupiter, and 900 Jupiters inside the Sun.

Pathfinder

• Where does the solar system fit into the universe? Go to pages 134–35 and 182–83.
• Are there any other solar systems? Go to pages 176–77.
• How did the rest of the universe get here? Go to pages 186–87.

Comet

Mercury
Distance from Sun:
36 million miles
(58 million km)
One day: 59 Earth days
One year: 88 Earth days

Jupiter
Distance from Sun:
484 million miles
(778 million km)
One day: 9.8 Earth hours
One year: 11.9 Earth years

Near-Earth asteroid orbit

Trojan asteroids

Mars
Distance from Sun:
142 million miles
(228 million km)
One day: 24.6 Earth hours
One year: 687 Earth days

Sun

Earth
Distance from Sun:
93 million miles
(150 million km)
One day: 23.9 hours
One year: 365.24 days

Venus
Distance from Sun:
67 million miles
(108 million km)
One day: 243 Earth days
One year: 225 Earth days

Asteroid belt

Trojan asteroids

Saturn
Distance from Sun:
888 million miles
(1,429 million km)
One day: 10.7 Earth hours
One year: 29.4 Earth years

Sun
Diameter:
865,000 miles
(1,392,000 km)

Neptune
Diameter:
30,778 miles
(49,530 km)

Saturn
Diameter:
74,904 miles
(120,540 km)

Mars
Diameter:
4,222 miles
(6,794 km)

Venus
Diameter:
7,521 miles
(12,104 km)

Pluto
Diameter:
1,429 miles
(2,300 km)

Uranus
Diameter:
31,766 miles
(51,120 km)

Jupiter
Diameter:
88,848 miles
(142,980 km)

Earth
Diameter:
7,927 miles
(12,756 km)

Mercury
Diameter:
3,032 miles
(4,879 km)

Charon, moon of Pluto

BIRTH OF THE PLANETS

The solar system was born from a swirling cloud of gas and dust. About five billion years ago, the cloud began to shrink. Under the force of gravity, most of the material fell toward the center of the cloud. Gas collected there, heated up, and became the Sun. Dust and gas left over in the cloud formed the planets. Here's how it happened.

CLOUD OF DUST AND GAS SHRINKS
Perhaps a nearby star explodes and squeezes the cloud like a snowball. The cloud starts shrinking. The Sun forms.

CLOUD BEGINS TO ROTATE
As it shrinks, the cloud begins to spin like a hurricane. It spreads into a flat disc around the new Sun.

DUST IN DISC FORMS ROCKY LUMPS
The dust particles in the disc begin to stick together and form billions of lumps of rocky material.

ROCKY LUMPS COLLIDE
These rocky lumps smash together and form thousands of objects as big as small planets.

THE SOLAR SYSTEM TODAY
The small planets collide for millions of years until only a few are left. These are the planets we know today, including mysterious Pluto.

Our Planet Earth

HAVE YOU EVER thought of Earth as speeding through space? We live on the third planet from the Sun. Like the other planets, Earth orbits the Sun. It also spins on its axis. But Earth is unique because it is the only planet with the right conditions for life.

Planets closer to the Sun are too hot for living things. Those farther from the Sun are too cold. Some planets have an atmosphere too poisonous to breathe—or no atmosphere at all. And some, like Jupiter and Saturn, have no solid surface to walk on. But here on Earth, you can breathe the air, see a blue sky, splash in a pool of water, or pick an apple from a tree. Earth is the only planet where you can do these things.

The world you see around you is constantly changing. Earth is a rocky planet like Mercury, Venus, and Mars, but it is much more active. Heat from deep inside our planet forces volcanoes to erupt, earthquakes to shake the surface, and the continents to shift slowly over time. Meanwhile, wind, rain, and ocean waves gradually reshape the landscape.

THE BIG MARBLE

In this view from the cargo bay of the space shuttle, the shuttle's tail points back toward our planet, which looks like a big, beautiful marble floating in space. The blue is the oceans, with their rippling waves and sea currents. The white is the clouds—puffy fair-weather clouds as well as raging hurricanes. The rich reds, browns, and greens are the deserts, plains, forests, and cities of our planet.

INSIDE EARTH

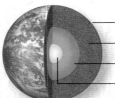

- Rocky crust
- Rocky mantle
- Liquid iron/nickel outer core
- Solid iron/nickel inner core

HANDS ON

Following Shadows

As Earth spins, the Sun appears to move across the sky and the shadows you see change. By following the shadows, you can tell that Earth is spinning and can even tell the time of day.

1. On a sunny day, push a wooden pole into the ground.
2. Every hour, use a Popsicle stick to mark where the pole's shadow falls. Write the hour on the stick.
3. Position several Popsicle sticks to make a sunclock.

Check the shadow of the pole over the next week or so and it will tell you the time.

A SHORT HISTORY OF EARTH

4.6 TO 4 BILLION YEARS AGO

Asteroids and comets rain down on the young Earth. The heat from their impacts keeps the surface red-hot and flowing with molten lava. Gases from volcanoes make a choking atmosphere. Primitive oceans form, only to boil off as vapor. Life is impossible.

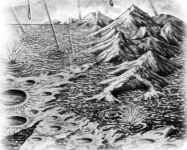

Asteroids pelt the young Earth.

3.8 BILLION YEARS AGO

The big impacts from asteroids and comets end. Earth cools off, and oceans form. The water comes from the debris of icy comets and from volcanic gases that condense into rain. Chemicals combine in the oceans to form single cells, the first life on Earth. Later, simple plants fill the air with oxygen.

Life begins in early ocean

Word Builders

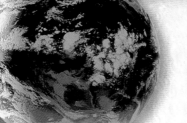

No single person named our planet. Many ancient people called the world after their god or goddess of the soil or fertility. The name **Earth** comes from the Anglo-Saxon word *eorthe,* meaning "land." But liquid water covers nearly three-quarters of the globe, so perhaps we should call our planet Ocean!

That's Amazing!

• The faster a planet turns, the shorter its day is. Three billion years ago, Earth turned much faster, and its day was only 18 hours long.
• Wind and rain have worn away most of Earth's impact craters. If Earth had no atmosphere to create weather, it would have as many craters as the Moon.

Pathfinder

• How would it feel to take off in the space shuttle? Go to pages 138–39.
• Is there any other life in the universe? Go to pages 144–45.
• Was the Moon once part of Earth? Go to page 153.
• Which other planet is the most like Earth? Go to pages 158–59.

NIGHT AND DAY

The spinning, or rotation, of Earth every 24 hours brings us night and day. To see how Earth's rotation works, spin around on a sunny day. First your face is lit up by the Sun. Then your face moves into shadow. The same thing happens to Earth. The part of Earth where you live faces the Sun during the daytime. As your place on Earth turns away from the Sun, it becomes night.

INSIDE STORY

The View from Space

The best part of traveling into space is the view back home. "It's hard to explain how magical this experience is," said astronaut Kathy Sullivan after her 1990 shuttle mission. "If you float up by the forward seats, you have six large windows providing a spectacular panorama of the Earth below. On my second shuttle flight, we could see all the way up to the Great Lakes from over the Gulf of Mexico. You can see rivers, cities, even airports. At night, you can even use the lights of highways and cities to locate your hometown, if you know your geography!"

Northern Summer Southern Winter   **Northern Winter Southern Summer**

Sun's rays

REASONS FOR SEASONS

Earth is a slightly tilted planet. Its axis doesn't point straight up and down in space, but leans over a little. For part of the year, the North Pole leans toward the Sun. This brings more sunshine and summer to the northern half of the planet. Six months later, when Earth is halfway around its orbit, the South Pole is tipped toward the Sun, bringing summer to the southern half of the world.

Life abounds in the oceans.

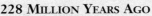

550 MILLION YEARS AGO

Hundreds of plant and animal species evolve in the oceans. Most die out, but a few of these strange early creatures evolve into fish and shellfish. Amphibians develop later and crawl onto land.

228 MILLION YEARS AGO

New reptile-like creatures walk on two hind legs across the land. These early dinosaurs evolve to rule Earth for 160 million years.

First dinosaurs appear.

200,000 YEARS AGO

The dinosaurs are long gone, and mammals now rule the world. The first modern humans appear.

First humans appear.

Diana, Roman Moon goddess   Apollo lunar module

Our Moon

IMAGINE WALKING ON the Moon. The Moon is about one-quarter the size of Earth and has only one-sixth as much gravity. You would weigh six times less on the Moon. That means you could jump six times higher than on Earth and bound around in giant leaps like a kangaroo.

There is one catch. You can't go outside without wearing a spacesuit. The Moon has absolutely no air. There's no oxygen to breathe. No liquid water. No plants. No life of any kind. Your spacesuit supplies everything you need to survive. It also keeps you at a comfortable temperature. In the sunshine, the Moon's surface can be as hot as boiling water, at 212°F (100°C). At night, temperatures can plunge to –240°F (–150°C). And lunar nights last two weeks.

After your moonwalk, you can admire your footprints in the powdery surface. With no wind or rain to wipe them away, they will still be there millions of years from now.

INSIDE THE MOON

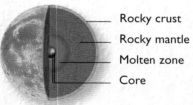

- Rocky crust
- Rocky mantle
- Molten zone
- Core

HANDS ON

Phasing the Moon

You can create the phases of the Moon. All you need is a dark room, a flashlight for the Sun, a basketball covered in aluminum foil for the Moon, and two friends.

Stand in the middle of the room to represent Earth. One friend stands a few steps in front of you with the basketball Moon held high. The other friend stands a few steps behind the Moon friend and shines the flashlight Sun on the ball all the time. As the friend with the Moon circles around you, you'll see how the Moon's phases occur.

MAPPING THE MOON
Spacecraft are once again exploring the Moon. In 1998, NASA placed the tiny Lunar Prospector robot probe in orbit around the Moon. It discovered ice at the north and south poles of the Moon. But you can't skate on this ice, because it is mixed in with the lunar rock and soil. One day, when people return to the Moon, they may tap this ice for water and rocket fuel.

Luna 9, 1966   *Surveyor, 1966–1968*   *Luna 16, 1970*

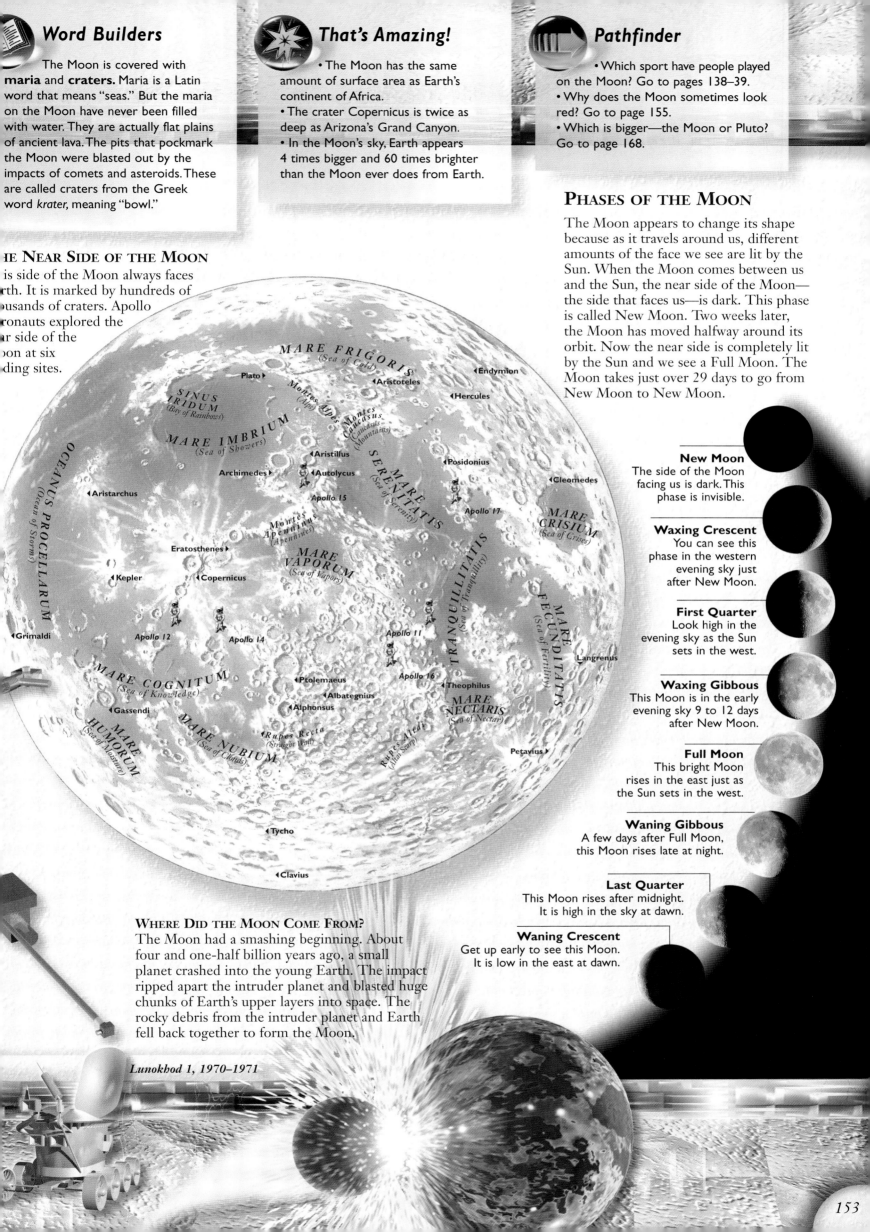

Word Builders

The Moon is covered with **maria** and **craters**. Maria is a Latin word that means "seas." But the maria on the Moon have never been filled with water. They are actually flat plains of ancient lava. The pits that pockmark the Moon were blasted out by the impacts of comets and asteroids. These are called craters from the Greek word *krater*, meaning "bowl."

That's Amazing!

• The Moon has the same amount of surface area as Earth's continent of Africa.
• The crater Copernicus is twice as deep as Arizona's Grand Canyon.
• In the Moon's sky, Earth appears 4 times bigger and 60 times brighter than the Moon ever does from Earth.

Pathfinder

• Which sport have people played on the Moon? Go to pages 138–39.
• Why does the Moon sometimes look red? Go to page 155.
• Which is bigger—the Moon or Pluto? Go to page 168.

THE NEAR SIDE OF THE MOON

This side of the Moon always faces Earth. It is marked by hundreds of thousands of craters. Apollo astronauts explored the near side of the Moon at six landing sites.

PHASES OF THE MOON

The Moon appears to change its shape because as it travels around us, different amounts of the face we see are lit by the Sun. When the Moon comes between us and the Sun, the near side of the Moon—the side that faces us—is dark. This phase is called New Moon. Two weeks later, the Moon has moved halfway around its orbit. Now the near side is completely lit by the Sun and we see a Full Moon. The Moon takes just over 29 days to go from New Moon to New Moon.

New Moon
The side of the Moon facing us is dark. This phase is invisible.

Waxing Crescent
You can see this phase in the western evening sky just after New Moon.

First Quarter
Look high in the evening sky as the Sun sets in the west.

Waxing Gibbous
This Moon is in the early evening sky 9 to 12 days after New Moon.

Full Moon
This bright Moon rises in the east just as the Sun sets in the west.

Waning Gibbous
A few days after Full Moon, this Moon rises late at night.

Last Quarter
This Moon rises after midnight. It is high in the sky at dawn.

Waning Crescent
Get up early to see this Moon. It is low in the east at dawn.

WHERE DID THE MOON COME FROM?

The Moon had a smashing beginning. About four and one-half billion years ago, a small planet crashed into the young Earth. The impact ripped apart the intruder planet and blasted huge chunks of Earth's upper layers into space. The rocky debris from the intruder planet and Earth fell back together to form the Moon.

Lunokhod 1, 1970–1971

Map labels:
MARE FRIGORIS (Sea of Cold)
Plato
Endymion
Aristoteles
Hercules
Montes Alpes (Alps)
SINUS IRIDUM (Bay of Rainbows)
Posidonius
Montes Caucasus (Caucasus Mountains)
MARE IMBRIUM (Sea of Showers)
Aristillus
Autolycus
MARE SERENITATIS (Sea of Serenity)
Cleomedes
Archimedes
Apollo 15
MARE CRISIUM (Sea of Crises)
Aristarchus
OCEANUS PROCELLARUM (Ocean of Storms)
Montes Apenninus (Apennines)
Eratosthenes
MARE VAPORUM (Sea of Vapors)
MARE FECUNDITATIS (Sea of Fertility)
Kepler
Copernicus
Langrenus
Apollo 12
Apollo 14
Apollo 11
TRANQUILLITATIS (Sea of Tranquillity)
Grimaldi
Ptolemaeus
Apollo 16
Theophilus
Albategnius
MARE NECTARIS (Sea of Nectar)
MARE COGNITUM (Sea of Knowledge)
Alphonsus
Gassendi
Petavius
MARE HUMORUM (Sea of Moisture)
MARE NUBIUM (Sea of Clouds)
Rupes Recta (Straight Wall)
Rupes Altai (Altai Scarp)
Tycho
Clavius

The Sun

THE SUN IS a star like those we see at night, but it is much closer to us. Without the Sun nearby, Earth would be as cold and lifeless as Pluto. Plants need sunlight to grow, and people and other animals need plants to survive.

The heat of the Sun also creates our weather. It powers the winds and evaporates water to make clouds and rain. Scientists think that even slight changes in the Sun's energy may warm or cool Earth's climate.

The Sun has been shining for five billion years. How does it make so much energy? With a surface as hot as 11,000°F (6,000°C), it looks as if the Sun is on fire, but it isn't burning in the same way as a piece of wood or a lump of coal. The Sun is actually a giant nuclear-fusion bomb. Deep in its superhot core, it smashes 600 million tons of hydrogen atoms together every second, turning them into heavier helium atoms. The energy released by this atom smashing escapes into space as light and heat.

NATURE'S LIGHT SHOW
Storms on the Sun blow a wind of particles into space. The particles sometimes rain down onto Earth's atmosphere and, like an electric current, za the air, causing a colored glow called an aurora. I you live in Canada, the northern United States, o Europe, or in southern Australia or New Zealand you can often see auroras in the sky. They look li rippling curtains of green, red, or pink light.

INSIDE THE SUN

— Photosphere
— Convective zone
— Radiative zone
— Hydrogen core

WARNING: Never look directly at the Sun—you could go permanently blind. If you want to watch a solar eclipse, you can buy the special filters you need to use at a science center or planetarium.

INSIDE STORY

Ancient Sunrise

You are one of hundreds of people gathered within a circle of giant standing stones called Stonehenge, in England. It is dawn on a quiet summer morning. There are no clocks or calendars, because the year is 1500 BC. Yet everyone knows that something special is about to happen. And there it is—the Sun is rising over a special stone in the distance. It does this only on one day a year—June 21, the summer solstice. Stonehenge, your giant stone calendar, is telling you the date.

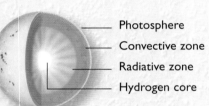

Incan Sun mask   *Mayan Sun temple*

Word Builders

The Roman goddess of the dawn was named Aurora. In the Northern Hemisphere, aurora displays are known as **aurora borealis,** which means "northern dawn." In the Southern Hemisphere, people call them **aurora australis,** meaning "southern dawn."

That's Amazing!

• In one second, the Sun sends out more energy than humans have consumed in all of recorded history.
• If you drove a car at highway speeds from Earth to the Sun, it would take 170 years to complete your journey.

Pathfinder

• Which other probe has looked at the Sun? Go to page 143.
• How does the Sun's gravity affect the planets? Go to pages 148–49.
• Is the Sun the only star with planets? Go to pages 176–77.
• Where is the Sun in our galaxy? Go to pages 182–83.

SPOTS ON THE SUN'S FACE

The Sun sometimes breaks out in spots. Within these dark blemishes, strong magnetic fields stop the Sun's gas from boiling and bubbling. The trapped gas cools and appears dark compared to the brilliant disc of the Sun. Scientists know that the number of sunspots peaks every 11 years, but they do not know how this cycle on the Sun affects Earth.

SOLAR WATCHDOGS

Satellites are constantly watching our star, the Sun. The Solar and Heliospheric Observatory (SOHO), shown here, has snapped thousands of Sun pictures. Other solar spacecraft include the Wind and the Advanced Composition Explorer (ACE) satellites, which sample the particles streaming from the Sun. A satellite called Polar keeps an eye on auroras.

GREAT BALL OF FIRE

The Sun is big—it contains 99.99 percent of all the matter in the solar system. You could pack a million Earths inside the Sun. In this image taken by the SOHO satellite, you can see a tongue of gas called a prominence shooting into space. Earth would be the size of a pinhead beside this giant prominence.

ECLIPSE SHADOWPLAY

SOLAR ECLIPSE

A total eclipse of the Sun is spectacular. Once every one or two years, the Moon comes directly between us and the Sun. Its shadow falls in a narrow band across Earth. People in this band see the Moon's dark disc cover the Sun for a few minutes. Only the faint outer atmosphere of the Sun, called the corona, remains visible.

Eclipse of the Sun

Earth

Moon

Sun's rays

Eclipse of the Moon

Moon

Earth

Sun's rays

LUNAR ECLIPSE

A total eclipse of the Moon can be seen over the entire night side of Earth. When the Full Moon passes through the dark inner part of Earth's shadow, the Moon goes dark for an hour or more. Sunlight filtering through our atmosphere turns the eclipsed Moon deep red.

Mercury and Venus

WELCOME TO THE solar system's hottest planets. Mercury and Venus both orbit much closer to the Sun's warmth than Earth does. But that's where any similarity between Mercury and Venus ends.

Mercury, the innermost planet, rushes around the Sun every 88 days. But it takes about two-thirds of that time—59 Earth days—just to spin around once on its axis. Its long day and short year combine so that sunrises occur 176 Earth days apart. At midday on Mercury, look for shade—temperatures soar to 800°F (430°C). At night, bundle up—the thermometer plunges to –290°F (–180°C).

There's no way to escape the heat on Venus, which is even hotter than Mercury. Everywhere, day and night, the temperature is a searing 860°F (460°C). That's hot enough to melt lead, tin, and zinc. Venus suffers from a greenhouse effect gone wild. A thick atmosphere of carbon dioxide traps solar energy and heats up Venus in the same way that a thick blanket keeps you warm at night. What's worse, acid rain falls from its clouds of sulfuric acid. Venus is a tough place to land a spacecraft. From 1970 to 1986, the Russian space program landed ten Venera probes on the surface of Venus. None of them lasted for more than an hour before malfunctioning.

HANDS ON
Spotting the Inner Planets

People from many lands have called Venus the evening star or morning star. Since Venus orbits near the Sun, it always appears just after the Sun sets and just before the Sun rises. If you see a dazzling object low in the sky during the early evening or morning, then that's probably Venus, outshining every other star and planet. Venus shines brightly because its thick clouds reflect the Sun's light.

Mercury is so near the Sun that it always appears just above the horizon, which makes it hard to see. In this photo, Mercury is lost in the tree branches, while Venus is the bright dot at the top of the photo.

VENUSIAN VOLCANOES
This image from the Magellan space probe shows Maat Mons, the highest of the 167 giant volcanoes on Venus. Maat Mons towers 26,000 feet (8,000 m) above the Venusian plains, so it is nearly as tall as Mount Everest. Maat Mons gradually built up over millions of years as lava poured from its summit. No one knows whether Venus's volcanoes still erupt.

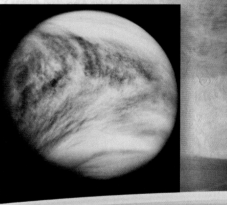

INSIDE MERCURY

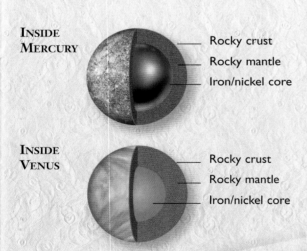

— Rocky crust
— Rocky mantle
— Iron/nickel core

INSIDE VENUS

— Rocky crust
— Rocky mantle
— Iron/nickel core

THE CLOUDY PLANET
Imagine yourself on Venus. The air around you is clear, but it shimmers in the intense heat. It's a dull day, like a heavily overcast day on Earth. The sky looks red and is covered completely by a smooth, dense haze. From Venus, you can never see the Sun during the day nor the stars at night.

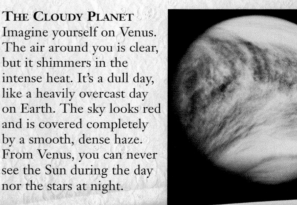

MAPPING A NEW WORLD
How do you map a planet always covered in clouds? From 1989 to 1993, NASA's Magellan probe beamed radar signals at the surface of Venus. The radio waves passed through the clouds, hit the surface, and bounced back to Magellan. Using the bounced-back radio waves, the probe helped create a picture of Venus's surface.

Rocket thrusters

Solar panels

Spacecraft turns to beam data to Earth.

Main antenna

Sulfuric acid clouds

Radar signals are sent to Venus.

Surface of Venu

Word Builders

• **Mercury** moves so quickly around the Sun that the Romans named it for the swift messenger of their gods, Mercurius.
• **Venus** is named for the Roman goddess of love and beauty. The planet was also called Ishtar by the Sumerians, Kukulkán by the Mayans, and Quetzalcoatl by the Aztecs.

That's Amazing!

• Mercury's dense core of iron and nickel is larger than our Moon.
• One impact feature on Mercury—Caloris Basin—is so big that it would stretch halfway across North America.
• Venus spins backward compared to all the other planets except Uranus. Perhaps a giant asteroid hit Venus and flipped it upside down.

Pathfinder

• Saturn's moon Titan is cloudy like Venus. How will scientists look at its surface? Go to page 143.
• Where are Mercury and Venus in the solar system? Go to pages 148–49.
• Does Mercury really look like the Moon? Go to pages 152–53.

THE CRATERED PLANET

Mercury looks like the Moon. Both are airless worlds covered with craters. Unlike the Moon, Mercury seems to lack any large lava plains. But we haven't seen all of Mercury close-up. Because of its flight path, Mariner 10, the only spacecraft to visit Mercury, could map only half the planet.

Data are received on Earth.

Data are sent to mission control.

Data are downloaded into computer.

The completed map of Venus

Deep-space tracking antenna

Scientist adds new data to map.

STRIPS OF VENUS

Magellan transmitted its radio pictures back to Earth. Each picture revealed a strip of Venus 10,000 miles (16,000 km) long from north to south but only 15 miles (24 km) wide. Mission scientists then pieced together the narrow strips into a map of Venus.

Mars

MARS IS THE planet most like Earth. A day on Mars is just 40 minutes longer than a day on Earth. Like Earth, Mars has seasons of summer and winter. And billions of years ago, Mars was almost as warm as Earth. Rivers flowed across the land. An ocean might have covered half the planet, and primitive life could have flourished. In 1996, scientists announced they had found fossils of bacteria, a simple form of life, inside a meteorite from Mars. Some scientists disagree with this claim. They think we have yet to find proof of life on Mars.

During your lifetime, astronauts will probably visit Mars. If you were one of these astronauts, you could walk around easily on Mars's dusty, red surface. You would need a spacesuit, though, because the air on Mars contains no oxygen, just carbon dioxide.

Your spacesuit would also keep you warm. On a summer day, Martian temperatures reach only 32°F (0°C), the freezing point of water, but at night they plunge to −110°F (−80°C), as cold as Antarctica in winter. During winter on Mars, prepare for bone-chilling temperatures colder than any place on Earth, about −190°F (−125°C). This is so cold that the air at the north and south poles of Mars freezes into caps of carbon dioxide ice.

INSIDE MARS

- Rocky crust
- Rocky mantle
- Iron core

CANYON DEEP, MOUNTAIN HIGH

Mars is a planet of towering volcanoes and gaping canyons. The tallest volcano is Olympus Mons. You would need to stack three Mount Everests on top of each other to reach the summit of this massive mountain. The longest canyon is Valles Marineris. Placed on Earth, Valles Marineris would stretch across North America. Arizona's Grand Canyon would be a scratch beside this mighty gash in the Martian crust.

VASTI
ARCADIA PLANITIA
Alba Fossae
Olympus Mons
Ascraeus Mons
AMAZONIS PLANITIA
Pavonis Mons
DAEDALIA PLANUM
Arsia Mons
Tharsis Montes
SY PLA
TERRA CIMMERIA
TERRA SIRENUM
Sirenum Fossae
PLAN

Chasma = long depression (like a canyon)
Mons = mountain
Montes = mountains
Fossae = long, shallow depressions (like grooves)
Patera = irregular or complex crater
Planitia = low plain
Planum = plateau or plain
Terra = extensive landmass
Tholus = small mountain or hill
Vallis, Valles = valley
Vastitas = extensive pla

INSIDE STORY

Mission to Mars

Imagine that you are the first astronaut on a mission to Mars. You slowly climb down the ladder of your lander. The Apollo astronauts took only three days to reach the Moon, but you have endured a six-month flight to get to Mars and, because of the planet's orbit, it will be two more years before you see home again. Without Earth's atmosphere to protect you, you've been exposed to harmful radiation from space. And your muscles and bones are weak after being weightless for so long.

Now you are about to become the first human to walk on Mars. The landscape looks like a beautiful red desert. The sky is an eerie shade of orange. You step onto the red sand. Billions of people on Earth are watching you on TV and listening for your first words. What do you say?

MARTIAN MOONS

Two little moons dart around Mars. Deimos, the outer moon, is only 9 miles (15 km) long, no bigger than a small city. Phobos, the inner moon, is a potato-shaped world 17 miles (27 km) long. Both moons may be ancient asteroids captured into orbit by Mars's gravity early in its history.

Deimos

Phobos

Word Builders

Given the red color of Mars's surface, it's not surprising that ancient people thought of blood and battles when they looked at the planet. The Babylonians called it **Nergal,** the star of death. The Greeks named it **Ares,** after their god of war. Today we know it as **Mars,** for the Roman god of war.

That's Amazing!

• If you could melt all the ice that exists on Mars, scientists think it would form an ocean between 33 and 330 feet (10 and 100 m) deep.
• Deimos's gravity is so weak you could launch yourself off this Martian moon by running fast and taking a giant leap.

Pathfinder

• Why did NASA send a rover to Mars? Go to pages 142–43.
• What did the bacteria-like markings in the Martian meteorite look like? Go to page 145.
• Are Phobos and Deimos like asteroids? Go to pages 160–61.

The Face, as photographed by Viking 1

The Face, as photographed by Global Surveyor

THE CASE OF THE FACE

In 1976, the Viking 1 orbiter photographed a mysterious feature that looked like a face. Was this evidence for life on Mars? In 1998, the Mars Global Surveyor probe photographed the feature with a much better camera. The sharp new images exposed the truth. The Face is really an eroded hill sculpted by winds, not by Martians.

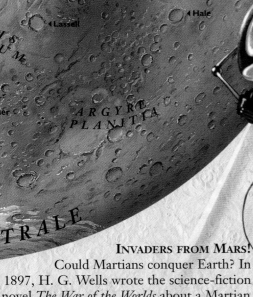

INVADERS FROM MARS!

Could Martians conquer Earth? In 1897, H. G. Wells wrote the science-fiction novel *The War of the Worlds* about a Martian invasion of Earth. A 1938 radio broadcast of the story scared thousands of people into thinking that Martians were really invading. We now know that Mars is too cold and its air is too thin to support advanced life. Martians do not exist.

Illustration from *The War of the Worlds*

MARS ON EARTH

So far, no astronauts have been to Mars, and no robot probes have returned with samples of Martian rocks. Yet scientists think they have found more than a dozen pieces of Mars on Earth. Here's how the rocks may have got here.

TAKEOFF

A small asteroid smashes into Mars. The force of the impact makes a crater and blasts pieces of Mars into space.

IN SPACE

Like a flurry of small asteroids, these Martian rocks go into orbit around the Sun for millions of years.

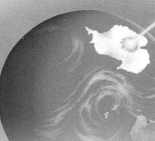

TO EARTH

Eventually some of the rocks collide with Earth. The rocks fall to the ground as meteorites. One particular Martian meteorite lands thousands of years ago.

ON ICE

In 1984, Roberta Score, a scientist searching for meteorites in Antarctica, finds the Martian rock resting on the ice.

Asteroids and Meteoroids

BETWEEN MARS AND Jupiter lies a region known as the asteroid belt. It contains tens of thousands of asteroids, but they are so far apart that you could fly through the belt and never see a single asteroid from your spaceship window. Almost all asteroids stay in the belt, but Trojan asteroids are farther out, in the same path around the Sun as Jupiter. Near-Earth asteroids wander close to the Sun and occasionally cross the orbit of Earth.

Astronomers think that asteroids are lumps of rock and metal left over from the early days of the solar system. The pull from Jupiter's gravity would have stopped the lumps from smashing together to form a planet. The largest asteroid, Ceres, is nearly as big as Texas in the United States, but most asteroids are the size of mountains.

Throughout the solar system, countless small rocks known as meteoroids orbit the Sun. The bigger chunks are usually pieces of asteroids shattered by collisions in the asteroid belt. The smaller specks are mostly dust particles shed by passing comets. Our planet collides with thousands of these meteoroids every day.

Hunting for Asteroids

"It was a cold night in December 1997 at the Spacewatch Telescope in Arizona," describes Jim Scotti. "I was alone in the dome when one asteroid appeared on the computer that was moving unusually fast." Jim Scotti had found a space rock called 1997 XF_{11}, one of about 200 asteroids known to come dangerously close to Earth. "Though the excitement of finding our first near-Earth asteroids has worn off, it's still satisfying to bag a new one."

WHAT A WHOPPER!
Sometimes chunks of space rock survive their fiery fall through the atmosphere and land on Earth. These are called meteorites. Most meteorites would fit in your pocket, but some are much larger. This meteorite is almost as big as a baby elephant. It was recovered from Greenland in 1897.

SHOOTING STARS
When a tiny meteoroid comes too close to Earth, it burns up high in our atmosphere. The burning meteoroid creates a brief streak of light in the sky. People often call this streak a shooting star, but the correct name for the streak is a meteor.

An astronomer who discovers an asteroid gets to name it. Many asteroids, such as Ceres, Pallas, and Juno, have been named for mythological figures. Some are named for famous astronomers. Four are named John, Paul, George, and Ringo, after the Beatles rock group. One is even named Mr. Spock after an astronomer's cat—and TV science-fiction character.

• Squeezing together all our solar system's asteroids would make a world about one-third the size of our Moon.
• The biggest meteorite ever found, the Hoba West meteorite in Namibia, Africa, is about 8 feet (2.5 m) long and weighs 66 tons (60 metric tons)—that's as heavy as nine elephants!

• What other rovers have explored space? Go to pages 142–43.
• Where do asteroids orbit? Go to pages 148–49.
• When can you see a meteor shower? Go to page 170.

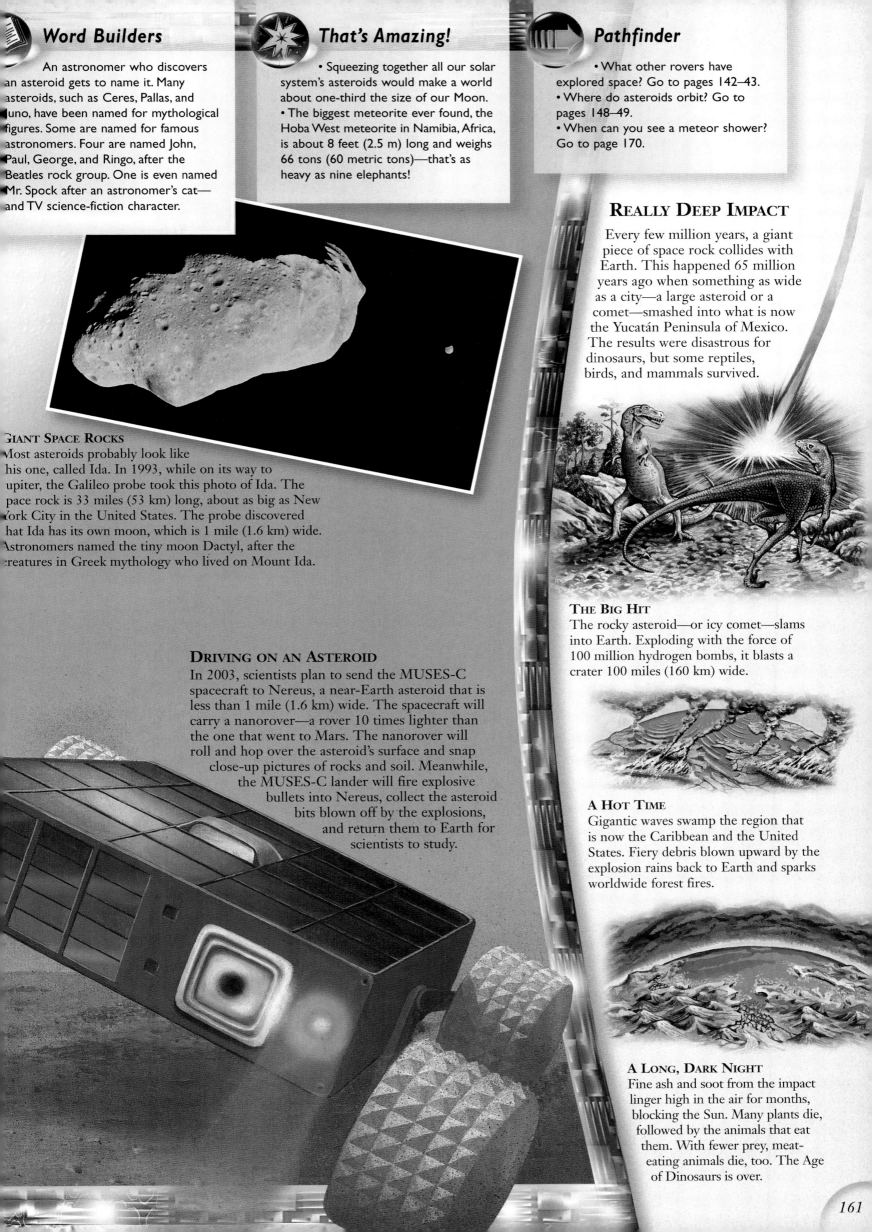

GIANT SPACE ROCKS
Most asteroids probably look like this one, called Ida. In 1993, while on its way to Jupiter, the Galileo probe took this photo of Ida. The space rock is 33 miles (53 km) long, about as big as New York City in the United States. The probe discovered that Ida has its own moon, which is 1 mile (1.6 km) wide. Astronomers named the tiny moon Dactyl, after the creatures in Greek mythology who lived on Mount Ida.

DRIVING ON AN ASTEROID
In 2003, scientists plan to send the MUSES-C spacecraft to Nereus, a near-Earth asteroid that is less than 1 mile (1.6 km) wide. The spacecraft will carry a nanorover—a rover 10 times lighter than the one that went to Mars. The nanorover will roll and hop over the asteroid's surface and snap close-up pictures of rocks and soil. Meanwhile, the MUSES-C lander will fire explosive bullets into Nereus, collect the asteroid bits blown off by the explosions, and return them to Earth for scientists to study.

REALLY DEEP IMPACT
Every few million years, a giant piece of space rock collides with Earth. This happened 65 million years ago when something as wide as a city—a large asteroid or a comet—smashed into what is now the Yucatán Peninsula of Mexico. The results were disastrous for dinosaurs, but some reptiles, birds, and mammals survived.

THE BIG HIT
The rocky asteroid—or icy comet—slams into Earth. Exploding with the force of 100 million hydrogen bombs, it blasts a crater 100 miles (160 km) wide.

A HOT TIME
Gigantic waves swamp the region that is now the Caribbean and the United States. Fiery debris blown upward by the explosion rains back to Earth and sparks worldwide forest fires.

A LONG, DARK NIGHT
Fine ash and soot from the impact linger high in the air for months, blocking the Sun. Many plants die, followed by the animals that eat them. With fewer prey, meat-eating animals die, too. The Age of Dinosaurs is over.

Jupiter, ruler of the Roman gods　　*Ganymede, cupbearer of the Greek gods*

Jupiter

VISITING JUPITER IN person would be hard to do. For one thing, you'd need a spaceship built like a balloon because there's no place to land. The biggest of all the planets, Jupiter is one huge ball of hydrogen and helium gases. These same gases make up the Sun, but Jupiter would need to contain 80 times more gas before it could shine like a star.

You'd also need to watch out for Jupiter's wild weather. Despite its size, this giant spins faster than any other planet—a day on Jupiter is less than 10 hours long. Jupiter's speedy spin helps whip the clouds into storms as big as a continent on Earth. Winds rage at up to 300 miles per hour (500 km/h). Superbolts of lightning crackle in the thunderclouds.

In 1995, the Galileo spacecraft started to orbit Jupiter, taking hundreds of pictures of the planet's storms, moons, and its faint, dusty ring. Galileo also sent a capsule, known as the Probe, into Jupiter's churning atmosphere.

TAKING THE PLUNGE

On December 7, 1995, the Galileo spacecraft cone-shaped Probe plunged into Jupiter's atmosphere at 50 times the speed of a bullet. Powerful winds blew the Probe hundreds of miles sideways as it descended through clouds of ammonia ice crystals. For an hour, its instruments sniffed and sampled the air, until Jupiter's fierce atmosphere first crushed and then vaporized the Probe.

INSIDE JUPITER

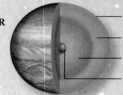

- Gaseous hydrogen
- Liquid hydrogen
- Metallic hydrogen
- Rocky core

COMET CRASH

In July 1994, 21 pieces of Comet Shoemaker-Levy 9 slammed into Jupiter one after the other. Telescopes around the world watched as the explosions scarred Jupiter's cloud tops with black spots as big as Earth. Months passed before Jupiter returned to normal.

Diameter:
1,951 miles
(3,140 km)

Diameter:
2,256 miles
(3,630 km)

JUPITER'S GIANT MOONS

Jupiter's powerful gravity controls a family of 16 moons. Twelve are the size of small asteroids— and some might actually be asteroids captured by Jupiter's gravity long ago. But four of Jupiter's moons are bigger than Pluto. The astronomer Galileo discovered these four giant moons in 1610. People still call them the Galilean satellites.

FIERY IO

Io is a world of volcanoes. Io's volcanoes not only erupt with molten rock, but they also pour liquid sulfur over the surface. The sulfur cools and hardens into a wildly colored crust of yellows, oranges, and reds. Some people think that this moon looks like a pizza.

Word Builders

Jupiter and its moons are called the **Jovian** system. **Jove** was another name for Jupiter, ruler of the Roman gods. If people are jovial, they are happy and fun-loving, like Jove himself. Most of the planet's moons are named after the god's many wives.

That's Amazing!

• Hurricanes on Earth last about two weeks. Jupiter's Great Red Spot has been raging for at least 300 years.
• Lightning bolts on Jupiter are 10 times more powerful than those on Earth.
• Metis, the innermost moon of Jupiter, zips around the planet so quickly that it could cross North America in just 2.5 minutes.

Pathfinder

• The astronomer Galileo found Jupiter's four large moons. What else did he discover? Go to page 136.
• What do scientists hope to find in Europa's ocean? Go to pages 144–45.
• What did Comet Shoemaker-Levy 9 look like? Go to page 171.

STRIPES AND SPOTS

Everywhere you look on Jupiter, you see clouds. There are white clouds of ammonia, blue clouds of water, and brown clouds of sulfur compounds. Jupiter's rapid spin wraps these clouds into long stripes around the planet. The Great Red Spot spins like a hurricane in the clouds. This giant storm system is big enough to swallow two Earths. Astronomers are still trying to work out how the spot formed.

Jupiter photographed by Voyager 2

Great Red Spot photographed by the Galileo spacecraft

HANDS ON
Following the Moons

To find Jupiter's four giant moons, you first need to find Jupiter. Call your local planetarium or science center, or check a web site such as *www.skypub.com*. Once you know where to look, you should be able to spot Jupiter by eye. Then you can use a pair of binoculars to find the moons, which look like tiny points of light. The moons move around Jupiter, so if you look again on another night, you'll see that they have shifted position. Sometimes a moon goes behind Jupiter, and you won't be able to see it at all. The pictures below show the positions of the moons on two different nights.

FLOATING IN THE CLOUDS

Imagine floating in Jupiter's atmosphere, where clouds come in a rainbow of colors. This image, taken by the Galileo spacecraft, has been processed in a computer. It shows what you would see if you were in between Jupiter's cloud layers.

May 5, 1998
| Callisto | Jupiter |
| Europa | Io |
| Ganymede |

May 6, 1998
| Io | Jupiter |
| Callisto | Ganymede | Europa |

ICY EUROPA

The Voyager 1 and 2 and Galileo spacecraft discovered that Europa is completely covered with a crust of ice. Below the ice may lurk a dark ocean of liquid water—perhaps the only other ocean in the solar system beyond Earth.

GIGANTIC GANYMEDE

Ganymede is so big that if it orbited the Sun instead of Jupiter, we would call it a planet. The biggest moon in the solar system, Ganymede is more than twice as large as Pluto and a bit larger than Mercury.

Diameter: 3,269 miles (5,260 km)

CRATERED CALLISTO

Thousands of craters pepper Callisto's icy surface. Apart from the occasional impact of a comet, this cold moon has hardly changed for billions of years.

Diameter: 2,983 miles (4,800 km)

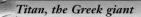

Saturn

IF YOU COULD approach Saturn, the most impressive sight would be the thousands of rings that circle the planet. Remove its rings and Saturn would look like a smaller version of Jupiter. Saturn is also a giant planet made of hydrogen and helium gases. It spins quickly, too, with a day lasting 10 hours and 40 minutes Earth time.

On closer inspection, you'd notice that Saturn's bands of clouds are less colorful than the clouds on Jupiter. This is probably because Saturn is farther from the Sun—and colder. Temperatures in Saturn's clouds of ammonia ice crystals hover at –210°F (–135°C). Winds blow even more strongly on Saturn than on Jupiter. In some places, Saturn's winds roar at 800 miles per hour (1,300 km/h), 11 times faster than a hurricane on Earth.

If you traveled around Saturn, you could count 18 moons. The giant is Titan, the second-largest moon in the solar system and the only one with a thick atmosphere. You wouldn't be able to see through Titan's dense, orange clouds, but in 2004 the Cassini spacecraft will send a probe plunging to its surface.

INSIDE STORY

The Planet with Ears

The year is 1656. Christiaan Huygens invites you to look through his telescope. It makes objects appear 50 times bigger. "You see what I have discovered?" asks Huygens. "Saturn is surrounded by a thin flat ring nowhere touching the planet." Wow! You *can* see the rings. Saturn had puzzled earlier observers, including Galileo, Fontana, and Riccioli, but their telescopes were so poor, Saturn looked like it had "handles" or "ears." Today, most backyard telescopes clearly show Saturn's rings.

Galileo's sketch, 1610   Fontana's sketch, 1646

Riccioli's sketch, 1648   Huygens's sketch, 1656

INSIDE SATURN

- Gaseous hydrogen
- Liquid hydrogen
- Metallic hydrogen
- Rocky core

- A Ring
- Cassini's Division
- B Ring
- C Ring

SCARFACE
A giant crater scars Mimas, a small inner moon of Saturn. Millions of years ago, a large object crashed into Mimas and carved out this crater. If the object had been any larger, it would have smashed the little moon into pieces. Mimas and most of Saturn's other moons are named after members of the Titans, a family of Greek supergods ruled by the giant Titan.

RING WORLD
Three main sets of rings orbit Saturn. The outer A Ring is separated from the B Ring by a dark gap called Cassini's Division, first seen by Giovanni Cassini in 1675. This gap is as wide as North America. The inner C Ring is darker than the others because it contains fewer ice particles to reflect sunlight.

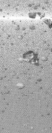

ICE BALLS COLLIDE
A large comet or asteroid smashes into an icy moon orbiting Saturn.

RUNNING RINGS AROUND SATURN

The rings of Saturn remain among the most beautiful yet mysterious objects in the solar system. How did the rings get there? And when did they form? One theory suggests the rings are only a few million years old and were formed by a cosmic collision. This is how it might have happened.

Word Builders

If you like **Saturdays,** you can thank Saturn. The day is named after the sixth planet, which was named after the Roman god of the harvest. It's easy to tell what objects **Sunday** (Sun-day) and **Monday** (Moon-day) are named after. But the other days? They're named after gods from Norse legends—Tiw **(Tuesday),** Woden **(Wednesday),** Thor **(Thursday),** and Frigg **(Friday).**

That's Amazing!

• Saturn's rings are no thicker than a six-story building. If you wanted to build a scale model, you'd need a sheet of paper eight city blocks wide but only as thick as a page in this book.
• Saturn would float on water—if you could find a big enough ocean!

Pathfinder

• How will scientists land a probe on Saturn's moon Titan? Go to page 143.
• Is there life on any of Saturn's moons? Go to pages 144–45.
• What other planets have rings? Go to pages 162–63 and 166–67.

INSIDE THE BLIZZARD

Saturn's rings are a blizzard of snowballs. From a distance, the rings look solid, but from close-up, you would see they are made of billions of ice chunks the size of hailstones and snowballs. If you could pack all the ring particles together, you could make a single giant snowball about 60 miles (100 km) across—the size of a small moon of Saturn.

SNOWY SMITHEREENS

The impact shatters the moon into a cloud of icy particles. These particles then orbit Saturn like a swarm of moonlets.

SPREADING OUT

Constant collisions among the icy particles grind most of them into even smaller pieces. Over the years, these particles spread out to form a broad ring around the planet.

SHEPHERD MOONS

Some of the icy particles that were not ground up remain as small moons that skim near the edge of the rings. Like sheep dogs herding a flock of sheep, the gravity of these shepherd moons keeps the ring particles in their places.

165

Uranus, Roman god of the sky   *Neptune, Roman god of the sea*

Uranus and Neptune

FOR THOUSANDS OF years, people thought the most distant planet was Saturn. Then, in 1781, William Herschel saw what he called a "curious nebulous star or perhaps a comet" through his telescope. He later realized it was the seventh planet, Uranus. Tiny wobbles in the path of Uranus led astronomers to look for a more distant planet that might be tugging at Uranus. Johann Galle and Heinrich D'Arrest spotted Neptune, the eighth planet, in 1846.

If you visited Uranus and Neptune, you'd find that in many ways they are like twins. Both are four times bigger than Earth. Each is circled by dark, thin rings and has an atmosphere choked with poisonous methane gas. This gas soaks up red light but scatters blue light back into space, making Uranus and Neptune look blue-green. Dive beneath the atmosphere and you'd discover a thick, slushy layer of ice and water.

Uranus and Neptune do have their differences. If you kept going past Neptune's slushy layer, you might come to a hot core. Astronomers think heat from this core rises, stirs up the cloud tops, and unleashes strong winds and large storms. The weather in Uranus's atmosphere seems calm by comparison. At the center of Uranus, you'd probably find a cold core.

THE VIEW FROM TRITON

Ringed Neptune looms large in the sky of Triton, the largest of Neptune's eight moons. Temperatures on Triton plunge to –390°F (–235°C). That's as cold as any moon or planet in the solar system. Despite the deep freeze, Triton's surface is dotted with geysers that spew out dark jets of supercold nitrogen ice and gas.

INSIDE URANUS
— Hydrogen, helium, and methane gases
— Water, ammonia, and methane slush
— Rocky core

INSIDE NEPTUNE
— Hydrogen, helium, and methane gases
— Water, ammonia, and methane slush
— Rocky core

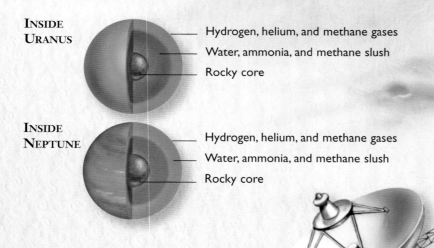

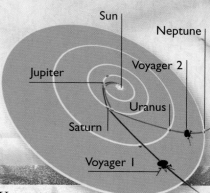

Sun
Neptune
Jupiter
Voyager 2
Uranus
Saturn
Voyager 1

INTERPLANETARY TRAVELER

Much of what we know about the four gas giant planets—Jupiter, Saturn, Uranus, and Neptune—was discovered by NASA's Voyager space probes. Launched from Earth in 1977, Voyager 1 and Voyager 2 explored Jupiter and Saturn in 1979, 1980, and 1981.

SAIL ON, VOYAGER

Voyager 1 visited only Jupiter and Saturn. It then flew away from the solar system, its main mission over. But Voyager 2's mission was to complete a grand tour of all four gas giant planets. It sailed past Uranus in 1986 and Neptune in 1989.

Word Builders

In 1997, astronomers discovered two new moons orbiting Uranus. They named the small moons **Sycorax** and **Caliban**, after two characters in *The Tempest*, a play by William Shakespeare. Sycorax is a witch, and Caliban is her beastly son. Most of the moons of Uranus are named for characters in Shakespeare's plays.

That's Amazing!

• Neptune's moon Triton is the only known moon in the solar system that orbits its planet in the opposite direction from the planet's rotation.
• Because Neptune's year—the time it takes to orbit the Sun—is 164 Earth years long, no one on Earth could live to be one Neptune year old.

Pathfinder

• What sort of missions were the Voyager missions? Go to pages 142–43.
• What are the other gas giants? Go to pages 162–63 and 164–65.
• Have other planets been found in modern times? Go to page 168.

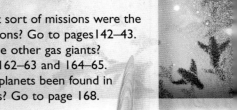

URANUS, THE SIDEWAYS PLANET

Compared to the other planets, Uranus is tilted over on its side. For much of Uranus's year, one of its two poles points at the Sun and its rings face the Sun. One theory for this strange position is that billions of years ago a giant asteroid whacked Uranus so hard that the planet toppled over.

Diameter: 31,766 miles (50,826 km)

MARVELOUS MOON MIRANDA

In 1986, Voyager 2 snapped close-ups of Uranus and several of its 17 moons. The inner moon Miranda looks strange, as if it has been smashed apart by an impact and then pulled back together by gravity into a jumble of icy blocks.

Diameter: 75 miles (120 km)

INSIDE STORY

Discovering the Rings

You're part of a team of astronomers flying on the Kuiper Airborne Observatory. A telescope pokes through the side of the airplane. Your target tonight—on March 10, 1977—is Uranus. You watch as a star is about to disappear behind the planet. An astronomer calls out, "Okay. We got one. We got a blip here." A colleague confirms the readings. "We got blips again. They're real." Something is causing the star to wink out just before it passes behind Uranus. "There's no clouds," someone reports. "Well, maybe this is a ring of Uranus. Hey, there's another one!" Your team has discovered something exciting—rings around Uranus—the first rings ever seen around a planet other than Saturn.

TRACKING THE GREAT DARK SPOT

Voyager 2 photographed the Great Dark Spot, a storm on Neptune as big as Earth. Scientists tracked this giant storm for many days. Five years later, when astronomers used the Hubble Space Telescope to look at Neptune again, the Great Dark Spot had disappeared.

HELLO FROM PLANET EARTH

Both Voyager 1 and Voyager 2 are now on their way to the stars. In case aliens find them, each probe carries recorded greetings from the people of Earth. The gold-plated record cover shows the position of Earth in the Milky Way Galaxy.

Pluto and Beyond

AT THE EDGE of the solar system lies Pluto, the smallest planet. From its cold surface, you would see the Sun as a brilliant star blazing in a black sky. Looming large in the sky is Charon, Pluto's moon. At 745 miles (1,200 km) across, Charon is half the size of Pluto. The two worlds are like a double planet dancing around the Sun. Both Pluto and Charon are made mostly of rock-hard ice.

Pluto's dim landscape is a patchwork of light, frost-covered regions and dark, frost-free regions. The frost covering is made of frozen nitrogen and methane chilled to –396°F (–238°C). The frost-free regions are a few degrees warmer. This difference in temperature stirs up cold winds in the thin nitrogen-methane air.

Astronomers once suspected that another planet orbited beyond Pluto. New calculations show that a tenth planet probably doesn't exist. But thousands of small icy comets orbit beyond Pluto, in a region called the Kuiper Belt. Some astronomers now wonder whether we should even call Pluto a planet—perhaps it really belongs to the Kuiper Belt. Instead of being the solar system's smallest planet, Pluto might be the largest object in the Kuiper Belt.

INSIDE PLUTO

— Water-methane-nitrogen ice

— Water ice

— Rocky core

INSIDE STORY

Discovering Planet X

Clyde Tombaugh discovered Pluto at 4:00 PM on February 18, 1930. The Lowell Observatory had hired Tombaugh to search for a ninth planet, known as Planet X. He photographed regions of the sky by night, and then examined each photo for unusual moving objects during the day. "Suddenly I spied a fifteenth-magnitude image popping out…. 'That's it,' I exclaimed to myself…. A terrific thrill came over me. Oh! I had better look at my watch and note the time. This would be a historic discovery." Tombaugh then walked down the hall to the office of the observatory director. "Trying to control myself, I stepped into his office as nonchalantly as possible. 'Dr. Slipher, I have found your Planet X.'"

HELLO, PLUTO!
Lop-eared Pluto first appe[...]
in a 1930 cartoon. Walt D[...]
named Mickey Mouse's do[...]
after the planet Pluto, wh[...]
had just been discovered.

FUZZY FACE
Our best view of Pluto, captured by the Hubble Space Telescope, shows fuzzy dark markings and bright polar caps. We won't see sharper views until the Pluto-Kuiper Express spacecraft explore the planet in 2013.

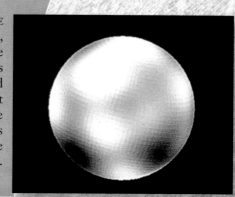

Word Builders

• In 1930, 11-year-old Venetia Burney of Oxford, England, suggested the new planet be named **Pluto**, for the Greek god of the underworld.
• When James Christy discovered Pluto's moon in 1978, he named it **Charon**, for the ferryman in Greek mythology who rowed souls across the River Styx to the underworld.

That's Amazing!

• Pluto's day (one rotation of Pluto on its axis) and month (one orbit of Charon around Pluto) are the same length—six Earth days and nine hours.
• The thin atmosphere of Pluto freezes into methane snow every winter.
• Signals from the Pluto-Kuiper Express spacecraft will take nearly six hours to reach Earth from Pluto.

Pathfinder

• Have spacecraft visited all the other planets? Go to pages 142–43.
• How big is Pluto compared to the Sun? Go to page 149.
• Pluto might look like Triton, one of Neptune's moons. What does Triton look like? Go to pages 166–67.
• What lies beyond the Kuiper Belt? Go to pages 170–71.

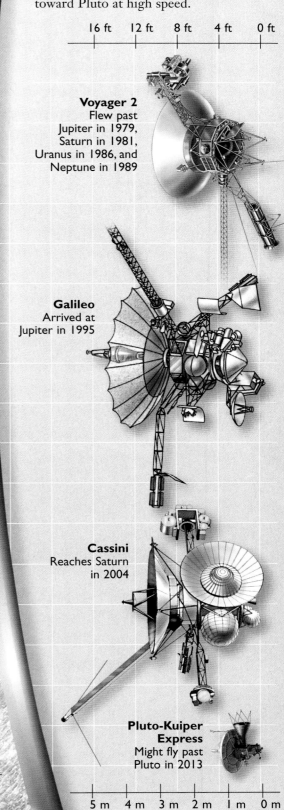

THE SPORTS CAR PROBE

The probes that visited Jupiter, Saturn, Uranus, and Neptune were as large as trucks. A probe as heavy as these would take decades to reach Pluto. But the two Pluto-Kuiper Express spacecraft will be like fast sports cars—small and light, so a rocket can shoot them toward Pluto at high speed.

16 ft   12 ft   8 ft   4 ft   0 ft

Voyager 2
Flew past
Jupiter in 1979,
Saturn in 1981,
Uranus in 1986, and
Neptune in 1989

Galileo
Arrived at
Jupiter in 1995

Cassini
Reaches Saturn
in 2004

**Pluto-Kuiper
Express**
Might fly past
Pluto in 2013

5 m   4 m   3 m   2 m   1 m   0 m

MISSION TO THE LAST PLANET

No spacecraft has ever visited Pluto, but that may change if the Pluto-Kuiper Express spacecraft are launched as scheduled. In 2013, after a journey of 10 years, a small spacecraft will fly past Pluto, the reddish world in this picture, and Charon, the gray world. A second spacecraft may follow six months later. Before flying on to explore icy objects in the Kuiper Belt, each spacecraft might send a little probe crashing into Pluto.

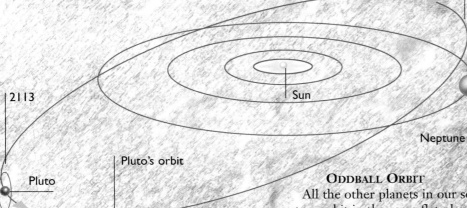

1989

2113

Pluto's orbit

Sun

Pluto

Neptune

ODDBALL ORBIT

All the other planets in our solar system orbit in the same flat plane, but little Pluto's orbit is tilted into a long, oval shape. For most of its 248-year orbit, Pluto is the outermost planet, but it sometimes crosses over the orbit of Neptune, making Neptune the outermost planet. From 1979 to 1999, Pluto was closer to the Sun than Neptune was. By 2113, Pluto will be at the most distant point on its orbit—more than 4.5 billion miles (7.3 billion km) from the Sun.

Comets

MOST COMETS STAY in the deep freeze of space. Some orbit in the Kuiper Belt, just beyond Pluto. Others are farther out, in the Oort Cloud—a swarm of millions of comets that extends partway to the nearest star. Sometimes, perhaps after colliding with another comet, a comet falls out of the deep freeze and into an orbit that takes it toward the Sun.

In the deep freeze, a comet is like a dirty snowball the size of a small city. As it nears the Sun's warmth, though, the comet begins to vaporize. Jets of gas and dust erupt from the nucleus, its frozen core. The gas and dust flow away from the nucleus to form long, wispy tails. Most comets take thousands of years to complete an orbit, but a few swing by the Sun every few years or decades.

Comets have hardly changed since the solar system formed, so scientists are keen to study any clues that they might contain about the birth of the solar system. Space probes can visit comets that are approaching the Sun. In 1986, the Giotto probe flew past Comet Halley's nucleus. From 2003 to 2008, the Contour probe will visit three comets. And in 2005, Deep Space 4 will collect a piece of Comet Tempel 1 and bring it back to Earth. In 2011, the Rosetta probe will drop a lander onto Comet Wirtanen's nucleus.

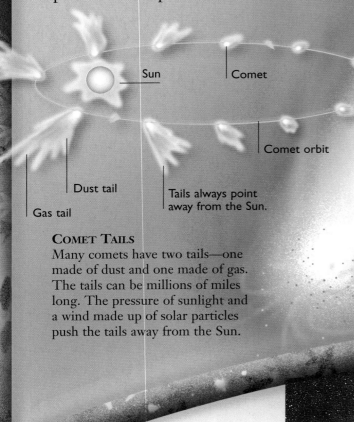

Sun

Comet

Comet orbit

Dust tail

Tails always point away from the Sun.

Gas tail

COMET TAILS
Many comets have two tails—one made of dust and one made of gas. The tails can be millions of miles long. The pressure of sunlight and a wind made up of solar particles push the tails away from the Sun.

HANDS ON

Raining Meteors

A meteor shower happens when Earth passes through a trail of dust from a comet. Some of the strongest meteor showers are the Perseids on August 12, the Orionids on October 22, the Leonids on November 17, and the Geminids on December 14. To observe a meteor shower, try to get away from bright lights and make yourself comfortable in a deck chair. If the Moon is not above the horizon, you could see 20 to 50 meteors in an hour. The meteors will appear to be streaming from one area of the sky—during the Geminid shower, for example, all the meteors seem to come from the constellation of Gemini.

FAMOUS COMETS

HALLEY
When comets travel close to Earth, we can see them in our sky. The famous Comet Halley appears every 75 or 76 years. It last flew past Earth in 1986 and will return again in 2061.

HYAKUTAKE
In March 1996, a comet that no one had ever seen before swept past Earth. It was only 9 million miles (14.5 million km) away, and its gossamer tail stretched nearly halfway across the sky.

Word Builders

If you discover a comet, it will be named after you—although you may have to share your comet with other people. Alan Hale and Thomas Bopp were scanning the sky miles apart when they discovered the same comet on the same night in 1995. Their discovery became known as **Comet Hale-Bopp.**

That's Amazing!

• Tons of comet dust float down to Earth every day. When you clean house, a few of the dust specks you sweep up may have come from comets.
• The Great Comet of 1843 had the longest tail of any comet—it stretched from the Sun to the orbit of Mars.
• During the year it was closest to the Sun, Comet Hale-Bopp gushed 9 tons of water into space every second.

Pathfinder

• Have other probes collected samples from space? Go to page 142.
• Are comet orbits the same shape as planet orbits? Go to pages 148–49.
• Where else can meteors come from? Go to page 160.
• What did Comet Shoemaker-Levy 9 look like when it crashed into Jupiter? Go to page 162.

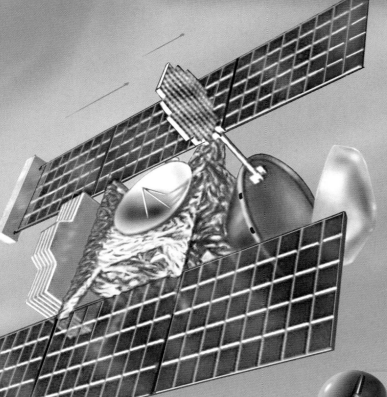

SWEEPING UP COMET DUST

If all goes as planned, a probe called Stardust will zoom through the head of Comet Wild 2 (pronounced *vilt 2*) in January 2004. A disc of spongelike material called aerogel will stick out of Stardust like a big flyswatter, ready to capture dust streaming from the comet's nucleus. In January 2006, Stardust will swing by Earth to drop a capsule containing the comet dust to scientists waiting in the Utah desert in the United States.

EVIL STARS

Throughout history, people have thought that comets were omens of disaster. The 900-year-old Bayeux tapestry records Comet Halley's appearance in 1066, before the Battle of Hastings in England. The Latin words say, "They are in awe of the star."

INSIDE STORY

Comet Sleuth

Astronomer Carolyn Shoemaker has found more comets than anyone else in history. She finds them by inspecting photographs taken through a telescope. Her first discovery came in 1983. "I was looking through films my husband Gene and I had taken. All of a sudden, there it was, and I knew it was a comet." Even after discovering 32 comets, each new find is a thrill. "I do try to contain myself for a while, until we find out if the comet is already known. But when I see a comet, my heart gives a big leap of joy."

SHOEMAKER-LEVY 9

In 1992, this comet traveled too close to the powerful gravity of Jupiter and broke into 21 pieces. Two years later, the pieces slammed into Jupiter, making dark spots on the planet.

HALE-BOPP

One of the brightest comets of the 20th century, Hale-Bopp graced Northern Hemisphere skies in March and April of 1997. This photo clearly shows its straight, blue gas tail and curving, yellow-white dust tail.

Our Universe

BEYOND OUR SOLAR system, the universe awaits. Visit the stars and see how they change throughout their lives. Search for stars that have their own families of planets. Enter a nebula—a huge cloud of gas and dust—and witness the birth of a star. Travel past the stars in our sky and look back at the spiral arms of our galaxy, the Milky Way. Keep moving and you'll reach another galaxy—one of 50 billion in the universe. But watch out—there might be a giant black hole at the galaxy's center. Finally, end your journey at the beginning of time and discover how our amazing universe began.

page **174**

Who sees a crocodile in the stars?

What is this star pattern called?

Go to **CONSTELLATIONS**.

page **176**

How is a star born?

How do astronomers find planets around stars?

Go to **SHINING STARS**.

page **178**

Why do stars explode?

Why do some stars regularly change their brightness?

Go to **CHANGING STARS**.

page **180**

What is happening inside this pillar of gas?

How did this bizarre shape form?

Go to NEBULAS.

page **182**

How is the Milky Way like a flying saucer?

What sort of galaxy is this?

Go to OUR GALAXY.

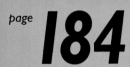

page **184**

What is shooting out of this galaxy?

What would happen if you fell into a black hole?

Go to GALAXIES AND BLACK HOLES.

page **186**

How did the universe begin?

How might the universe end?

Go to THE EXPANDING UNIVERSE.

Constellations

CAN YOU SEE pictures in the stars? People have long imagined that particular groups of stars form the outlines of beasts, heroes, and gods—like dot-to-dot drawings. These star groups are called constellations. Most stars in a constellation are actually light-years apart in space—they just look close together in our sky.

Different people have imagined different pictures in the same group of stars. The ancient Greeks saw the stars of Orion as a hunter, but the Egyptians thought the same stars formed Osiris, the god of light. In China, the same stars were the warrior Tsan. The New Zealand Maoris see a canoe in Orion's stars, while an Amazon tribe sees a giant crocodile. Constellations once helped people sail ships and make calendars. Today, finding star patterns will help you learn your way around the sky.

Astronomers divide the sky into 88 constellations. Most come from Greek myths, but a few were named in modern times. You can't see all 88 constellations at once—the ones you see depend on where you live, what time of night it is, and where Earth is in its orbit around the Sun.

NORTHERN SKY STAR CHAR[T]

If you are in the Northern Hemisphere—areas such as the United States, Canad[a] Europe, and Japan—these are the bright sta[rs] you can see at some time during the year. T[o] use the map, face south and turn it so th[e] current month is at the bottom, near you. Th[e] stars you can see in the sky are in the lowe[r] half of the map. The ones near the horizo[n] are at the map's edge. Thos[e] overhead and behin[d] you lie toward th[e] map's cente[r]

ORION STEPS ONTO THE SKY
Orion the Hunter climbs into a northern January sky. The three stars of Orion's belt point down to Sirius, the night sky's brightest star, rising through the trees.

ORION THE HUNTER
In Greek mythology, Orion was the son of Neptune and a great hunter. When Orion boasted that he would hunt down every animal in the world, Gaia, the Earth goddess, sent a scorpion to sting and kill him.

THE BIG DIPPER
The Big Dipper is a pattern of seven stars in Ursa Major, the Great Bear. In Great Britain, this pattern is known as the Plough. Germans call it the Great Wagon and Three Horses.

Word Builders

As Earth orbits the Sun each year, the Sun appears to travel through a band of 12 constellations called the **zodiac.** The name comes from the Greek word *zoidiakos,* meaning "circle of animal signs." Seven zodiac constellations are named for animals, such as Cancer the Crab. Four others resemble people, such as Aquarius the Water Bearer. Libra the Scales is the only one that doesn't resemble a living creature.

That's Amazing!

• On a clear, moonless night far from city lights, the stars seem too many to count. But if you did, you'd count about 2,000 stars that you can see at any moment with just the unaided eye.
• Most constellations are so old that no one knows who named or thought of them. From drawings on clay tablets, we know that 5,000 years ago, Sumerians saw some of the same pictures in the sky that we do today.

Pathfinder

• Do you need a telescope to see constellations? Go to page 136.
• What are the stars made of? Go to pages 176–77.
• What object can you see in the constellation of Orion? Go to page 181.
• To which galaxy do the constellation stars belong? Go to pages 182–83.

SOUTHERN SKY STAR CHART

These are the Southern Hemisphere's bright stars, ones you can see from Australia, New Zealand, South America, and southern Africa. Face north and turn the map so the current month is at the bottom. Stars near the horizon are at the edge of the map. Stars overhead and behind you lie toward the map's center.

HANDS ON

Following the Stars

When you first look up at the night sky, it can seem overcrowded with stars. Concentrate on the brightest stars, and you'll soon match them up with the charts on these pages.

To identify even more stars and constellations, you can use a planisphere—a round map of the night sky with a top disk that you turn to the current date and time. You can also learn about stars by using a star atlas, a book of detailed star maps. Starmapping computer programs let you print out a map of the night sky for any particular time and place. For your stargazing sessions, dress warmly—you'll be standing still for a long time. Bright lights can ruin your night vision and make it hard to see the stars, so find a dark observing spot and cover your flashlight with red cellophane.

LEO THE LION
People have seen Leo as a starry lion since ancient times. The six bright stars that look like a backward question mark trace out the lion's head. Leo is one of the 12 constellations of the zodiac.

SCORPIUS THE SCORPION
Many different people saw Scorpius as a scorpion. In Greek mythology, this is the scorpion that killed Orion. These mortal enemies are opposite each other in the sky—as one rises, the other sets. Scorpius is another zodiac constellation.

175

Shining Stars

DURING THE DAY, you can see one star in the sky—our Sun. At night, with the Sun's glaring light gone from the sky, you can see hundreds of other stars. They are balls of hot hydrogen gas like our Sun, but they are so far away that each appears as a sparkling point of light.

Stars come in many colors and sizes. Our Sun is a yellow star with a surface temperature of 11,000°F (6,000°C). That's hot—but white and blue stars are hotter. Orange and red stars, on the other hand, are cooler. Stars can be average size like our Sun, or they can be giants or dwarfs. If the Sun were the size of a beachball, bright giant stars would be monster balloons as wide as a small town, while dim dwarf stars would be as small as green peas.

A few stars, like the Sun, travel through space alone, but most are multiple stars that are made up of two or more stars dancing about each other. Like the Sun, some stars have families of planets. If you lived on a planet that orbited a multiple star, you would see more than one sun in the sky.

ALIEN SOLAR SYSTEMS

Astronomers thought other solar systems would look like ours—with small, rocky planets close to a star, and cold gas giants far out. They were surprised to discover solar systems where huge Jupiter-like planets orbit as close to their star as Mercury does to our Sun. Whether these alien solar systems also have small, rocky planets like Earth remains unknown.

HANDS ON

Why Stars Twinkle

Do you know why stars twinkle? Try this experiment.

❶ Wad up small pieces of aluminum foil to make stars. Place the stars on a piece of dark cardboard.

❷ Pour water into a large glass bowl until it is three-quarters full. Place the bowl on top of the silver stars.

❸ Make the room dark and shine a flashlight into the bowl.

❹ Tap the side of the bowl several times. The water will move, and the stars will look smudged for a moment.

In the same way that the light shining off the foil moves when the water does, starlight passing through Earth's atmosphere travels through layers of moving air that bend the light back and forth. This makes the stars look as if they are twinkling. If you traveled up to the Hubble Space Telescope, beyond Earth's atmosphere, the stars would shine steadily.

A SHORT HISTORY OF A STAR

Stars are born, live for billions of years, and then die. Throughout their lives, stars change size and temperature as they use up their hydrogen supply. Here is the life cycle of an average star like the Sun.

A NEBULA COLLAPSES...
A cloud of gas and dust called a nebula starts shrinking. Squeezed by gravity, its center heats up.

...A STAR IS BORN...
The nebula's center becomes so hot that it crushes hydrogen into helium, releasing energy. The star begins to shine.

...AND LIVES...
For billions of years, the star stable, radiatin light and heat.

Word Builders

• Some star names are Greek—**Arcturus** (and the word Arctic) comes from the Greek word *arktos*, meaning "bear." **Sirius,** from the Greek word *Seirios,* means "the brilliant one."
• Other star names are from Arabic words—**Betelgeuse** is from *yad al-jauza,* meaning "the hand of the giant," while **Rigel**, from *rijl*, means "foot."

That's Amazing!

• An Apollo spacecraft took just three days to travel to the Moon, but it would take 850,000 years to reach the nearest star.
• If you could bring one teaspoon of white dwarf matter to Earth, it would weigh as much as a large truck.

Pathfinder

• Why are we looking for planets around other stars? Go to pages 144–45.
• What makes the Sun a special star? Go to pages 154–55.
• How can you identify the stars? Go to pages 174–75.
• Which stars end their life with a bang? Go to pages 178–79.
• Can you see where stars are born? Go to pages 180–81.

INSIDE STORY

Planet Hunters

How do you find alien planets? "Just as a leashed dog can jerk its heavier owner around in circles, a planet can swing its star around," explain Paul Butler and Geoff Marcy. The duo were among the first to find planets around other stars. After 10 years of work at Lick Observatory in California, they detected tiny wobbles in the motions of stars caused by the tug from Jupiter-like planets. The discoveries made them famous. "We got calls from every newspaper, magazine, and TV station there was." The team is now using the Keck and the Anglo-Australian telescopes to hunt for Earth-like planets around 800 nearby stars like the Sun. "Within three to six years," predicts Marcy, "we'll know whether our solar system is special."

GREAT BALLS OF STARS

Picture a sky blazing with so many stars that the night is never dark. That's what you'd see from the center of one of our galaxy's globular clusters. Each cluster is a ball of a million ancient stars.

SPRINKLED STARS

The Pleiades, or Seven Sisters, are only 50 million years old—so young that the dinosaurs never saw them. They are one of hundreds of young open clusters that are sprinkled around the spiral arms of our galaxy.

...AND BLOWS OFF GAS...

The unstable, aging star blows off its outer layers in explosions. The layers turn into a colorful cloud of gas—a planetary nebula—surrounding the star.

...THEN BALLOONS...

Eventually, the star's hydrogen fuel begins to run out. It swells to become a red giant star.

...THEN SHRINKS

What's left of the star shrinks to the size of Earth. This hot white dwarf will shine for billions more years.

Changing Stars

OUR SUN SHINES steadily year after year, but not all stars are so stable. Some old stars change size every few days or weeks, becoming brighter as they balloon and dimmer as they shrink. These are known as pulsating variables.

Other stars change because they belong to double star systems. Some double stars are so close together that one star pulls gas away from the other. The more ravenous star collects enough gas from the other star to set off an explosion known as a nova. After the explosion, the star collects gas again. Some hungry stars collect so much gas that they blow apart as a supernova, one of nature's most powerful explosions. The star is completely destroyed.

Supernovas can also occur at the end of a giant star's life. Giant stars burn so furiously that they last only a few million years. When their fuel runs out, they explode, crushing their deep core into a neutron star or a black hole. Neutron stars are extremely dense city-size spheres that spin very rapidly. Black holes are infinitely dense and swallow up anything that comes close to them—even light.

LOOK OUT! THIS STAR'S ABOUT TO BLOW!

Eta Carina is near the end of its life. In 1841, this giant star blew off two puffballs of gas, which have been getting bigger ever since. They are seen here in a 1993 photo from the Hubble Space Telescope. Sometime in the next few thousand years, the star will blow apart as a supernova. When it does, it will look as bright as Venus in our sky.

INSIDE STORY

Supernova Watcher

"I was contemplating the stars when I noticed a new star, surpassing all the others in brilliancy, shining directly above my head. I was so astonished at the sight I doubted my own eyes." The new star, discovered by Tycho Brahe in 1572, was a surprise because people thought that stars never changed. By careful observations, Tycho Brahe proved that his supernova lay far beyond the Moon in the realm of the stars. All that remains today of Tycho's star is a gas cloud called a supernova remnant (left). It can be seen only by X-ray telescopes.

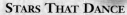

STARS THAT DANCE
Eclipsing stars revolve around each other as if they are dancing. When one star hides behind the other, its light is cut off, and the pair looks dim in our sky. When the star comes out, the pair looks bright again.

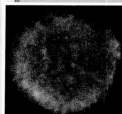

STARS THAT INFLATE
Every few days or weeks, pulsating stars puff up, cool off, and shrink. Then they heat up and balloon in size again. Astronomers have discovered thousands of these variable stars in the sky. By timing their pulsations, astronomers can calculate how far away the stars are.

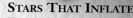

Word Builders

One eclipsing star that appears to dip up and down in brightness is named **Algol,** from the Arabic word *al-ghul* for "ghoul." In Greek mythology, Algol is the winking eye in the snake-haired head of a woman called the Gorgon. It was thought that anyone who looked at her would turn to stone.

That's Amazing!

• As they spin, some neutron stars flash pulses of radio beams. When astronomers detect these pulses, they call the star a pulsar.
• A supernova releases as much energy in a few days as the Sun will release in its lifetime of 10 billion years.

Pathfinder

• How did variable stars expand the universe? Go to page 135.
• Which supernova remnant looks like a crab? Go to page 181.
• Find out more about black holes. Go to pages 184–85.

SUPERNOVAS

Supernovas are stars that self-destruct, blowing apart in titanic explosions and spewing out clouds of starstuff. Two kinds of stars can explode as supernovas.

OVERWEIGHT STARS

A blue giant star swells to a red supergiant. The bloated star runs out of fuel in its core. In an instant, the core collapses into a dense neutron star or black hole.

Stage 1
Massive blue star

Stage 2
Red supergiant star

Stage 3
Boom! Supernova explosion

Stage 4
Debris expands away from neutron star.

HUNGRY STARS

The gravity of a white dwarf star sucks gas away from its companion star. The white dwarf becomes too heavy to support itself and collapses. A burst of nuclear fusion tears the hungry star to bits, flinging star debris into space.

Stage 1
White dwarf drags material from red giant.

Stage 2
White dwarf becomes too heavy.

Stage 3
Pow! Supernova explosion

Stage 4
Star is destroyed, and star debris blows into space.

ALL IS QUIET...

It was just an ordinary star, one of millions in a nearby galaxy, the Large Magellanic Cloud.

...THEN BANG!

On February 23, 1987, astronomers watched the star explode and become brighter than any supernova since 1604. No one knows when the next supernova will appear.

NGC 604, star-birth nebula *Cat's Eye, star-death nebula*

Nebulas

THE UNIVERSE CONTAINS more than stars and planets. The space between the stars is sprinkled lightly with atoms of gas and specks of dust. Like water vapor in our atmosphere, some of this starstuff collects into clouds called nebulas. Gravity packs some nebulas so tightly that stars condense from the cool, dark clouds, like raindrops forming in rain clouds.

Once stars form, they become chemical factories. Deep inside their atom-smashing cores, stars turn hydrogen and helium atoms into dozens of other chemical elements. At the ends of their lives, stars blow planetary nebulas and supernova remnants into space. These star-death nebulas carry the elements made inside stars back into space, where they eventually find their way into other nebulas.

Like cosmic recycling plants, these other nebulas, enriched by the stuff from older stars, form new stars, new planets—and new life. The oxygen, carbon, iron, and all the other elements in your body came from stars that lived and died billions of years ago. You are made of starstuff recycled through swirling nebulas.

INSIDE STORY

Star Photographer

"We can't hear the stars, nor smell nor taste them, nor can we reach out and touch them. Indeed we can barely see them," explains David Malin as he loads an enormous glass photographic plate. Using the Anglo-Australian Telescope as a giant camera, he's taking a portrait of a nebula so faint the exposure will last an hour or more. Why go to the effort? For Malin, the answer is easy. "Astronomical images are proof of the beauty and endless variety of nature. Photographs are also a tool of discovery. An hour's photography can reveal more than the eye and telescope together can ever see." The photos below of the Trifid and Horsehead nebulas are two of Malin's "cosmic landscapes."

FOUR TYPES OF NEBULAS
GLOWING NEBULAS
Bright nebulas are lit up like neon signs by stars deep inside them. The stars' energy makes the gas glow in shades of red, green, and blue. This bright nebula, the Trifid, is 3,500 light-years away. Stars are still forming inside it.

DARK CLOUDS
Other star-forming nebulas are made of dark, dusty clouds that block the light from distant stars. What shape can you see in this dark nebula Here's a hint—it's called the Horsehead Nebula.

Word Builders

Nebula is the Latin word for "cloud." When astronomers first used telescopes, any fuzzy patch in the sky that did not look like a star was called a nebula. We now know that many of what the early astronomers called nebulas are not gas clouds in our galaxy. They are really galaxies made up of billions of stars.

That's Amazing!

• The clouds around the Orion Nebula contain enough gas to make 10,000 Suns.
• Two elements—hydrogen and helium—make up 99 percent of the universe. The other 1 percent—the elements that make planets, living things, and us—first developed inside stars.

Pathfinder

• Where is the Hubble Space Telescope? Go to pages 136–37.
• How can a nebula turn into a solar system? Go to page 149.
• What sort of star ends up as a planetary nebula? Go to pages 176–77.
• How does a supernova remnant form? Go to page 179.

HANDS ON
Find the Orion Nebula

The Orion Nebula is a cloud of dusty gas where new stars are forming. The young stars make the nebula glow.

To find the Orion Nebula, start by looking for the constellation of Orion the Hunter, using the star charts on pages 48–49. In the center of Orion is a row of three bright stars, the Hunter's belt. Beneath the belt is the Hunter's sword, made up of three fainter stars.

If you look through binoculars, you'll see that the sword's middle star is much fuzzier than the others. In fact, it is not a star at all—it's the Orion Nebula. In photos the nebula looks red, but through binoculars it looks ghostly gray. That's because our eyes can't see the true colors of stars and nebulas.

THE EAGLE NEBULA, A STELLAR NURSERY

The Eagle Nebula, 7,000 light-years away, is filled with young stars. A photo taken by David Malin shows the entire nebula (above). The Hubble Space Telescope peered deep into the nebula. Its sharp image (left) reveals pillars of gas and dust towering 1 light-year high. At the tips of the pillars, blobs of gas the size of our solar system contain new stars being born. Our Sun and planets formed out of a similar nebula five billion years ago.

BLOWING STAR BUBBLES

Dying stars often blow off their outer layers to make bubbles of gas, like this Hourglass Nebula. Because these nebulas looked like dim planets through early telescopes, astronomers named them planetary nebulas.

STELLAR GRAVEYARDS

The Crab Nebula is what remains of a supernova star that people saw explode in AD 1054. Supernova remnants like the Crab help enrich a new generation of stars.

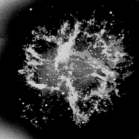

Our Galaxy

IF THE SOLAR system is your cosmic neighborhood, then the Milky Way galaxy is your sprawling city of stars. This city is made up of 200 billion stars and is so wide that a light beam takes 100,000 years to travel from one side to the other. Star-studded spiral arms spin around the city center, a dense core, or nucleus, that is packed with stars. Our Sun lives in the galactic city's suburbs, in a spiral arm roughly halfway out from the center of the galaxy.

All the stars you see in the sky—every constellation and all the star clusters and nebulas you can see through telescopes—belong to our galaxy. Far away lurks something that you can't see. Using infrared and radio telescopes to probe the center of the Milky Way, astronomers have found stars and gas frantically swirling around a very small, dense, dark object—perhaps a massive black hole.

Just as there are many cities in the world, our galaxy is one of many star-cities in the universe. All the other galaxies are far away—light from the nearest big star-city, the Andromeda galaxy, takes 2.8 million years to reach us.

YOUR STAR CITY

If you could travel to a place far above the Milky Way, you would see a view like the one shown below—a glowing nucleus of old yellow stars surrounded by a swarm of globular star clusters. Spiral arms studded with young blue stars sweep away from the nucleus. The galaxy would appear motionless because it turns too slowly for human eyes to detect any movement.

Spiral arms

Direction of rotation

INSIDE STORY

Discoverer of Dark Matter

"My earliest recollection," explains American astronomer Vera Rubin, "is of sitting in the back of a car at night and asking my father why the Moon is going where we are going. I can still recall the excitement of the question. Today the excitement I get from asking questions is no less." Vera Rubin's curiosity led her to a remarkable discovery—galaxies are surrounded by clouds of invisible dark matter. Astronomers now think that 90 percent of the matter in the universe is dark, but the identity of the dark matter is a mystery. "Still more mysteries of the universe remain hidden," Rubin says. "Their discovery awaits the adventurous scientists of the future willing to ask some really far-out questions."

MILK IN THE SKY

In the night sky, we can see the spiral arms of our galaxy. They look like a pale ribbon of light arcing across the sky. We call this hazy band the Milky Way—the same name that we give to our entire galaxy.

Word Builders

Our galaxy's name, the **Milky Way,** is an English translation of the Latin words *Via Lactea,* meaning "road of milk." The word **galaxy** comes from the Greek word *gala,* meaning "milk." Greek legend tells that the hazy band of light across the night sky was made of milk spilled by the baby Hercules.

That's Amazing!

• Since the first dinosaurs appeared 228 million years ago, the Sun has made only one orbit of our galaxy.
• At the center of the Milky Way, there might be a black hole that weighs as much as a million Suns.

Pathfinder

• How does the Milky Way fit into the universe? Go to pages 134–35.
• What did Galileo see when he looked at the Milky Way through a telescope? Go to page 136.

A GALAXY MENAGERIE

Like animals in a zoo, many kinds of galaxies populate the universe. Most belong to four main species.

SPIRAL GALAXY
In spirals like the Whirlpool galaxy, several arms of brilliant stars reach out from a densely packed core. Stars in the arms turn around the core.

BARRED SPIRAL
Like the Great Barred Spiral, some galaxies have arms that start from the ends of unusual bars. Our Milky Way galaxy may be a barred spiral.

ELLIPTICAL GALAXY
Elliptical galaxies are like cosmic beehives, with billions of stars swarming in every direction. Some elliptical galaxies, such as M87, have grown to monstrous size by devouring other galaxies.

IRREGULAR GALAXY
Not all galaxies have tidy shapes. Some are messy collections of stars. The Small Magellanic Cloud is an irregular galaxy that orbits the Milky Way.

HANDS ON
Observing the Milky Way

The best place to see the Milky Way is in the country, far from city lights. And the best time is a night near New Moon in summer, autumn, or winter.

If you look at the Milky Way through binoculars, you'll see that it's made up of thousands of stars. In July or August, look for the most crowded part of the band, around the constellation of Sagittarius. Here, you are looking toward the heart of our galaxy. Can you see the dark lanes of dust and gas that cut through the glowing star clouds? These lanes hide the Milky Way's center.

Globular cluster

Nucleus

Possible black hole in center

Sun

THE DARK SIDE OF THE GALAXY
From a side view, our galaxy would look like a flying saucer. Stack two CDs on top of each other and stick a marble in the hole, and you have a good scale model of the Milky Way. The galaxy's flat disc and bulging core may be surrounded by a halo of dark matter that we can't see.

Galaxies and Black Holes

THE UNIVERSE IS like a huge block of Swiss cheese! The 50 billion galaxies in the known universe are not neatly spaced. They clump together into clusters that can contain thousands of galaxies. The clusters bunch into superclusters around bubblelike regions of empty space.

Galaxies are sometimes drawn so close together by one another's gravity that they pull one another out of shape or even collide, triggering bursts of star birth. Large galaxies can even swallow up smaller galaxies. The Milky Way might one day gobble up its neighbors, the Magellanic Clouds.

Every galaxy might contain black holes. Our galaxy alone might have thousands that were created by supernova explosions. But not all black holes are made from single stars. At the center of many galaxies, there are black holes that have swallowed millions of stars. Some galaxies produce such an astonishing amount of energy that they each must have a supermassive black hole at their center. Luckily for us, even the closest black holes are too far away to swallow our Sun.

POWERHOUSE GALAXIES
Quasars might be supermassive black holes fed by the densely packed matter in young galaxies. From a region the size of our solar system, a quasar (right) gives off more energy than an entire galaxy.

COLLIDING GALAXIES
Galaxies can collide, rip apart, then burst to life with new stars. In the wreckage of the Antennae galaxies' impact (left), billions of young blue stars are starting to shine.

WHIRLPOOL OF DESTRUCTION
Journey to the center of a galaxy, and you might find an accretion disc—a whirlpool of stars, gas, and dust spinning around a black hole. The hole itself emits no light, but you can see the radiation given off by the doomed matter as it is torn apart. The hungry hole can't swallow all its food—any gas it doesn't eat shoots away in high-speed jets.

NGC 4261
In a galaxy known only by its catalog number, NGC 4261, Hubble captures an image of an accretion disc—the whirlpool around a black hole. You can see hints of a jet shooting from the center of the disc.

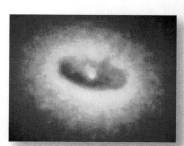

LOOKING FOR BLACK HOLES

The sharp cameras of the Hubble Space Telescope have peered deep into the centers of other galaxies. While black holes remain hidden, their swirling discs and high-speed jets give them away.

Word Builders

• As long ago as 1784, English astronomer John Michell realized objects could be so dense that light could not escape from them. But the first person to actually use the words **black hole** was physicist John Wheeler in 1967.
• **Quasar,** coined in 1963, is short for "quasi-stellar radio source."

That's Amazing!

• If our Sun turned into a black hole (although scientists think it can't), the planets would still orbit it. You must get very close to a hole to be sucked in.
• Crush Earth to the size of a marble, and it would become a black hole.

Pathfinder

• What instruments are used to find black holes? Go to pages 136–37.
• When can a star turn into a black hole? Go to pages 178–79.
• Why do astronomers think there is a black hole in the center of our galaxy? Go to pages 182–83.

INSIDE STORY

Down a Black Hole

Oh, no! As you journey through interstellar space, you're falling feet first into a black hole. If you look up, you can see the entire future of the universe flash by in an instant. But the hole is so small that its gravity is pulling on your feet harder than it is on your head. You're being stretched into spaghetti. Ouch! If you had fallen into a bigger black hole, the gravity wouldn't have stretched you quite so much. But some scientists think that the radiation inside any black hole would still get you.

To leap safely across the universe, you'd need to find a wormhole—a cosmic tunnel that connects remote regions of space. Wormholes are popular devices in movies, but no one knows if they really exist. Good luck in your search!

HEADING TOWARD ANDROMEDA
Our Milky Way and the Andromeda galaxy are the biggest members of the Local Group, a small cluster of about 30 galaxies. Here you can see Andromeda with its two tiny neighboring galaxies. Andromeda and the Milky Way are speeding toward each other. Five billion years from now, they might collide and form one gigantic elliptical galaxy.

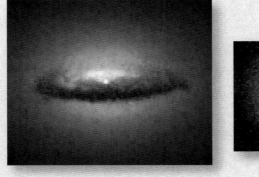

M87
A jet of gas that has squirted away from a spinning black hole shoots out of the giant galaxy M87. Its hungry hole has swallowed three billion Suns' worth of starstuff.

NGC 7052
In a galaxy 190 million light-years away, Hubble reveals a dusty disc rapidly spinning around a hole 300 million times heavier than our Sun.

NGC 6251
The galaxy NGC 6251 is in the constellation of Ursa Minor, the Little Bear. In this Hubble portrait, the white spot is light shining from superhot gas near a black hole in the galaxy.

The Expanding Universe

DID YOU EVER wonder how our universe began? The Big Bang theory suggests that our universe was born about 15 billion years ago. Though it sounds like science fiction, the theory explains that our universe began when a tiny bubble broke away from another weird universe made of other dimensions, where space and time did not exist. As the bubble broke away, time began. The bubble exploded and grew superhot. As it cooled, it formed all the matter and energy we see today.

The explosion is still happening—we see all the galaxies rushing away from one another. Like a balloon blowing up, space is getting bigger, carrying galaxies farther apart. This expansion of the universe was discovered in the 1920s. Then in the 1960s, cosmic background radiation—the dim heat of the Big Bang— was detected. These are two strong pieces of evidence for the Big Bang theory.

Like all theories, the Big Bang changes with new ideas and new evidence. One idea proposes that our universe may be one of many universes connected together. Another idea, called inflation, suggests that our universe is so enormous that if it were the size of Earth, then the part of the universe we can see would be smaller than a speck of dust. One thing is certain—the universe is filled with so many mysteries, we will never run out of amazing things to discover.

THE BEGINNING OF THE UNIVERSE

A bubble of time and space, searing at a temperature of trillions of trillions of degrees, blows up like a cosmic balloon. As it expands, it cools. Tiny particles called electro and quarks condense into an atomic soup. The soup congeals to make particles called neutrons and protons. Then atoms of hydroge and helium form. Gravity clumps these atoms together to form the first stars and galaxies.

Time = 0 secon
Bang! Time a
space beg

Time = 1 billion trillion trillionth of a second
Matter (electrons and quarks) forms.

Time = 300,000 years
Atoms (hydrogen and helium) form.

Time = 1 billion years
First stars and galaxies form.

INSIDE STORY

Space and Time Mastermind

"I am still trying to understand how the universe works," says Stephen Hawking, speaking through his computer. His body is paralyzed by a muscle disease, but Stephen Hawking has used his mind to explain how space and time began. Explaining the Big Bang, he says it's "a bit like the North Pole of the earth. One could say that the surface of the earth begins at the North Pole." Time itself began in the Big Bang—so just as it makes no sense to ask what is north of the North Pole, it makes no sense to ask what happened before the Big Bang.

WRINKLES IN SPACE

By peering into radiation that has been traveling for billions of years, the Cosmic Background Explorer satellite gazed back in time to 300,000 years after the Big Bang. The blue areas pictured here are cool, lumpy regions of the young universe. Out of these wrinkles, superclusters of galaxies formed.

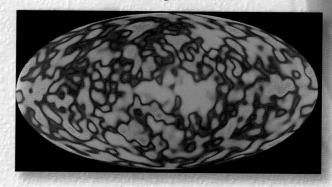

Word Builders

The label **Big Bang** was first used in 1950 by Fred Hoyle, who had devised his own Steady State theory of the universe. He was opposed to the Big Bang theory and made up the name to make fun of it. Maybe the name suggested by the Calvin and Hobbes cartoon characters would be better— Horrendous Space Kablooie!

That's Amazing!

• Just after the Big Bang, in the tiniest fraction of a second, the universe grew 100 trillion trillion trillion trillion times bigger.
• The universe contains roughly as many stars as there are grains of sand on all the beaches of the world.

Pathfinder

• Who discovered that the universe is expanding? Go to page 135.
• Is there life anywhere else in the universe? Go to pages 144–45.
• How was the solar system born? Go to page 149.
• How are stars created? Go to pages 176–77.

HANDS ON
Balloon Universe

You can make your very own universe.

❶ Blow up a round balloon until it is about as big as an orange, and hold the end so air can't escape.

❷ With a felt-tip marker, draw about 20 galaxies on the balloon. They can be spirals, ellipticals, and irregulars. Make them about the same distance apart.

❸ Look in a mirror and keep blowing up the balloon. Can you see the galaxies moving away from each other?

Like the balloon, the universe is expanding, and all its galaxies are moving farther apart.

THE UNIVERSE'S FATE

Though there are other theories about the beginning of the universe, none explains it as well as the Big Bang theory does. But how will the universe end? Scientists think there are two possibilities. Which is right? New telescopes may provide the answer, or they may reveal evidence that our universe behaves in ways we haven't even imagined yet.

A BIG CRUNCH?
Just as a ball thrown into the air falls back to Earth, the universe may stop expanding and begin falling back together. Trillions of years from now, all matter and energy may squeeze into a hot "big crunch."

A UNIVERSE WITHOUT END?
Perhaps there isn't enough matter and gravity to stop the universe expanding. In trillions of years, space may become dark as galaxies collapse into black holes. Then the black holes would dissolve into scattered particles.

Time = 15 billion years
Today's universe has 50 billion galaxies.

Glossary

asteroid An object made of rock and/or metal that orbits the Sun. Also known as a minor planet. Most asteroids orbit in the asteroid belt between Mars and Jupiter.

astronomy The scientific study of the solar system, our galaxy, and the universe.

atmosphere A layer of gas that surrounds a planet, moon, or star.

atom A tiny bit of matter. An atom is the smallest piece of all the different elements, such as hydrogen, oxygen, and iron. Atoms are made of even smaller particles—electrons, protons, and neutrons.

aurora A colored glow in the sky that occurs when particles from the Sun rain down onto Earth's atmosphere. Also known as the northern or southern lights.

axis An imaginary line through the center of a planet, moon, or star. A planet, moon, or star spins, or rotates, around its axis.

bacteria The simplest forms of life on Earth, made of single cells. Bacteria were perhaps the first forms of life to develop.

Big Bang theory The theory that the universe formed when a tiny bubble of energy exploded about 15 billion years ago.

billion A thousand million. In numerals, it is written as 1,000,000,000.

black hole An infinitely dense object with such powerful gravity that even light cannot escape. A black hole can form when a massive star explodes as a supernova. Supermassive black holes have swallowed millions of stars.

cluster A gathering of stars or galaxies bound together by gravity. Loosely bound groups of several hundred young stars are called open clusters. Tightly bound groups of hundreds of thousands of old stars are called globular clusters. Galaxies form galactic clusters.

comet An object made of dust and ice that orbits the Sun. As a comet nears the Sun, its ice melts and forms tails of dust and gas.

constellation One of the 88 official star patterns seen in the night sky.

convective zone A region within a star where hot material moves up to cooler regions and back down again, much like the movement of boiling water.

core The central region of an object. Earth has a core of nickel and iron. The Sun makes its energy through nuclear fusion in its core.

crater A round scar left on a planet or moon where a comet or asteroid has crashed into it.

crust The outer layer of a rocky planet, moon, or asteroid.

day The time a planet or moon takes to spin around once on its axis.

eclipse When one object passes in front of another, blocking or dimming the other object's light. A solar eclipse occurs when the Moon comes between Earth and the Sun. A lunar eclipse occurs when Earth is between the Sun and the Moon.

eclipsing star A pair of stars that revolve around each other and appear to dim and brighten regularly. When one star moves behind the other, its light is cut off and it looks dim. When the star comes out, it looks bright again.

galaxy A group of billions of stars and nebulas, held together by gravity.

gas giant A large planet made mostly of hydrogen. The solar system's gas giants are Jupiter, Saturn, Uranus, and Neptune.

gravity The force that attracts one object to another. Gravity holds planets and moons in orbit and also holds us on the ground.

horizon The imaginary line in the distance where the ground seems to meet the sky.

Hubble Space Telescope A large telescope that orbits above Earth's atmosphere. The Hubble provides the sharpest pictures of stars and galaxies ever taken.

infrared energy Invisible radiation that travels in slightly longer waves than visible light does. You feel infrared radiation as heat when you are near a fire or heater.

Kuiper Belt A region beyond Pluto where thousands of small icy comets orbit the Sun.

lava Molten rock that comes out of a volcano or through a crack in a planet's or moon's surface.

light-year The distance that a beam of light travels in one year—5.9 million million miles (9.5 million million km).

Local Group A cluster of about 30 galaxies including our galaxy, the Milky Way.

lunar Associated with the Moon, as in "lunar surface" or "lunar eclipse."

magnetic field The region of space in which an object exerts a magnetic force.

mantle The layer inside a rocky planet beneath the crust and above the core.

meteor The bright streak of light created when a meteoroid enters Earth's atmosphere and burns up. Meteors are often called shooting stars.

meteorite A meteoroid that lands on the surface of a planet or moon.

meteoroid A small rock or piece of metal that travels through space. Larger meteoroids are usually pieces of shattered asteroids. Smaller meteoroids are mostly dust particles shed by comets.

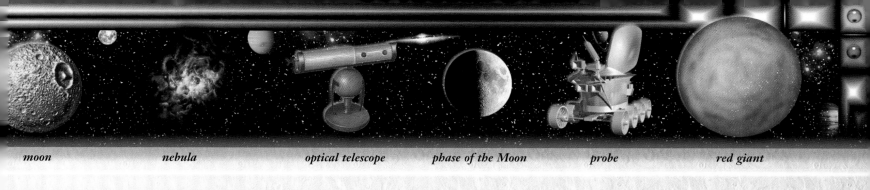

Milky Way The galaxy that contains our solar system and all the stars you can see in the night sky. Also, the hazy band of stars that arcs across the sky.

moon A natural object that orbits a planet.

near-Earth asteroid An asteroid that travels close to the Sun and crosses the orbit of Earth.

nebula A cloud of dust and gas in space. A nebula can be bright or dark.

neutron star An extremely dense, city-size star that is left when a supernova star explodes.

nova An explosion caused when a star collects too much gas from its companion star. After the nova, the star starts collecting gas again.

nucleus The core of a comet or galaxy.

Oort Cloud A swarm of millions of comets that extends from the Kuiper Belt partway to the nearest star.

optical telescope A telescope that collects visible light.

orbit The path of an object, such as Earth, as it moves around another object, such as the Sun. Also, to move around another object under the control of its gravity, as in "a planet orbits the Sun."

phases The changes in the appearance of an object, such as the Moon, as we see more or less of it lit up by the Sun.

photosphere The visible surface of the Sun or another star.

planet A big object, such as Mars, that orbits a star, such as the Sun. Because it does not produce its own light like a star does, a planet can be seen only because it reflects sunlight.

planetary nebula A cloud of gas formed when a dying star blows off its outer layers.

poles Two opposite points on the surface of a spinning planet, moon, or star. The axis of a planet, moon, or star passes through the poles.

probe A spacecraft that escapes Earth's gravity and explores the solar system. Probes have been sent to study planets, moons, asteroids, comets, and the Sun.

pulsar A neutron star that rotates very fast, sending out regular pulses of radio waves.

pulsating variable Stars that change size every few days or weeks, becoming brighter as they balloon and dimmer as they shrink.

quasar Short for "quasi-stellar radio source," the core of a distant young galaxy that emits an incredible amount of energy.

radar astronomy The study of solar system objects by bouncing radio waves off their surfaces.

radiation The process that carries energy through space as waves or particles.

radiative zone The deep region of a star that transfers energy to the convective zone.

radio energy Invisible radiation that travels in longer waves than infrared light does.

red giant A large, cool star in a late stage of its life.

rocky planet A small planet made mostly of rock. The solar system's rocky planets are Mercury, Venus, Earth, and Mars.

satellite A spacecraft or moon that orbits a larger object. Artificial satellites are sent into orbit around Earth to study Earth and space.

solar system A group of planets, comets, asteroids, meteoroids, and dust orbiting a central star. Our solar system is made up of nine planets and countless comets, asteroids, meteoroids, and dust specks orbiting the Sun.

space The airless region beyond Earth's atmosphere through which the planets, stars, and galaxies travel.

space shuttle A reusable NASA spacecraft that carries people and cargo into orbit around Earth.

space station A large artificial satellite that orbits Earth and can be occupied by people for long periods of time.

spiral galaxy A large galaxy with several starry arms reaching out from a dense core. It resembles a pinwheel.

star A large ball of hydrogen gas that produces light and heat. The Sun is a star.

supernova An extremely powerful explosion of a star. Supernovas occur when a giant star runs out of fuel and explodes as a supernova, or when a star collects so much gas from its companion star that it blows apart.

supernova remnant The gaseous remains of a star that has exploded as a supernova.

Trojan asteroids Two groups of asteroids that orbit the Sun in the same orbit as Jupiter.

ultraviolet energy Invisible radiation that travels in slightly shorter waves than visible light does. The Sun's ultraviolet radiation causes sunburn.

universe Everything that exists—all the galaxies, black holes, stars, nebulas, moons, planets, comets, asteroids, meteoroids, and dust scattered throughout space.

white dwarf A small, very hot star near the end of its life.

X-ray energy Invisible radiation that travels in shorter waves than ultraviolet light does.

year The time a planet takes to complete one orbit around the Sun.

Index

Acknowledgements

The Human Body

The publishers would like to thank the following for their assistance in the preparation of this bcok: Mallory Baker, Barbara Bakowski. Herman Beckelman, Robert Beckelman, James Clark, Robert Goodell Jr., Steve Otfinoski, Jason Prentice, Lloyd Prentice, Dina Rubin, Jennifer Themel, Stephen Vincent, Michael Wolfman, D.D.S, Vinnie Zara..
Our special thanks to the following children who feature in the photographs: Michelle Burk, Simon Burk, Elliot Burton, Clay Canda-Cameron, Lisa Chan, Anton Crowden and Henry (the dog), Amanda Hanani, Mark Humphries, Gina Lamprell, Louis Lamprell, Bianca Laurence, Kyle Linnahan, Daniel Price, Rebecca Price, Poppy Rourke, Zoe Rourke, Jeremy Sequeira, Julian Sequeira, Gemma Smith. Gerard Smith, Chrisopher Stirling, Lucy Vaux, Craig Wilford, Amanda Wilson.

PICTURE CREDITS (t=top, b=bottom, l=left, r=right, c=center, e=extreme, f=flap, F=Front, C=Cover, B=Back). (TPL=The Photo Library, Sydney, SPL=Science Photo Library.) **AdLibitum** 7b, 8br, 9c, 9bl, 10bl, 14bl, 17r, 17b, 163, 22/23b, 22tl, 22cl, 22bl, 23tr, 23b, 24tr, 24br, 25tl, 26c, 26br, 263, 28cr, 28b, 29bl, 29br, 30bl, 30br, 30br, 32bl, 33bl, 33br, 34tr, 34bl, 35tl, 36c, 36tr, 36br, 37bl, 38/39c, 38tr, 38br, 40tr, 40cl, 40bl, 51c, 42tr, 42cr, 44c, 49br, 50br, 51tr, 53c, 56tl, 56cl, 56bl, 63br (M. Kaniewski). **AP/AAP** 21br, 62tr, 62bl. **Auscape** 39bl (Chassenet-BSIP), 39br (Estiot-BSIP), 27tr (Laurent-Bouhier-BSIP). **Baxter Immuno Aktiengesellschaft** 58bl. **E.T. Archive** 60tr. **The Granger Collection** 50bl. **The Image Bank** 56crt, 62bc (Flip Chalfant), 33cr (J. P. Kelly), 59cr (J. Stuart). **McLean Hospital** 19cr. Private photograph usage by permission of M. Rourke 38tc. **TPL** 30cr (E. Anderson), 39cl (D. Bosler) 13b (D. Becker) 21tr (SPL/D. Besford), 61tr (SPL/Dr A. Brody), 10br (SPL/Dr J. Burgess) 30bl (M. Clarke)51br (D. Day) 55bl (M. Delmasso) 21bl (Hulton-Deutsch), 39cl (Lori Adamski Peek), 16b (Z. Kaluzny), 53 (V. Michaels), 33t (NIH/Science Source), 35bl, 46tr (S. Peters), 10tr, 37tr, 42cb, 43cl, 51, 59cb (SPL), 52bl (SPL/O. Burriel), 24/25c (SPL/Prof. P. Cull), 36tl (SPL/M. Dohrn), 46cr, 49cl, 59t (SPL/Eye of Science), 62c (SPL/K. Gulbrandsen), 51cr (SPL/M. Kage), 37tl, 47c, 61br (SPL/Dr P. Marazzi), 42cl, 48br 55cr, 59b (SPL/Prof. P Motta), 26bl (SPL/Motta/Anatomy/Sapienza), 20b (SPL/A. Pasieka), 53c (SPL/Salisbury Hospital), 26tr (SPL/A. Syred), 62tl (SPL/G. Tompkinson), 15br (SPL/H. Young), 12bl (D. Struthers) 15tr (U.B.H Trust), 31bl (USDA/Science Source), 46tl (C. Thatcher). **Rainbow** 52br (H. Morgan). **University of Chicago** 56tr. **Warren Museum/Harvard Medical School** 20c.

ILLUSTRATION CREDITS
Susanna Addario 9tl, 11br, 18/19c, 18t, 18bl, 18br, 19tr, 19bl, 20/21c, 20t, 20cl, 21cr. **Martin Camm** 14tl. **Amy and Sam Collins/Art and Science Inc**. 35tr, 42t, 42br, 42/43c, 43b, 48crt, 48bl, 54/55c, 54t, 54b, 55br. **Marcus Cremonese** 6tr, 8cr, 8r, 9br, 12/13c, 12t, 13tr, 13cr, 13br, 14/15c, 14b, 15b, 30r, 48crb, 49cr, 49bl, 52t, 52l, 53cr, 52br, 53l, 58/59c, 59r, 60/61c, 60t, 61cr, 61bc, 64t, 64bl, 65tr, 65tc, 65bl. **Dr. Levent Efe** 57b. **Christer Eriksson** 9tr, 10tl, 10tr, 22/23c, 22bl, 22br, 23r, 23bl, 23br, 31c, 65br. **Peg Gerrity** 9cr, 28t, 28c, 28r, 29c, 48tr, 50t, 50/51c, 51bl. **Gino Hasler** 6br, 16bl, 16c, 24br, 25b, 26tc, 26tr, 27l, 27cr, 27br, 34cr, 34br, 38l, 39tr, 40/41b, 40tl, 40tr, 40cr, 49tr, 56r, 57r, 58c. **Karen Hinton** (Cochlear Limited, Australia) 25tr. **Frank Knight** 9cl, 26tl. **Jeff Lang** 24t. **Stuart McVicar** (Digital Manipulation) 8tr, 10/11c, 62/63c. **Siri Mills** 8cr, 16/17c, 17bl, 64br. **Spencer Phippen** 35br, 46/47c. **Claudia Saraceni** 14tc, 32/33c. **Peter Schouten** 14tr. **Marco Sparciari** 6cr. **Kate Sweeney** 7tr, 35cl, 44/45c, 44/45b, 44t, 44br, 45b. **Thomas Trojer** 32/33c. **Rod Westblade** 36/37b.

Rocks and Minerals

The publishers would like to thank the following experts and institutions for their assistance in the preparation of this book: Barbara Bakowski, Brian Chase, James Clark, William Henika, Steve Otfinoski, Ross Pogson, Virginia Polytechnic, Dina Rubin, Cynthia Shroba, Ph.D., Jennifer Themel.
Our special thanks to the following children who feature in the photographs: Michelle Burk, Simon Burk, Elliot Burton, Lisa Chan, Amanda Hanani, Andrew Tout.

PICTURE CREDITS (t=top, b=bottom, l=left, r=right, c=center, e=extreme, f=flap, F=Front, C=Cover, B=Back) (APL=Australian Picture Library, BPK=Bildarchiv Preussischer Kulturbesitz, DWSPL=D.W. Stock Photo Library, FLPA=Frank Lane Picture Agency, NGS=National Geographic Society, NMNH=National Museum of Natural History, Washington, NHM=Natural History Museum, NSP=Natural Science Photos, TPL=The Photo Library, Sydney, SPL=Science Photo Library.) **Ad-Libitum** 68tr, 71tr, 72tl, 72tr, 72l, 72bl, 72br, 73bl, 73br, 80c, 83c, 84bl, 84br, 85tl, 86tr, 86bl, 90br, 91cl, 91cr, 92tr, 96/97c, 96bl, 100tl, 100tr, 100bc, 101ct, 101cb, 103t, 105tl, 106b, 111tl, 111tr, 116bl, 118tr, 127br, 99c, 114bl, 114br, 118c, 118br, 119tl, 120bl (M. Kaniewski). **The Age** 123r (S. O'Dwyer). **American Museum of Natural History** 101br, 117br. **APL** 87tl (D&J Heaton), 79b (H.T. Kaiser),77tl (J. Penisten), 79c (S.Vidler). **Association Curie et Joliet-Curie** 114l. **K. Atkinson** 78t. **Auscape** 122r (J. Ferrero), 84r (F. Gohier), 82tr (M & K Krafft), 82/83b (T. Till). **Australian Museum** 117tr, 119r (Nature Focus). **BPK** 109c (Margarete Busing). **The Bridgeman Art Library** 101tr, 108tr. **R. Coenraads** 97br, 99tl, 99tr, 120tr. **Corel Professional Photos** 103br. **DWSPL** 123l (M. Fenech). **The Field Museum, Chicago**, IL 89br. **FLPA** 87cr (M. Nimmo). **Gannett Suburban Newspapers** 89tr (S. Bayer). **Icelandic Photo** 80tr (Mats Wibe Lund/Sigurg. Jonasson). **Jeff. L. Rottman Photography** 96tl. **Jim Stimson Photography** 86/87c. **The Kobal Collection** 74ct. **Mary Evans Picture Library** 81tr, 96l, 113r, 118bl. **The National Gallery Picture Library, London** 100l. **NASA** 110tr, 110bl. **NGS** 114t (J. L. Amos). **NHM** 89c, 98br, 99br, 124bl. **NMNH** 78bl, 92/93c, 102bl (C. Clark), 100/101c. **North Wind Pictures** 85tr, 121tr. **NSP** 94tr (O. C. Roura). **TPL** 85r (O. Benn), 124tr (S. Fraser), 110br (G.B. Lewis), 111br (Dr. K Macdonald), 103b (NASA), 116tr (P. Hayson), 113c (A. Husmo), 106c (P. Robinson), 74t, 76tr (SPL), 112bl (SPL/C. Caffrey), 75cb (SPL/ Geoscape). **Photo Researchers Inc.** 92l (T. McHugh), 84/85c (C. Ott), 93br (G. Retherford). **Planet Earth Pictures** 88tr (E. Darack). **G.R "Dick" Roberts** 94l. **Scottish National Portrait Gallery** 87tr. **J. Scovil** 88l, 88br, 93c, 94cr, 94br, 95l, 95r, 96t, 97t, 98l, 102c, 102cr, 103tl, 103cl, 103bl, 124br. **B. Shelton** 124cr. **Tiffany & Co**. 98tr. **Tom Stack & Associates** 81br. **Tom Till Photography** 83t. **Visuals Unlimited** 108c (J. Greenberg), 121br (D. Thomas). **Werner Forum Archive** 82bl. **William Mallat Photography** 115bl.

ILLUSTRATION CREDITS
Susanna Addario 68cr, 69tr, 70br, 76tl, 78tl, 96tc, 103r, 104tcr, 106tr, 108tl, 108tc, 127tr. **Andrew Beckett/ illustration** 72/73c, 70tr. **Anne Bowman** 105bl, 105br, 124tl, 124tc, 124tr, 125tl. **Chris Forsey** 68br, 70tcr, 70bcr, 74/75c, 74t, 74/75b, 75r, 76/77c, 78/79c, 78bl, 79r, 80/81c, 80/81b, 104cr, 104bcr, 105cr, 110/111c, 110tl, 110tc, 110b, 111bl, 112/113c, 112tl, 112tc, 112tr, 112bl, 112br, 113bl, 113br, 122/123c, 122tl, 122tc, 122tr, 122etr, 122br, 123bl, 123br, 126tl, 126bc, 126br. **Ray Grinaway** 71tl, 71cl, 71cr, 71br, 74bl, 82tl, 82bl, 82br, 83tl, 84tl, 84tc, 84tr, 86tl, 86tc, 86tr, 88tl, 88tc, 88tr, 89tl, 90tl, 90tr, 90tcr, 90cr, 90bcr, 91tl, 91bl, 92tl, 92tc, 92tr, 92b, 93tr, 93b, 94tl, 94tc, 94tr, 94bl, 94br, 95cr, 95bl, 95bc, 95br, 96tr, 97r, 98tl, 98tc, 100bl, 100br, 101bl, 101br, 101c, 102tl, 102tc, 102bl, 103tr, 103cr, 103r, 103br, 105tr, 109tc, 109r, 118tl, 118tc, 118tr, 119r, 119b, 124br, 125c, 126tc, 126tr, 127tr, 127bc. **Frank Knight** 124bl. **David McAllister** 106bl, 106br, 107c, 107bl, 107br. **Stuart McVicar** (digital manipulation)77tr. **Oliver Rennert** 76tr. **Claudia Saracini** 80tc. **Michael Saunders** 78tc, 78tr, 78b, 80tr, 83tr, 83cr, 83br, 84br, 85bl, 85br, 86/87b, 88br, 89bl, 89br, 91tr, 98tr, 98b, 99bl, 99br, 103r, 104tr, 105cl, 106tl, 106tc, 106r, 108tr, 120/121c, 120tl, 120tc, 120tr, 120b, 121bl, 121br, 125r, 126bl, 127tc, 127tr. **Kevin Stead** 91br, 102tr. **Sharif Tarabay/illustration** 116/117c, 116/117b, 116tl, 116tc, 116tcr. **S. Trevaskis** 108bl. **Thomas Trojer** 103c, 104br, 114/115c, 114tl, 114tc, 114tr, 115r. **Rod Westblade** 76tc. **Ann Winterbotham** 80tl.

Space

The publishers would like to thank the following people for their assistance in the preparation of this book: Barbara Bakowski, James Clark, Dina Rubin, and Jennifer Themel. Our special thanks to the following children who feature in the photographs: Michelle Burk, Simon Burk, Amanda Hanani, Mark Humphries, Bianca Laurence, Jeremy Sequeira, Gemma Smith, Amanda Wilson, Max Young.

PICTURE CREDITS (t=top, b=bottom, l=left, r=right, c=center, e=extreme, f=flap, F=Front, C=Cover, B=Back) (AAO=Anglo-Australian Observatory, AAT=Anglo Australian Telescope, APL=Australian Picture Library, ASP=Astronomical Society of the Pacific, TPL=The Photo Library, Sydney, SPL=Science Photo Library.) **AAO** 54c (D. Malin), 172cl, 178b, 180br, 181cr, 183tcr. **AAP Image** 138r, 141bl, 143b. **AAT** 183bcr (D. Malin), 180bl, 183br. **Ad-Libitum** 138ct, 138cb, 145br, 148b, 150bl, 176l, 187t, 137l, 152b, 175r (M. Kaniewski). **APL** 160c (Woodfin Camp), 168bl. **ASP** 137tr, 155t, 163bc, 169br, 174br, 182bl. **Austral** 168c (FOTO). **Alan Dyer** 146cbr, 154tr, 155tr, 174bl. **E.T. Archive** 178c. **Akira Fujii** 134cr, 147ebl, 153r, 155br, 163bl, 171bc, 181tr, 188c. **IAC Photo** 137cr (D. Malin). **Image Select** 135r. **Mary Evans Picture Library** 148tr. **David Miller** 156tr. **NASA** 135br, 163cl, 164bl, 178/179c (JPL Photo), 182bc (Leiden Observatory/W. Jaffe), 182bl, 183bc, 183br (STScl), 138r, 151r, 156c, 157r, 159tr, 171bl. **Newell Color** 132tr, 134cl, 173tl, 181bl. **Novosti** 139c. **The Image Bank** 154bl (S. Krongard). **TPL** 177cr, 185c (J. Chumack), 137bl (T. Craddock), 173tc, 180/181c (I. M. House), 185c (Jodrell Bank), 134bl (Nigel Press), 177cl, 182r (SPL/L. Dodd), 143c, 154/155c (SPL/ ESA), 170br (SPL/G. Garradd), 147tl, 159bc (SPL/D. Hardy), 170bl (SPL/Magrath/Nielsen), 137c (SPL/ Magrath Photography), 134br, 140l, 141c, 145c, 157c, 159tl, 161t, 162bc, 162br, 163cl, 167cr, 167bl, 186br (SPL/ NASA), 137br, 178bl (SPL/Max-Planck-Institute), 167bc (SPL/ D. Parker), 160l (SPL/J. Samford), 145t (SPL/Dr. S. Shostak), 186bl (SPL/Dr. R. Stepney), 151tl, 173cr, 181br, 184br (SPL), 167r (SPL/US Geological Survey), 183tr (SPL/US Naval Observatory), 135bl, 152c (World Perspectives), 171cl. **Tom Stack & Associates** 57c (B. & S. Fletcher), 21br, 41br. **UA News Services** 34tr (L. Stiles). **UC Berkeley** 177tr (G. Marcy).

ILLUSTRATION CREDITS
Julian Baum/Wildlife Art Ltd 146cr, 152tr, 152cr, 152bl, 152bc, 152br, 153bl, 153br, 162/163c, 163br, 189tr. **Gregory Bridges** 158bl. **Tom Connell/Wildlife Art Ltd** 132br, 132ebr, 133tl, 133tr, 138/139c, 138tl, 138tcl, 138tcr, 138tr,138bl, 138bc, 138br, 139bl, 139bc, 139br, 140/141c, 140tl, 140tr, 140bl, 140bc, 140br, 141tl, 141r, 188br, 189bl, 189bcl, 189bcr. **Christer Eriksson** 133bl, 133br, 144/145c, 144/145b, 144tl, 144tc, 144tr, 189bel. **Chris Forsey** 130bc, 158/159c, 158bc, 172etr, 172tr, 172r, 174t, 174bl, 175bl, 175br, 176b, 188bel, 189etr, 189br. **Murray Frederick** 146ctr, 147tr, 150br, 151bl, 151bc, 151br, 161tr, 161cr, 161br. **Lee Gibbons/ Wildlife Art Ltd** 147cb, 164/165c, 164r, 164bc, 164br, 164bl, 165br, 173tr, 182/183c, 182tl, 182tr, 182bl, 182br, 183b, 188tr, 188bcl. **Ray Grinaway** 150tl, 152tl, 154tl, 154tc, 154tr, 154bc, 154br, 156tl, 156tc, 158tl, 160tl, 162tl, 162tc, 164tl, 164tc, 166tl, 166tc, 168tl. **David A. Hardy/Wildlife Art Ltd** 130tr, 130cr, 130br, 132etr, 133cl, 133cr, 134t, 134tl, 134tc, 135c, 142/143c, 142tl, 142tc, 142tr, 142bl, 142br, 143t, 143r, 146tr, 147bl, 148/149c, 148t/b, 149r, 149b, 150/151c, 150cl, 152cl, 153c, 154cl, 156cl, 156bl, 158cl, 162cl, 164l, 166/167c, 166l, 166bl, 166br, 168/169c, 168t, 168l, 169t, 169r, 169bc, 170/171c, 170tl, 170tc, 170tr, 170l, 170c, 172b, 172br, 173bl, 173bc, 173br, 174/175c, 178tl, 178tc 178tr 178bl, 178br, 179r, 180tl, 180tr, 184/185c, 184tl, 184tc, 184tr, 185r, 186/187cb, 186tl, 186tc, 186tr, 186bl, 186br, 187tr, 187br, 188etr, 188tl, 188tc, 188bl, 188bcr, 188ber, 189tel, 189tl, 189ber. **Robert Hynes** 167tr. **Peter Mennim** 164c. **Oliver Rennert** 136/137c. **Trevor Ruth** 147ct, 162c. **Marco Sparaciari** 130tcr, 132ctr, 132cbr, 136tl, 136tc, 136tr, 136r, 136bl, 136bc, 136br, 137etr, 137ecr, 137ebr, 146br, 156/157b, 156bc, 158tc, 158tr, 158bc, 158br, 159tr, 159r, 159br, 189tcl. **Chris Stead** 172rc, 176/177c. **Kevin Stead** 188etl. **Cliff Watt** 163cr. **Tony Wellington** 160/161c, 160tc, 160bl, 160br. **Rod Westblade** 150t, 155c, 157bl. **David Wood** 151r, 155cr, 176t.

Don't miss these other Pathfinders science collections:

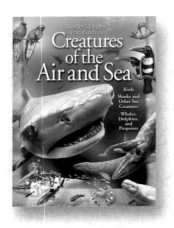

Creatures of the Air and Sea

Did you know that hummingbirds can fly backward? That there is a shark so small it can fit into the palm of your hands? Or that some dolphins are pink? Facts like these are at your fingertips every time you open this collection of three complete Reader's Digest Pathfinders—***Birds, Sharks and Other Sea Creatures***, and ***Whales, Dolphins, and Porpoises***

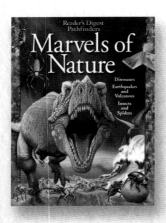

Marvels of Nature

Did you know that some dinosaurs had feathers? That a single volcanic eruption can change the weather around the world? Or that most spiders are really good guys—they eat so many insects that they are nature's pest control experts? Facts like these are at your fingertips every time you open this collection of three complete Reader's Digest Pathfinders—***Dinosaurs, Earthquakes and Volcanoes***, and ***Insects and Spiders***.

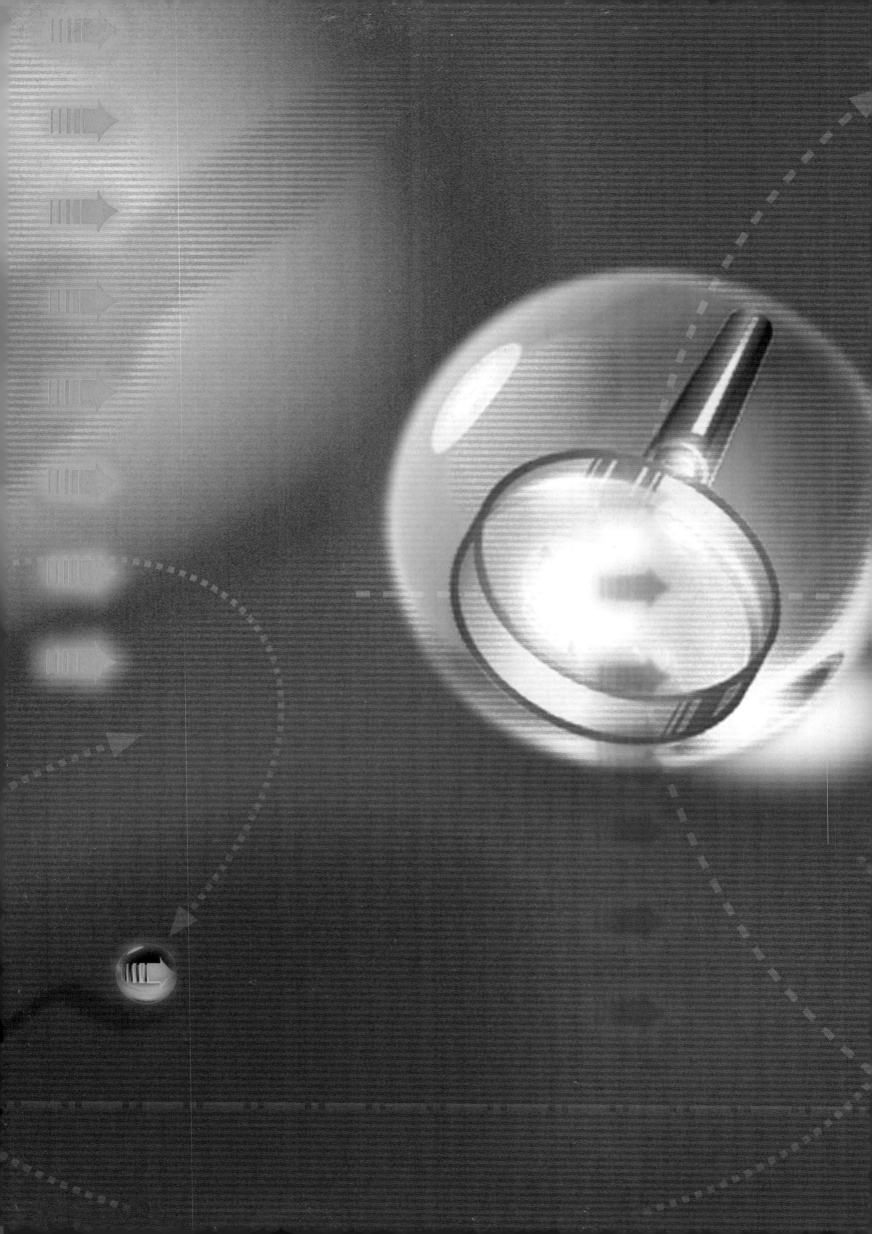